IMAGES
of America

APEX

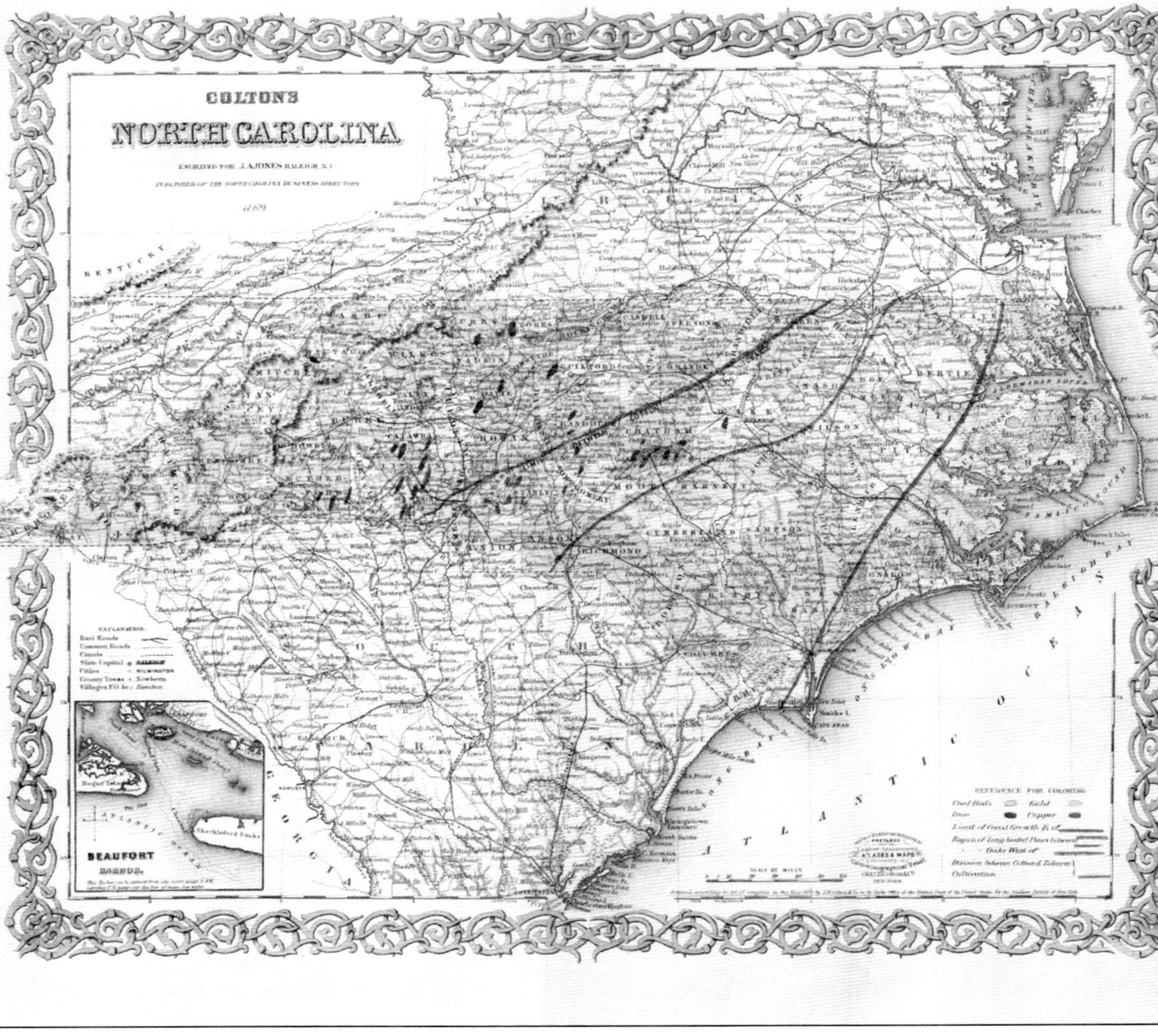

An 1869 J. H. Colton Map of North Carolina. This state map shows the division lines of the cotton and tobacco cultivation and the region of oak and long-leafed pines. The small circles in Chatham County represent the iron and coal beds. The map also shows the early progress of the Chatham Railroad, which starts in Raleigh but does not quite reach Apex. (Courtesy of the North Carolina State Archives.)

On the Cover: Apex Mule and Supply Company. It was opened in 1909 by J. W. "June" Lassiter, Lindsay S. Olive, Percy Olive, Sidney W. Stone, and W. B. Johnson. Two years later, they added a fancy and heavy grocery store department that was run by Adolphus G. Bell. Eventually, Bell relocated his business to the Sellars Building. This photograph was taken in 1921. From left to right are Adolphus G. Bell, Jack "Tink" Pearson, and Sam Branch. (Courtesy of Woodrow W. Maynard and Ann Grebing.)

IMAGES
of America

APEX

Sherry Monahan

ARCADIA
PUBLISHING

ISBN 978-0-7385-6638-2

Published by Arcadia Publishing
Charleston, South Carolina

Printed in the United States of America

Library of Congress Control Number: 2009928200

For all general information contact Arcadia Publishing at:
Telephone 843-853-2070
Fax 843-853-0044
E-mail sales@arcadiapublishing.com
For customer service and orders:
Toll-Free 1-888-313-2665

Visit us on the Internet at www.arcadiapublishing.com

For Aunt Juanita . . . who is dancing in heaven.

Contents

Acknowledgments

No book can ever be written alone. Authors depend on family and friends who kindly listen to our ups and downs, and experts who assist us in various aspects of research. This book required me to reach out to strangers who I asked to let me into their lives—both past and present. This writing journey has shown me how generous, kind, and friendly people can be.

I have so many people to thank and a short space to do it in. This list is alphabetical so I do not leave anyone out. Thanks to Danny Berrier, who is the keeper of history for the Apex United Methodist Church; to Jacque Burgess for photographs and whose spirit and liveliness are an inspiration; to Bob Crowley, who suggested I write this book; to Kim Cumber of the North Carolina State Archives, who helped me look for old photographs; to Debbie Douglass, who not only shared photographs, but put out a call to residents when I was short on images; to Georgia Evangelist, town clerk of Apex, for her time, knowledge, and dedication to preserving history; and to Ann Grebing (and Ron, too) for photographs and whose knowledge of Apex history is unsurpassed. Sue-Lynn Hinson of the Apex Volunteer Fire Department provided photographs and history. Additionally, thanks to Diane Long and Susan Mills for wonderful photograph collections. Sue Sennert of the Salem Baptist Church shared two amazing photographs, and Tommy Stephens and Janet Davis shared their father's collection of photographs that he took over the years while working at the *News and Observer*. Lastly, thanks to the staff at the Apex Baptist Church for their precious photograph gems and to Richard Winter for the postal history.

I also have to thank my husband, Larry, who listens, cooks dinner, and supports me as I pursue this crazy love of writing.

Lastly, I want to thank my editor, Lindsay Harris at Arcadia. I know some authors thank their editors because it is the right thing to do, but mine is genuine. Lindsay has offered support, guidance, and a kind ear when things looked their worst. Her cheery voice on the other end of the phone helped me through some trying times. By the end of each call she had me laughing. I am thankful for everything she has done.

Introduction

Apex's history is unique in that it is mainly remembered and told by longtime residents with deep family roots and by historians fortunate to speak with those residents. The information in this book comes from those who were willing to share their knowledge and photographs, and from archival materials from various sources.

As early as the 1830s, the Apex vicinity was occupied. Patrick W. Dowd, an ordained Baptist minister, bought 1,500 acres that encompassed the northern part of Apex. It is believed he called the area Shepherd's Vineyard because of the sheep and the muscadine grapevines growing all over the area. He married a Tarboro socialite named Martha Austin and had a stately mansion built for her on the land. A local family by the name of Mann built the mansion. Ten years later, Dowd established the Salem Meeting House, which is now the Salem Baptist Church.

In the beginning, Apex was nothing more than a hunting destination the locals called Log Pond. This area was noted for its deer hunting, and the 1911 *Apex Journal* even claimed there was a deer stand near the pond. It was never incorporated or showed up on any map, but the locals knew where it was. In fact, part of Center Street runs right through the old log pond today. Other nearby communities, like Green Level and Holly Springs, were already evidencing community life and growth.

As with many towns, progress in other areas affected the Log Pond area. Supposed coalfields in Chatham County spurred frenzied talk, and plans for a railroad began. Chatham County historians believe this was just a ruse to get a railroad to their neck of the woods. Others state it was because of the Civil War. The Confederates likely saw the railroad as a military enterprise to obtain the coal and were probably the true force behind the railroad. The war itself got in the way, and funds to have the railroad built dried up. The Chatham County railroad lay dormant until after the war, and around 1870, Apex became a station stop. Q. I. Hudson was the first railroad agent.

How Apex got its name is closely related to the railroad and its terrain. The town sits atop a natural ridge, and it is believed railroad surveyors found the site to be the highest point along their survey. The *Apex Journal* wrote in 1911 that "the town is ideally situated on a ridge that is the highest point between along the Seaboard Air Line Railway, which runs from Hamlet to Norfolk." It is interesting to note the newspaper referred to Apex as a town since the census referred to it as the village of Apex.

The main part of downtown Apex was largely owned by John McClenahan Ellington and Hilliard Bell. In 1867, Ellington (also known as John McC. Ellington) and Bell divided their land, with Ellington taking 160 acres of the east side of old Haywood Road, which is now Salem Street. Bell kept 160 acres on the west side. Shortly after the division, Ellington began selling town lots. Bell sold his land to Henry C. Olive and G. W. Atkinson shortly after splitting with Ellington.

Ellington was the first to take advantage of the railroad when he began a lumber business. Other timber products included turpentine, tar, and pitch. H. C. Olive followed right behind when he started a tobacco factory on what was once called Factory Hill. While Olive's first venture did not fare well, he went on to become one of Apex's most prominent citizens. He was also involved early on with cotton.

By 1871, Daniel Mann had his general store established and also applied for a post office franchise. In October 1871, Mann was granted a contract from the U.S. Post Office Department. Shortly after the post office was established, so was the town. On February 23, 1873, Apex was incorporated. The first mayor was H. C. Olive, and town commissioners included Alvin N. Betts, John McC. Ellington, W. L. Ellington, and Q. I. Hudson. On February 28, 1873, the Apex town charter was ratified, and William F. Utley was named the first town marshal. However, it was not until 1875 that Apex created the ordinances the marshal needed to enforce. Utley was not your ordinary marshal—he was a Civil War veteran who enforced the law with one leg.

It is interesting to note that the first two ordinances established dealt with disorderly houses and drunkenness, and things citizens were not allowed to do on Sunday. In its early stages, Apex was pretty free, and the town had liquor establishments, houses of ill fame, gambling, and drunkenness. The *Apex Journal* carried a story that was written by Rev. J. M. White: "Barrooms were established and did their accustomed work. For some years drinking and carousing were common. . . . Some of its best citizens seeing with sorrow the moral ruin that was coming on the village wanted to get rid of the bars as the cause of evil." Some argued that closing the bars in town would kill Apex's life and prosperity. Reverend White countered by noting that men would say anything when they want to satisfy their own needs.

Despite the arguments, Apex passed their ordinances, but like anywhere else, it had residents who broke them and were fined or arrested for violating town ordinances. Bibulous citizens who roamed the streets found themselves confined to the basement of H. C. Olive's store, which served as a jail. When they sobered up, they rang a bell and someone came to let them out. Eventually, Apex began to emerge as a town with rules and morals.

Churches had already established themselves in Apex and the White Oak Township, thus leading to a more civilized community. Apex had numerous churches either in town or in nearby communities. Church buildings were established in the Apex vicinity as early as the 1840s. Those in and near Apex included the Apex Baptist Missionary Church, which began in 1873, and the Salem Baptist Church in 1840, which belonged to Patrick Dowd. Others were the Apex United Methodist Episcopal in 1870, Union Chapel Baptist in 1869, and the Christian Home United Church of Christ in 1866. There were several other churches in nearby communities, including Olive Chapel, New Hill, and Green Level.

The Apex community also saw the Chatham Railroad reorganized into the Raleigh and Augusta Air Line Railroad in 1875. At this time, Apex boasted several businesses, two schools, a steam cotton gin, and a sash and blind factory. According to the *Sentinel* newspaper, Apex's population was 600. However, since the U.S. Census shows Apex's population as 231 in 1880, the 600 number likely included the entire White Oak Township. It was not uncommon to see misquoted census numbers because some counts included the people in the county or township in which the town was situated.

Apex businessmen were thinking big in 1898 when they organized the Apex Industrial Association. The townspeople were also thinking, but not about the industrial environment. They were more concerned with the privy problem. They passed an ordinance that required residents and business owners to use lime or some other disinfectant when cleaning out privies. They were also required to bury the contents at least 10 inches.

The beginning of the 20th century saw many events that affected the progress of Apex and its 346 residents. In 1901, one of the largest buildings in Apex was erected by Charles Sellars and, by 1906, was occupied by Watkins-Seymour's Hardware; Bennett and Weaver; B. H. Pate, Inc., who had a meat market; and Dr. Romulus W. Stephens Sr., who performed dentistry.

The year 1905 was a pivotal one for Apex. In February, a devastating fire swept through the town. It leveled nearly 80 percent of the wooden structures in downtown. Even as the embers continued to glow, the townspeople began the arduous task of rebuilding—but with brick this time. The fire also caused Apex to develop a firefighting plan and building ordinance to address any future issues. The firefighting plan was a bucket brigade, and the building ordinance addressed using brick instead of lumber.

Children's education had been a part of Apex early on, but it was not until 1906 that a permanent school was built to educate Apex's youth. The Apex graded school was constructed at a cost of $7,000 and had 125 students its first year.

It was also during this time that the railroad was extended to Durham, which opened new markets for anyone along the route. One event that demonstrated Apex's permanency was the establishment of the Merchants and Farmers Bank. As one might guess, this served the farmers, merchants, and local businessmen in town. In addition, L. S. Franklin and E. W. Franklin started the *Apex Journal* on July 4, 1905.

Having the extended railroad and new bank allowed businessmen to enter a new market—tobacco. Some felt this was the opportune time for them to enter this market because a tobacco disease called Granville wilt crippled tobacco farmers in Person and Granville County. The first auction house to open was the Golden Leaf Tobacco Lead Warehouse. The town of Apex saw wagonloads of tobacco coming to town. In 1906, the Planters Warehouse was built. That year also saw the building of a brand new railway station. Apex now had two warehouses and three prize houses (a place where tobacco is packed), and was marketing about two million pounds annually.

The tobacco auction houses in Apex soon joined the latest farming wave in the U.S.—cooperative pricing. The decision eventually collapsed the Apex auction houses because buyers took their business to other auction houses not in the co-op.

Cotton had been a local crop in Apex for years, but it was not until 1910 that it got in to the cotton market. Its first year saw more than 3,000 bales of cotton brought to town and sold. In 1911, the *Apex Journal* wrote, "Pretty soon Apex is going to be the most prominent cotton market throughout this section of the country." They also had their very own "ginning man," M. C. Sorrell. He was not affiliated with the cotton mills or dealers and offered to buy local cotton and cottonseed at a fair price.

The month of June 1911 brought another fire to Apex, but this one was not nearly as destructive as the 1905 disaster. Only nine businesses were destroyed and few others damaged. In September, the town requested issuing bonds for town improvements, which would include the new town hall.

At this time, Apex boasted three hotels, two banks, several boardinghouses, a marble yard, a furniture store, two lumberyards, a knitting mill, a canning factory, a livery stable, two undertakers, a newspaper, two large department stores, one drugstore, two meat markets, two fish mongers, a hardware store, two restaurants, a dry-goods store, five grocery stores, a farm supply store, four churches, and many other establishments to support a population of about 680. It even had its own tonic. The Apex Manufacturing Company started making Rogers' Famous Chill Tonic in 1899, and it was selling quite well to the local druggists in 1911. The company advertised the tonic as, "Guaranteed to cure chills and fever and all malarial and bilious troubles." It contained quinine, iron, cascara sagrada (a laxative), and aromatics.

It was also around this time that Apex began to transform into a sophisticated town. Town ordinances began addressing the appearance of Apex. Some that were passed included cleaning up the streets, laying water pipes, installing streetlamps, grading and paving roads, and installing gas tanks.

The year 1914 brought some notable changes to Apex. First, the train depot burned and had to be rebuilt. Later that year, G. C. Norris requested permission to show moving pictures at the town hall in the theater upstairs. Progress was seen in the mayor's office when a telephone was installed there. The town speed limit was also increased from 8 miles per hour to 15.

Apex continued on a steady path, with various types of businesses coming and going. In 1927, a new type of business began operating in Apex when Agri-Insecticides and Chemicals opened its doors. It was just the first of many to take advantage of the local minerals and conveniently situated railroad.

Also in 1927, A. B. Hunter recommended to the town board that a fire company be organized. The board passed resolutions appointing members and officers of the original department to serve a two-year period. Shortly thereafter, the town also passed several resolutions to obtain firefighting equipment and facilities.

In late 1927, Whitson Benton was appointed as night fireman. He was to sleep in the firehouse and was paid $2.50 per month. By December 1927, a room was built and furnished as living quarters. In 1928, the fire department is listed on the Sanborn map showing 18 volunteers and was located in the bottom of the town hall building.

However, by the late 1930s, there was no official fire department in Apex, and the firefighting squad consisted of anyone who heard the alarm and was willing to offer his services. In 1938, nineteen men from Apex met to address concerns about the lack of sufficient fire protection. The Apex Volunteer Fire Department was chartered in 1939, and some of its charter members included Charles A. Baucom, Romulus Stephens, Bruce Benton, and Sidney Seymour.

In 1956, Apex celebrated the completion of a new three-bay firehouse, which currently sits on Salem Street.

Apex has changed since its early beginnings, yet there are still things about the town that remain the same. The train still passes through, but it no longer picks up passengers, and the old town hall is now a cultural arts center. Apex continues to be a popular main-street community where locals and visitors alike stroll the streets and patronize the many businesses that dot Salem Street.

One

In the Beginning

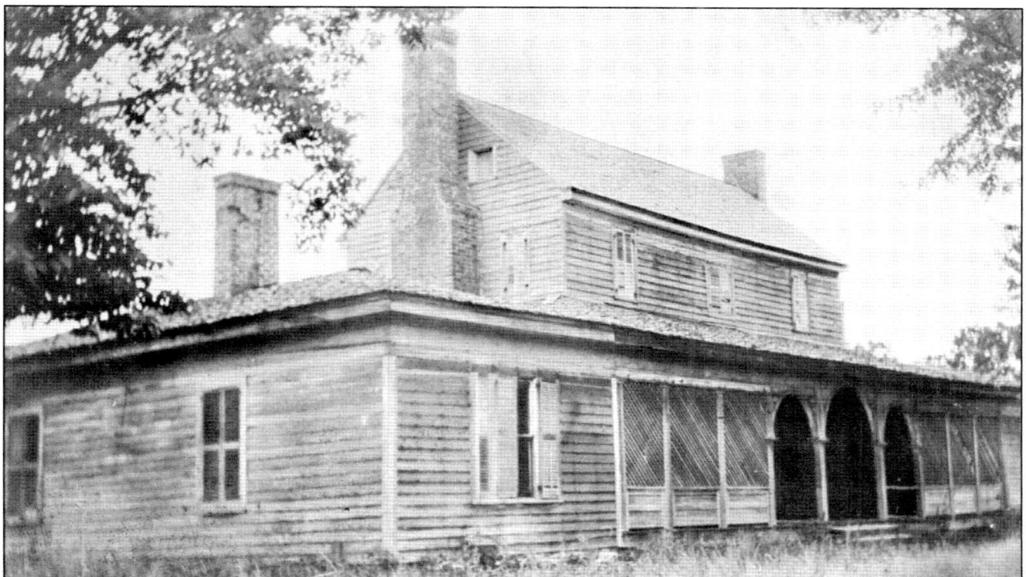

Shepherd's Vineyard. Patrick W. Dowd was an ordained Baptist minister with the Salem Baptist Church. When he married Tarboro socialite Martha Austin, he took her to the country. He made sure she was happy by building her a large plantation home on his 1,600 acres. Part of that land is where northern Apex is today. (Courtesy of the North Carolina State Archives.)

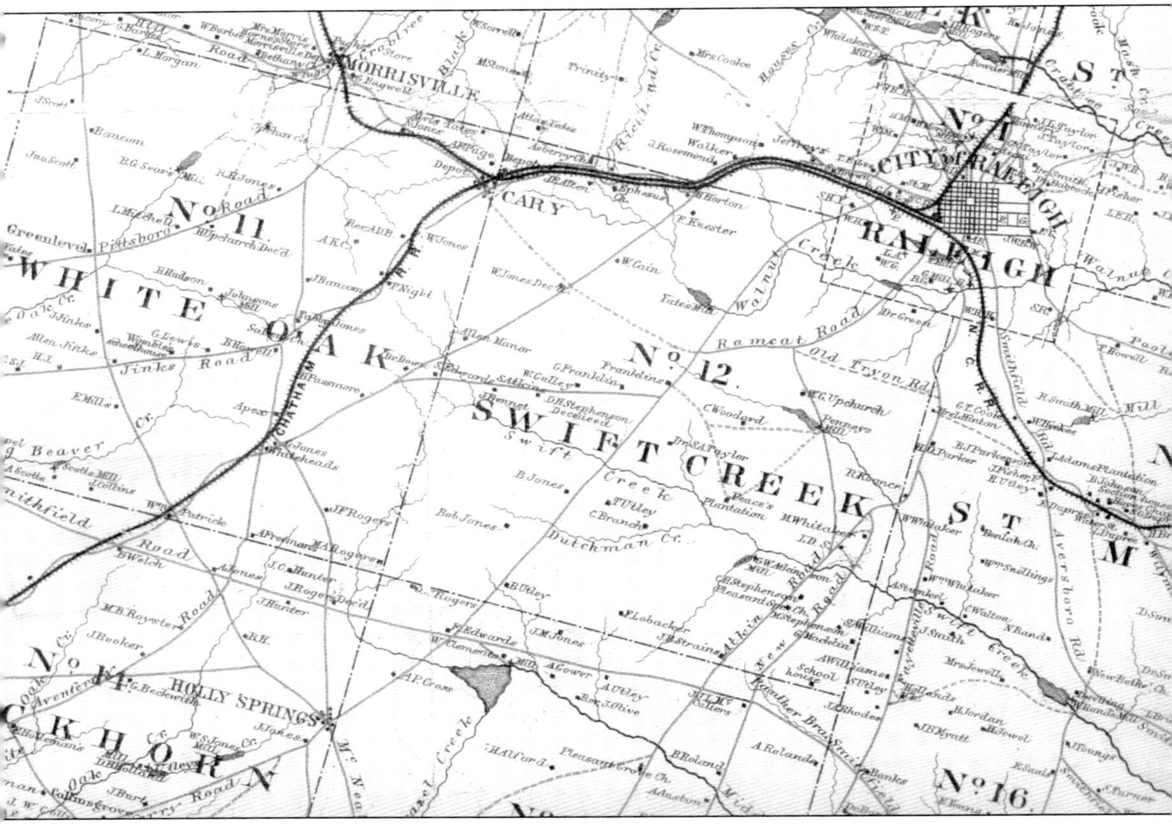

AN 1878 NORTH CAROLINA RAILROAD MAP. It was not until 1870 that Apex became a station stop along the Chatham Railroad. Construction began in 1857 and reached about halfway between Cary and Apex by 1861. Construction was halted when the Civil War began, but in 1862, the Confederate government realized the need to complete the railroad to gain access to coal and iron for the war effort. Work progressed slowly, and by the end of the war, the line had barely reached to a mile beyond Apex. By 1875, the railroad was chartered under a new name to allow for further lines. The Chatham Railroad was now known as the Raleigh and Augusta Air Line Railroad. By 1904, the Raleigh and Augusta was merged with the Seaboard Air Line. Today the railroad is known as the CSX Transportation line. (Courtesy of the North Carolina State Archives.)

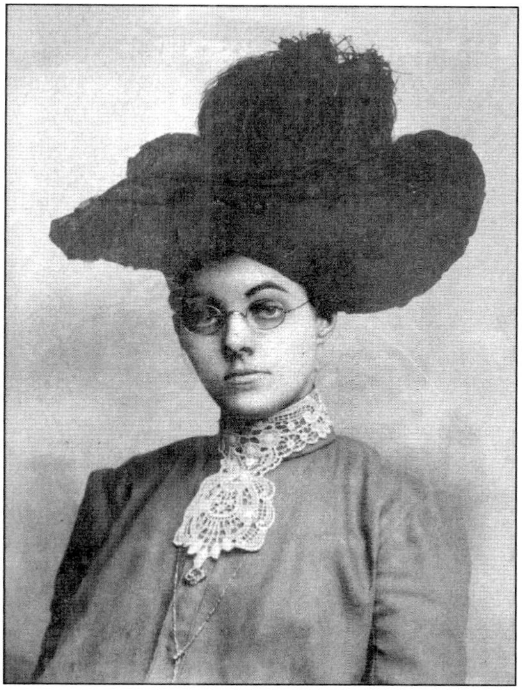

ADELINE MARY MANN. Adeline, or Aunt Allie as she was called, was Daniel Mann's first child. She was born in 1836 and eventually married Henry Rhodes. Daniel Mann applied to the U.S. Postal Department to obtain permission to start Apex's post office. He also served as the first postmaster in 1873. Prior to that, he married Susannah Womack, and they had seven children. They were Adeline Mary, born in 1836; Silas Quentin, born in 1838 and married to Amelia Lela Robards; William Saunders, born in 1839 and married to Elizabeth "Bettie" Bell; Caswell Simeon, born in 1842 and married to Mary Rogers; Ara Ann, born in 1848 and married to Adolphus C. Mills; Jasper Joseph, born in 1849 and married to Rosa ?; and Adolphus T., born in 1854 and married to Vera Prince. (Both, courtesy of Diane Long.)

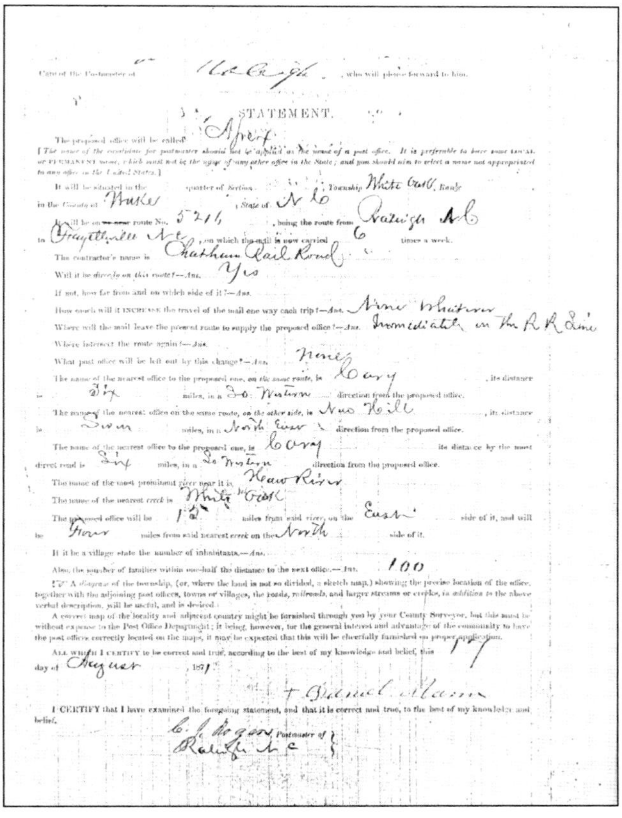

Care of the Postmaster at Raleigh, who will please forward to him.

STATEMENT.

The proposed office will be called Apex

[The name of the candidate for postmaster should not be applied as the name of a post office. It is preferable to have some local or PERMANENT name, which must not be the name of any other office in the State; and you should aim to select a name not appropriated to any office in the United States.]

It will be situated in the quarter of Section , Township White Oak, Range , in the County of Wake, State of N C

It will be on route No. 5211, being the route from Raleigh N C to Fayetteville N C, on which the mail is now carried 6 times a week.

The contractor's name is Chatham Rail Road

Will it be directly on this route?—Ans. Yes

If not, how far from and on which side of it?—Ans.

How much will it INCREASE the travel of the mail one way each trip?—Ans. None whatever

Where will the mail leave the present route to supply the proposed office?—Ans. Immediately on the R R Line

Where intersect the route again?—Ans.

What post office will be left out by this change?—Ans. None

The name of the nearest office to the proposed one, on the same route, is Cary, its distance is Six miles, in a So. Western direction from the proposed office.

The name of the nearest office on the same route, on the other side, is New Hill, its distance is Seven miles, in a North Western direction from the proposed office.

The name of the nearest office to the proposed one, is Cary its distance by the most direct road is Six miles, in a So Western direction from the proposed office.

The name of the most prominent river near it is Haw River

The name of the nearest creek is White Oak

The proposed office will be 12 miles from said river, on the East side of it, and will be Four miles from said nearest creek on the North side of it.

If it be a village state the number of inhabitants.—Ans.

Also, the number of families within one-half the distance to the next office.—Ans. 100

A diagram of the township, (or, where the land is not so divided, a sketch map,) showing the precise location of the office, together with the adjoining post offices, towns or villages, the roads, railroads, and larger streams or creeks, in addition to the above verbal description, will be useful, and is desired.

A correct map of the locality and adjacent country might be furnished through you by your County Surveyor, but this must be without expense to the Post Office Department; it being, however, for the general interest and advantage of the community to have the post offices correctly located on the maps, it may be expected that this will be cheerfully furnished on proper application.

ALL WHICH I CERTIFY to be correct and true, according to the best of my knowledge and belief, this 17 day of August, 1871.

Daniel Mann

I CERTIFY that I have examined the foregoing statement, and that it is correct and true, to the best of my knowledge and belief.

C. J. Rogers, Postmaster of Raleigh N C

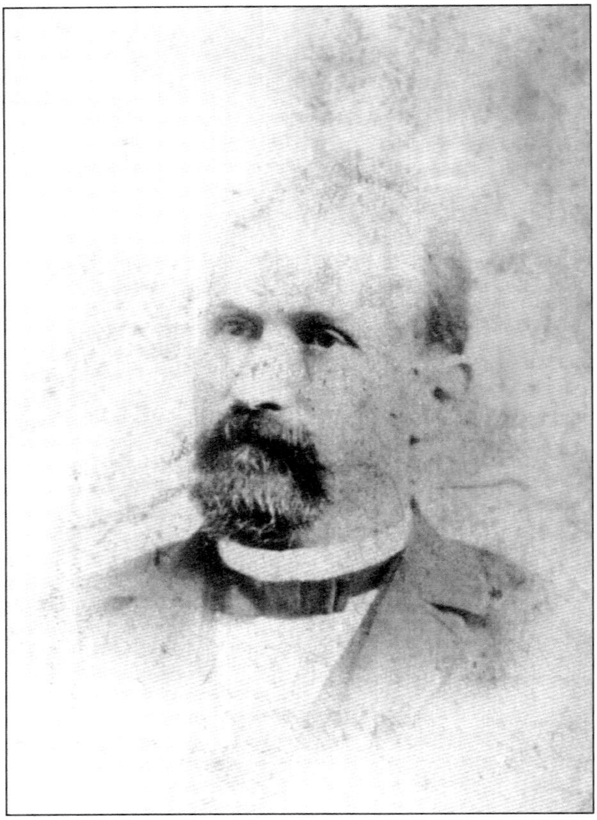

Henry Calvin Olive. H. C. was one of the first men to invest in Apex's future. In 1868, he and G. W. Atkinson purchased 160 acres in downtown Apex. They sold lots to hopeful businessmen and entrepreneurs. Olive became Apex's first mayor and was a soldier in the Confederate army. Olive was passionate about education and served as the chairman of the board of education and also as a state senator. He accomplished all this by the age of 50, when he suffered an untimely death in 1898. Just prior to his death, Olive organized the H. C. Olive Company. His three sons were all involved in his businesses at early ages. His eldest son, Lindsay, ran the company, while his brothers followed their own interests. The mercantile business netted about $3,000 in 1898 and, by 1910, was doing over $30,000. (Both, courtesy of Ann Grebing.)

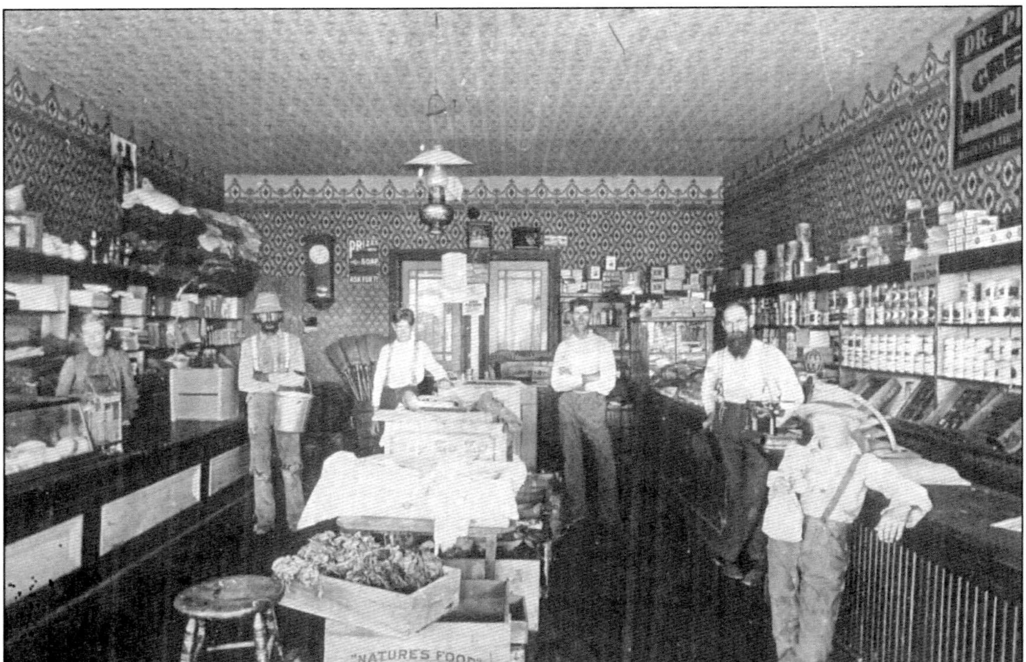

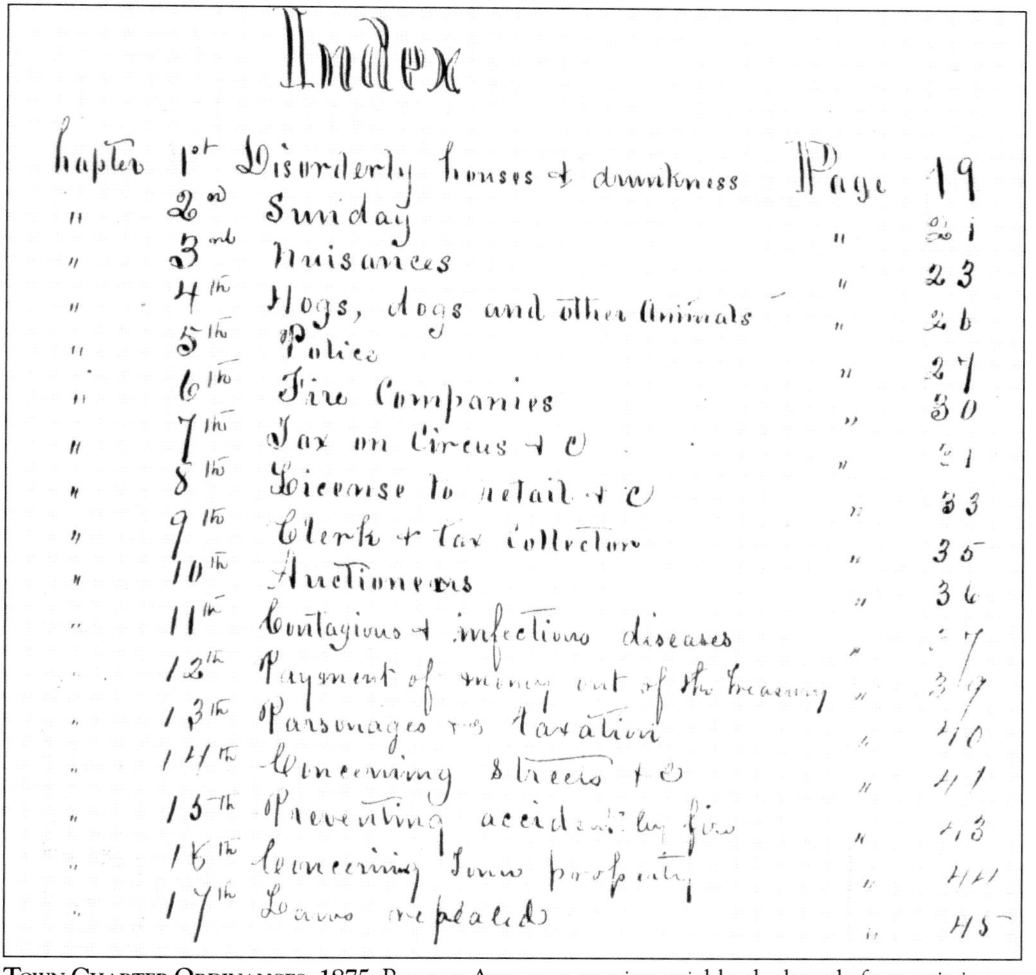

Index

TOWN CHARTER ORDINANCES, 1875. Because Apex was growing quickly, the board of commissioners drafted town ordinances. The first ordinance addressed disorderly houses and drunkenness. The first section stated, "Every person who shall keep a disorderly house, or house of ill fame, within the limits of the Town of Apex . . . shall forfeit and pay ten dollars for every day the house is so kept." (Courtesy of the Town of Apex.)

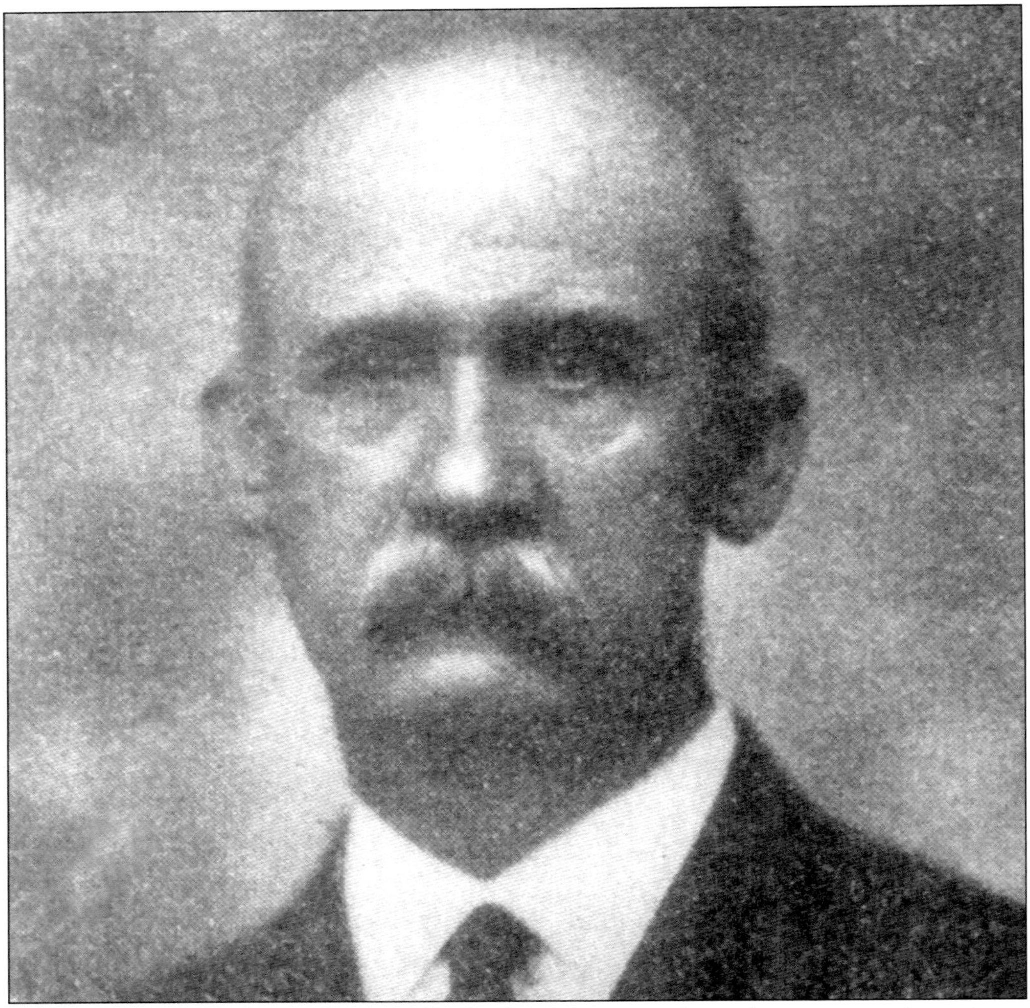

William Francis Utley. Utley was a lumber businessman and merchant in town, but prior to that he served in the Civil War until he lost his right leg. Although he was a one-legged marshal, Utley had no trouble enforcing newly formed ordinances, including No. 2, which stated one could not play games on Sunday. Any proprietor of a 5-pin alley, 10-pin alley, or other sport ground permitting games to be played on Sunday forfeited $25. (Courtesy of Ann Grebing.)

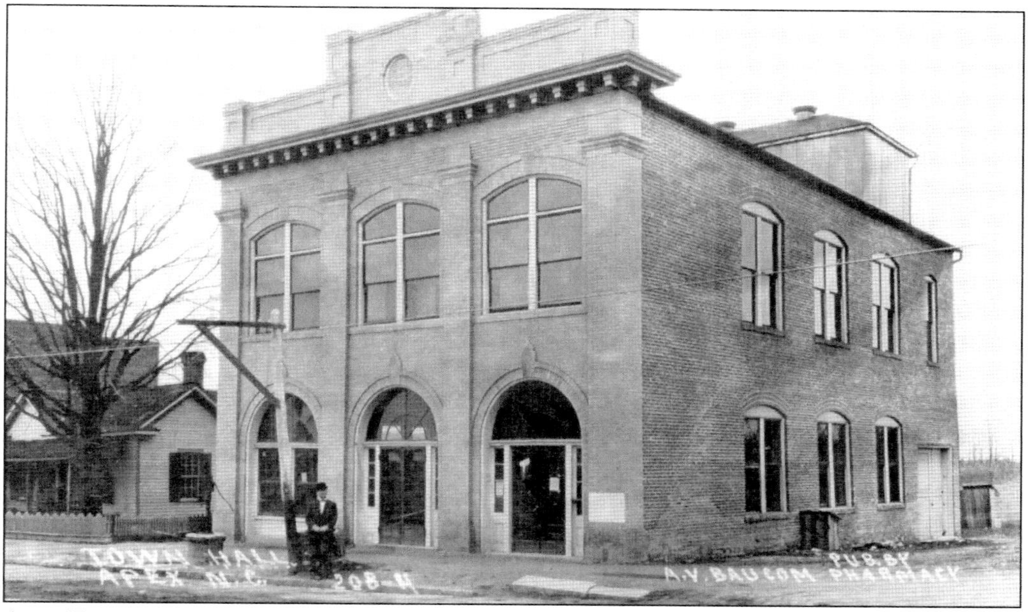

Apex Town Hall. As Apex continued to grow, city officials realized they needed a town hall. In 1912, a modern building was erected, which cost $7,500. It was two stories high and contained five market stalls, four prisoner cells, the mayor's office, a space for firefighting apparatus, and an auditorium with seating for about 200. The tower contained the town clock and a fire bell. The auditorium was used for plays, meetings, and a movie theater, which showed thrillers and comedies. There was also a piano so music could be played when the films broke down and were being repaired. It remained the town hall until 1979, when a new building was erected. (Above, courtesy of Ann Grebing; right, courtesy of the Town of Apex.)

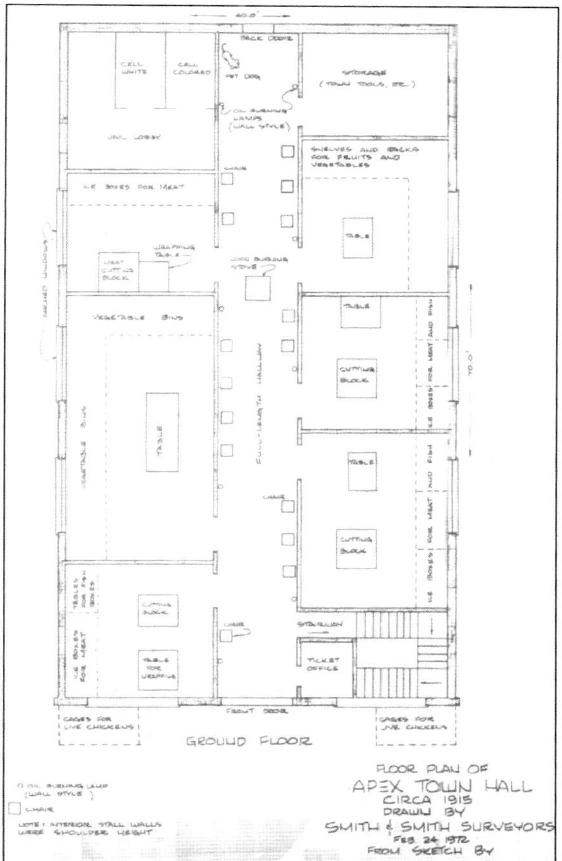

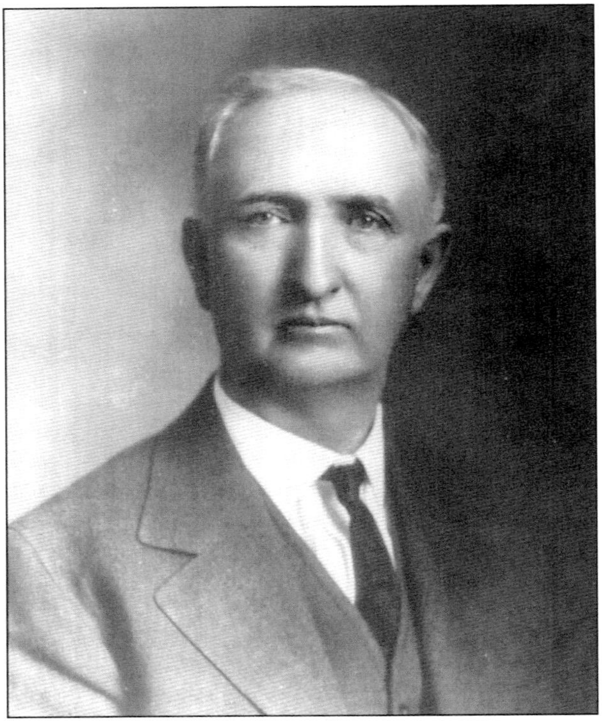

ADOLPHUS B. HUNTER. A. B. came to Apex in 1878 and was associated with W. H. Harward in the steam cotton gin they operated. They later partnered in a general store called Harward and Hunter. In 1898, they peacefully dissolved their partnership. Hunter eventually ended up with his own business and was influential in many others in town. He served in the North Carolina House of Representatives and as mayor. (Courtesy of Ann Grebing.)

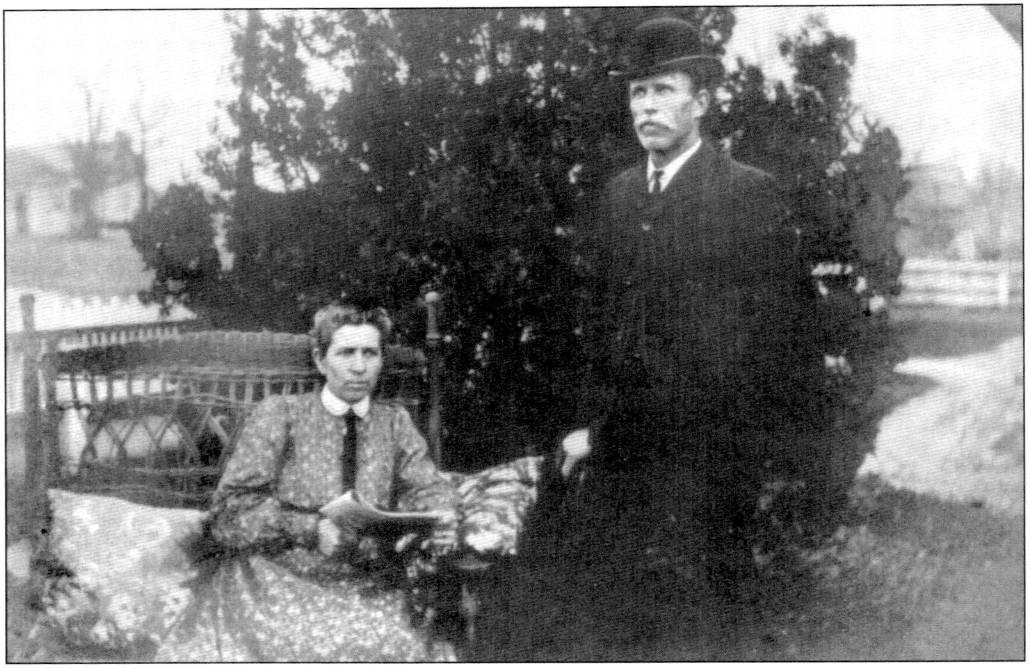

WILLIAM HENRY AND BURLENA HARWARD. W. H. was one of the first to buy part of Apex's downtown from Ellington. Harward and A. B. Hunter not only owned businesses in town, they also owned several vacant lots. Harward was also the president of the Merchants and Farmers Bank. Burlena Harward was the president of the Woman's Club in Apex in 1916. (Courtesy of Ann Grebing.)

Two

In and About Town

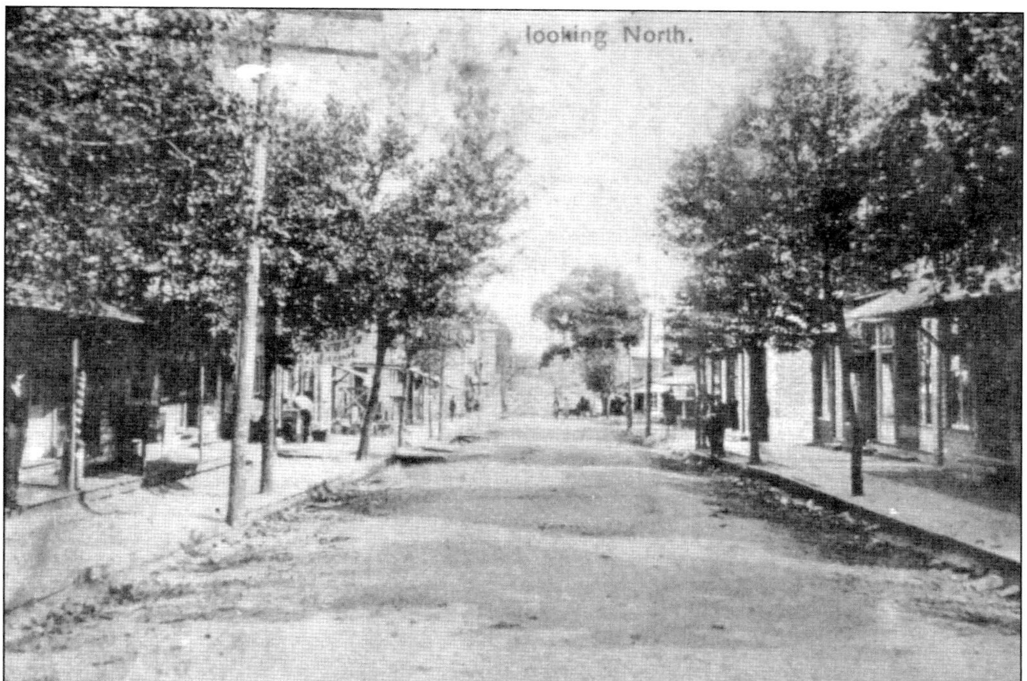

Salem Street, around 1900. This photograph shows Salem Street around 1900 looking north. It was taken before the 1905 fire, which destroyed a large portion of the downtown area. The buildings shown here are made of wood. Note all of the trees on the street. During this time, the streets were graded to make them smoother for horses, wagons, and pedestrians. (Courtesy of Ann Grebing.)

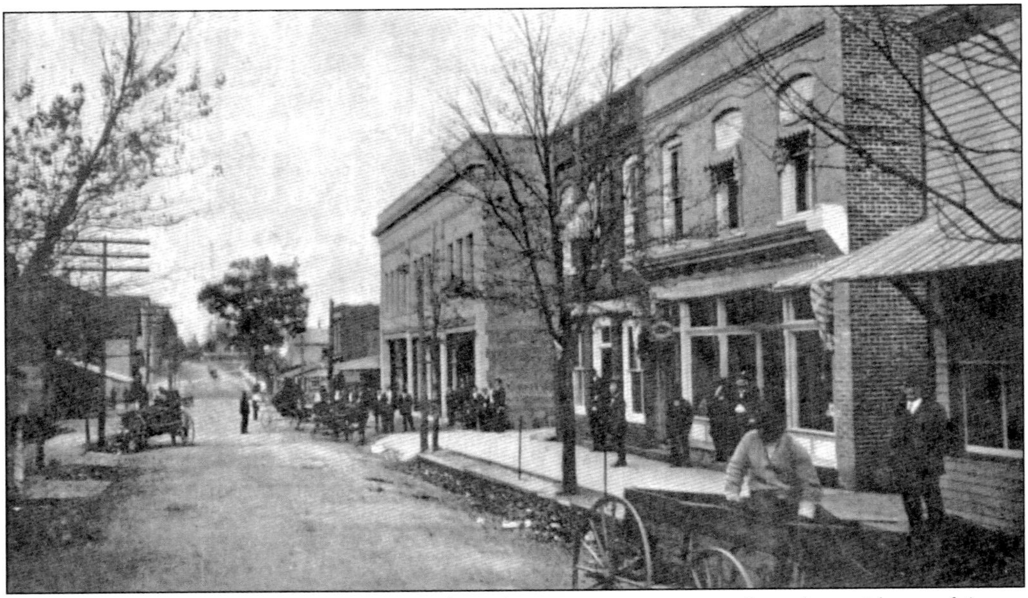

North Salem Street, around 1910. When the census man counted up the residents of Apex, he counted 680 people. This North Salem Street scene shows several of those men conducting business in the distance. Because photography during this time was unusual, there are several men who appear to be watching the photographer. (Courtesy of Ann Grebing.)

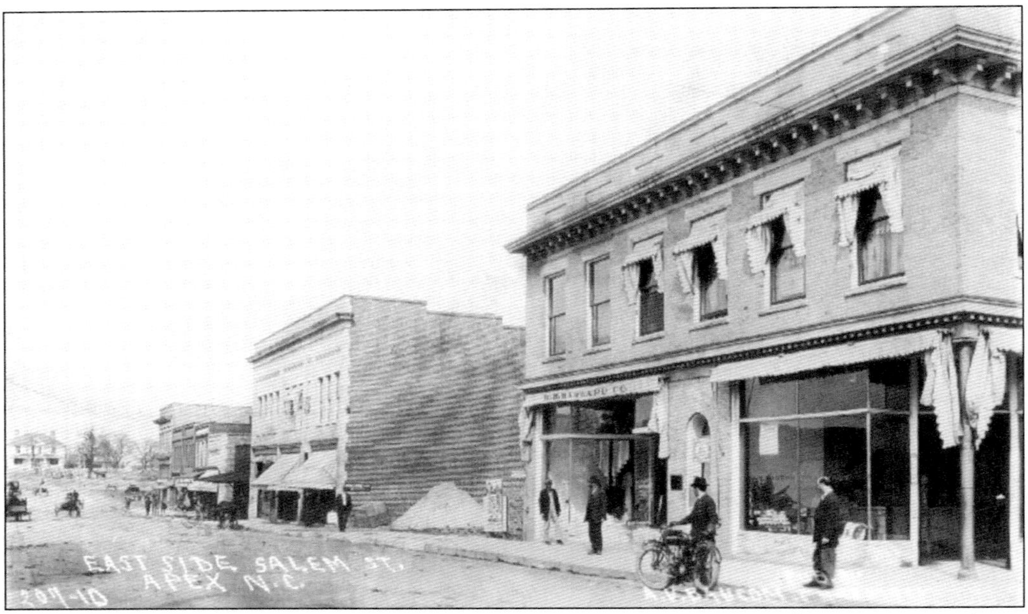

Salem Street, 1920s. These are nearly the same photographs, just taken a few years apart. This is the later view of North Salem Street looking to the north. Note the signs for the W. H. Harward Company and A. V. Baucom Pharmacy. (Courtesy of the Apex Volunteer Fire Department.)

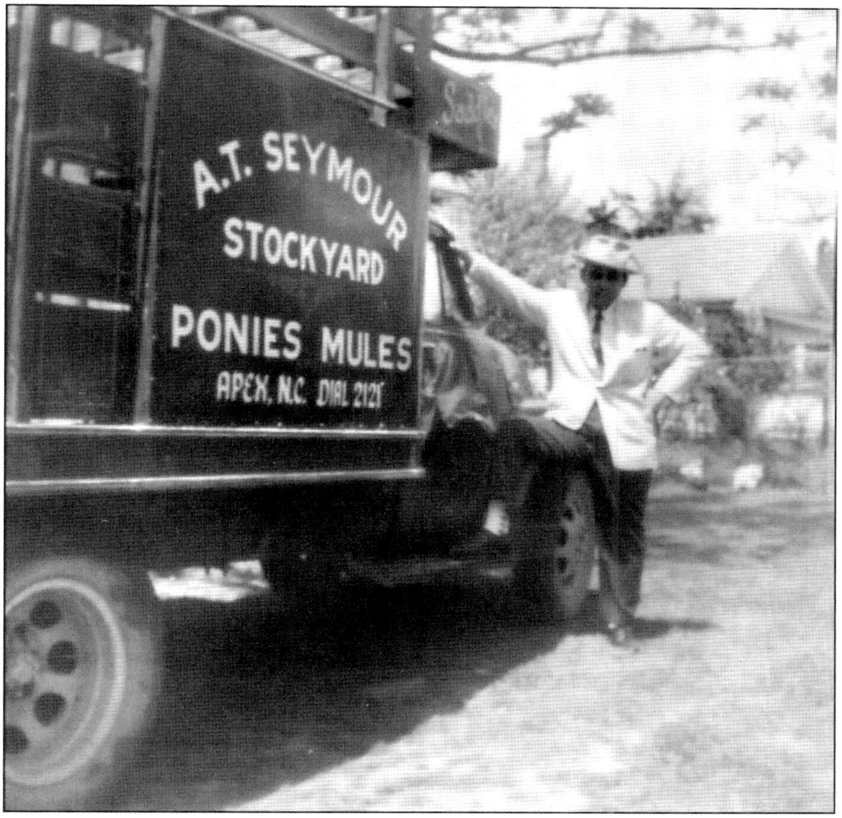

ALPHAEUS TEMPLE SEYMOUR. A. T. was born in Sanford in 1882. He arrived in Apex in 1910 and partnered with Samuel Watkins. They had the largest hardware store in town. They began their business in the Sellars building but quickly moved to their own building. They sold Benjamin Moore paints; Colt and Smith and Wesson pistols; and Winchester and Remington rifles. They also carried enamelware and stoves for the kitchen, farming items like barbed wire, and building materials, including cement, brick, shingles, and plaster. Later the two split, and A. T. opened up A. T. Seymour's Stockyards, where he sold horses and mules. (Both, courtesy of Susan Mills.)

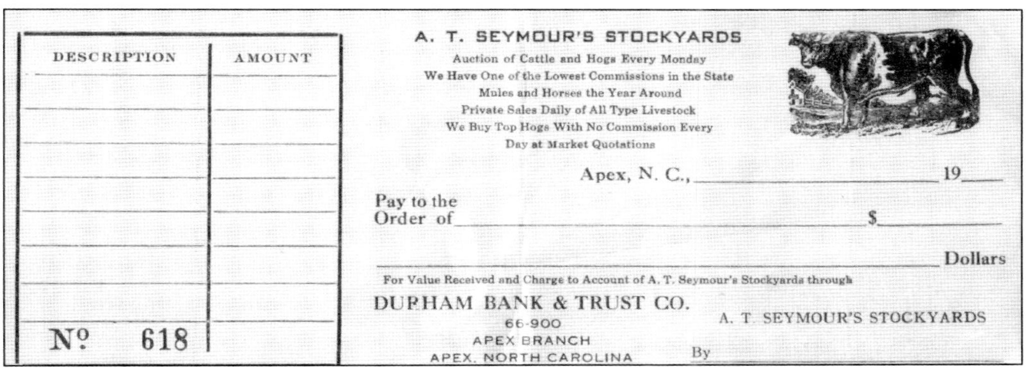

DESCRIPTION	AMOUNT
Nº 618	

A. T. SEYMOUR'S STOCKYARDS
Auction of Cattle and Hogs Every Monday
We Have One of the Lowest Commissions in the State
Mules and Horses the Year Around
Private Sales Daily of All Type Livestock
We Buy Top Hogs With No Commission Every
Day at Market Quotations

Apex, N. C., ____________ 19____

Pay to the
Order of ____________ $____________

____________ Dollars

For Value Received and Charge to Account of A. T. Seymour's Stockyards through

DURHAM BANK & TRUST CO.
66-900
APEX BRANCH
APEX, NORTH CAROLINA

A. T. SEYMOUR'S STOCKYARDS

By ____________

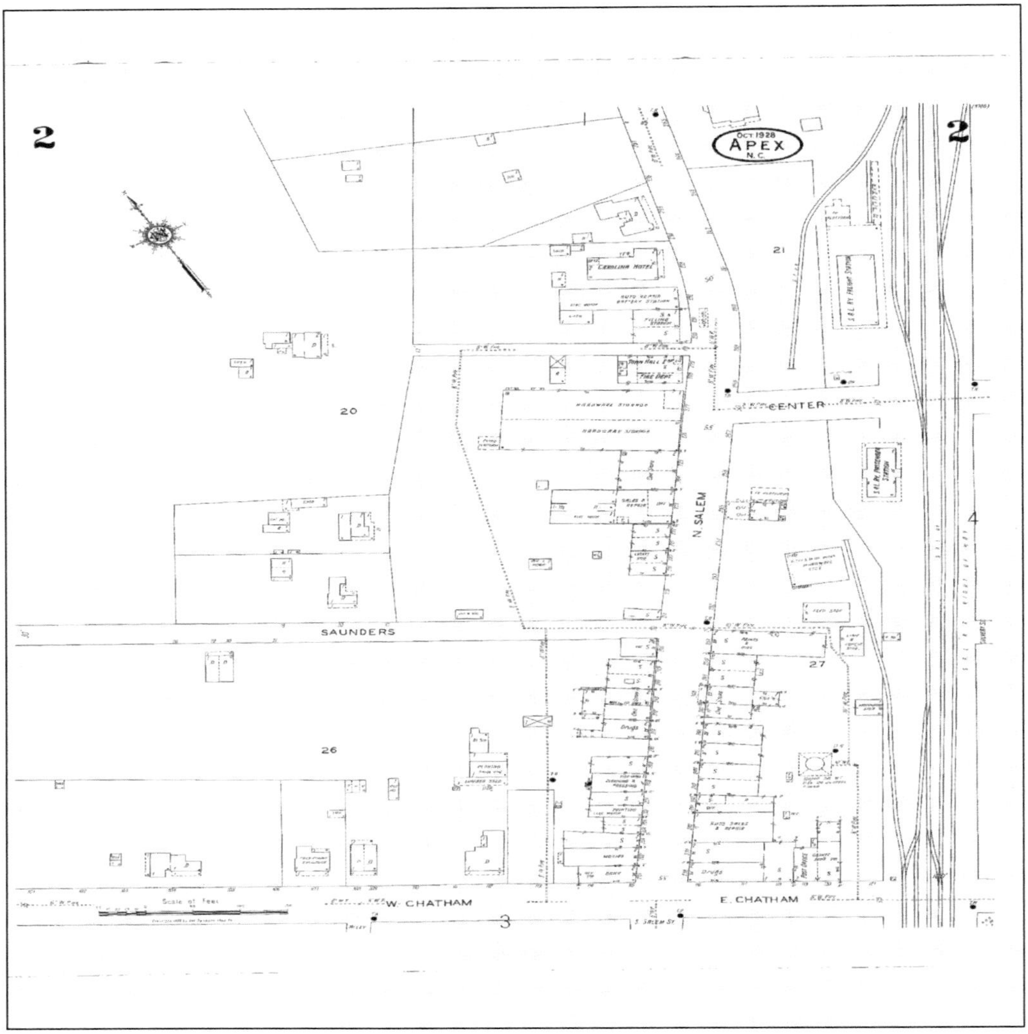

APEX SANBORN FIRE MAP, 1928. Founded in 1867 by D. A. Sanborn, the Sanborn Map Company was the primary American publisher of fire insurance maps for nearly 100 years. Extensive information on building use is given, ranging from symbols for generic terms such as stable, garage, and warehouse, to names of owners of factories and details on what was manufactured in them. In the case of large factories or commercial buildings, even individual rooms and their uses were recorded on the maps. Other features shown include pipelines, railroads, wells, dumps, and heavy machinery. The map details Apex's growth and improvements. It showed that the Apex Fire Department had 18 men, one chief, and one paid man on duty day and night. To fight fires, Apex had one American LaFrance truck consisting of a 600-gallon-per-minute pumper and 500 feet of hose. (Courtesy of the Wake County Public Library.)

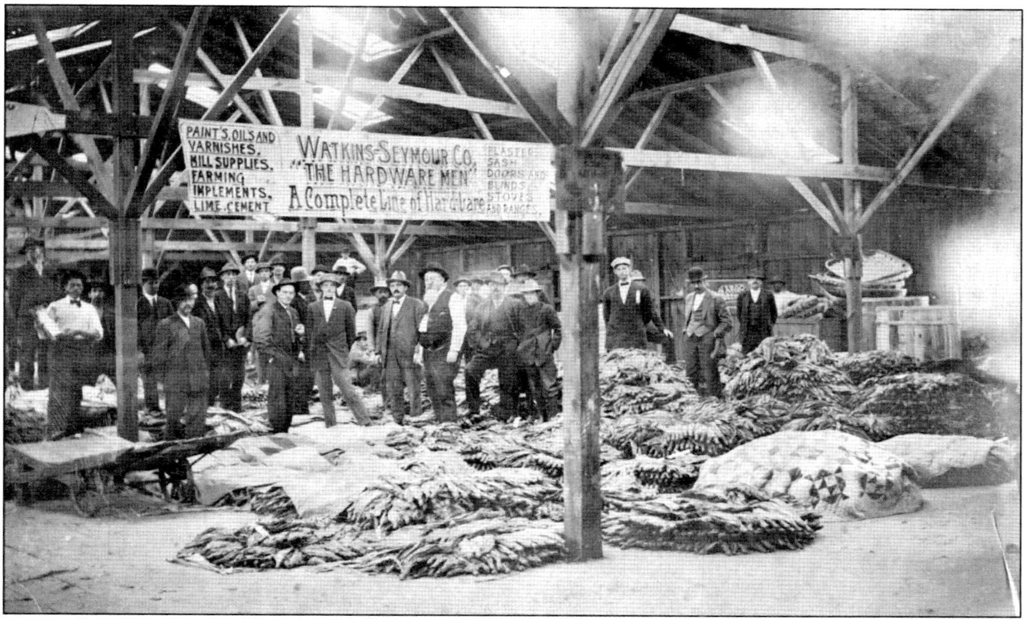

PLANTERS' WAREHOUSE. In 1900, W. B. Johnson and Sidney W. Stone formed the Planters' Warehouse for the purpose of auctioning tobacco. In 1911, Johnson sold his share of the business to Stone. Johnson then partnered with S. B. Currin at the Golden Leaf Warehouse. Stone wanted everyone to know that he was now the sole owner of the warehouse, so he took out an advertisement in the *Apex Journal.* "I do not feel it is necessary for me to introduce myself to the public as you all know me. . . . I was born on a farm and know what it means to raise a crop of tobacco. . . . Bring your first load of tobacco on to the Planters' Warehouse and you will find that Apex is the market and the Planters' Warehouse the place to sell your tobacco." (Both, courtesy of the Wake County Public Library.)

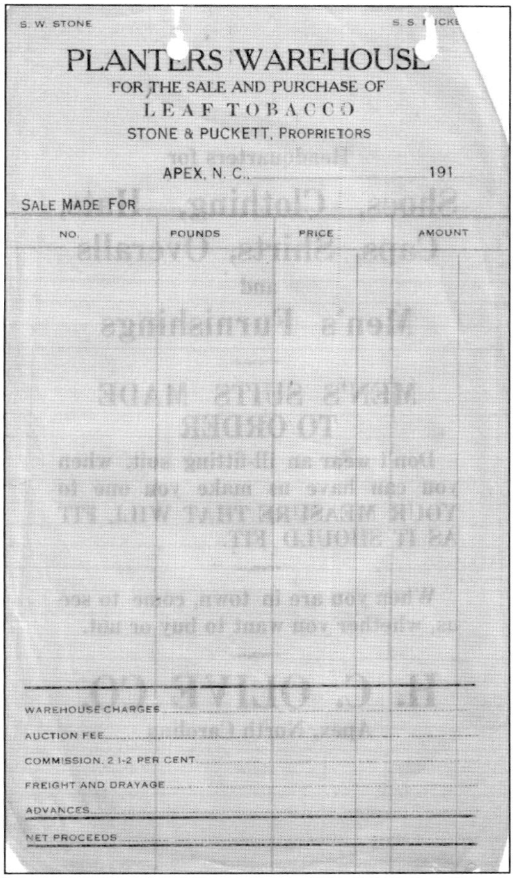
S. W. STONE S. S. [illegible]

PLANTERS WAREHOUSE
FOR THE SALE AND PURCHASE OF
LEAF TOBACCO
STONE & PUCKETT, PROPRIETORS

APEX, N. C., 191

SALE MADE FOR

NO.	POUNDS	PRICE	AMOUNT

WAREHOUSE CHARGES
AUCTION FEE
COMMISSION, 2 1-2 PER CENT.
FREIGHT AND DRAYAGE
ADVANCES
NET PROCEEDS

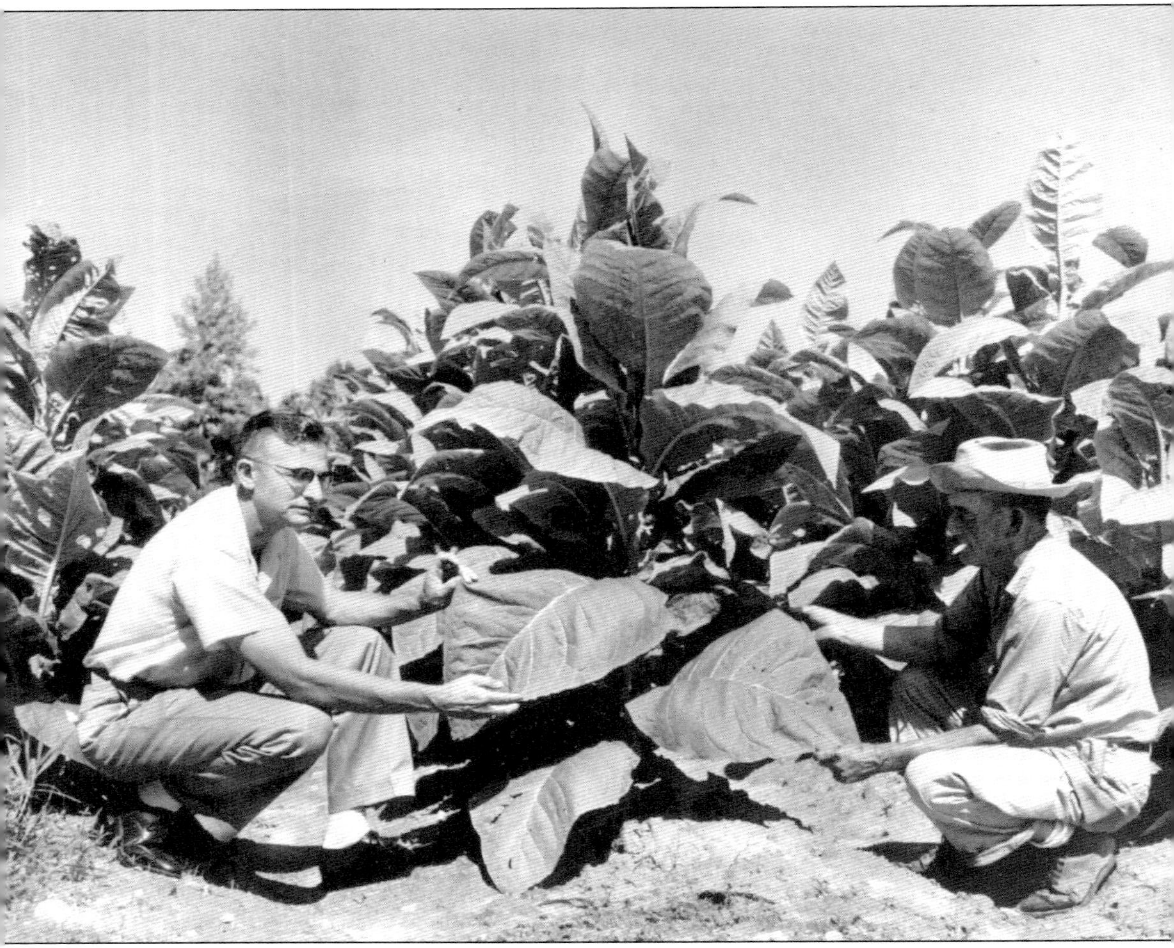

Tobacco. Local farmers inspect a tobacco crop. In 1911, Apex claimed it had gained a reputation for growing the best bright-leaf tobacco in the world. When the 1911 market opened, it brought more than 20,000 pounds with an average price of 12¢ per pound. (Courtesy of Bob Crowley.)

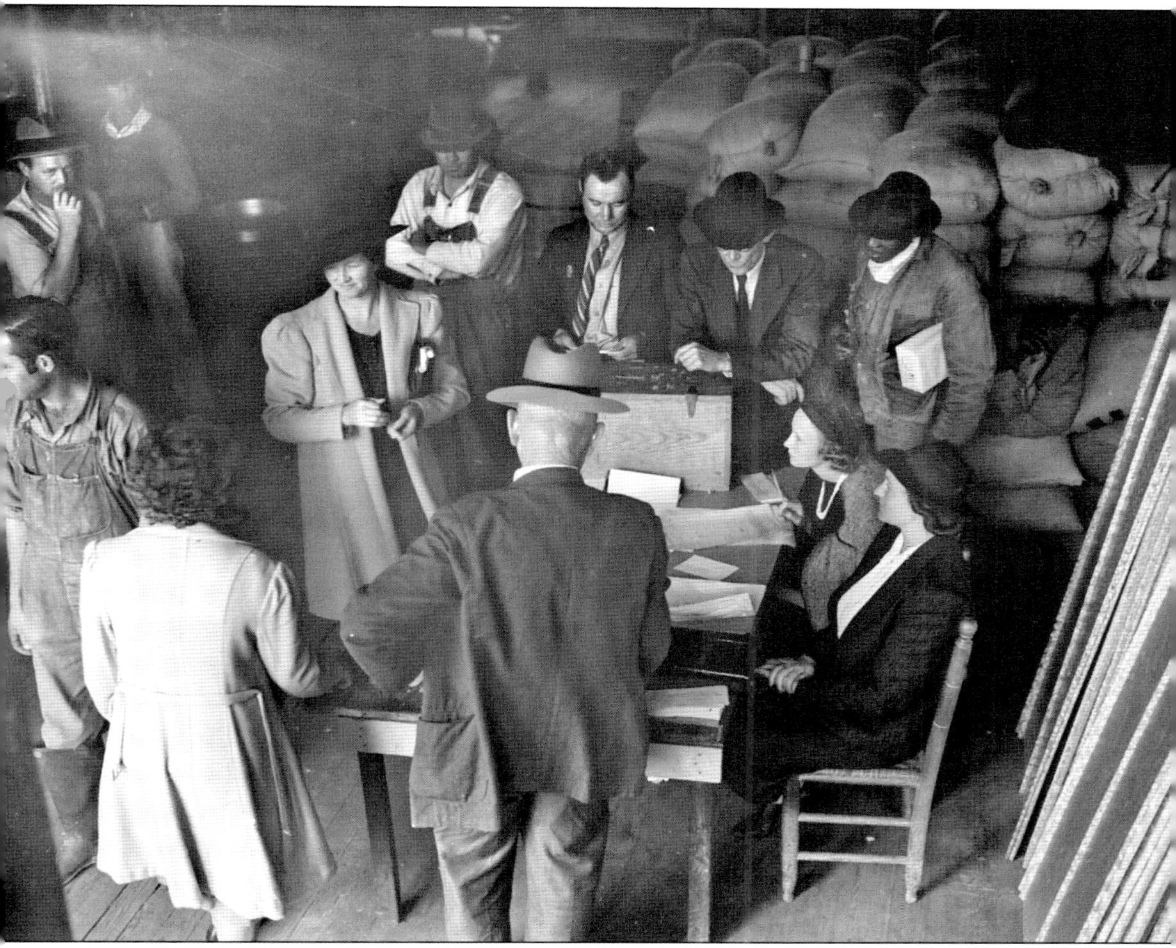

VOTING ON TOBACCO CONTROL. In 1939, the state's conservation and development team traveled all over North Carolina in an effort to promote and bring business to the state. This photograph was taken in Apex while people voted on tobacco control. (Courtesy of the North Carolina State Archives.)

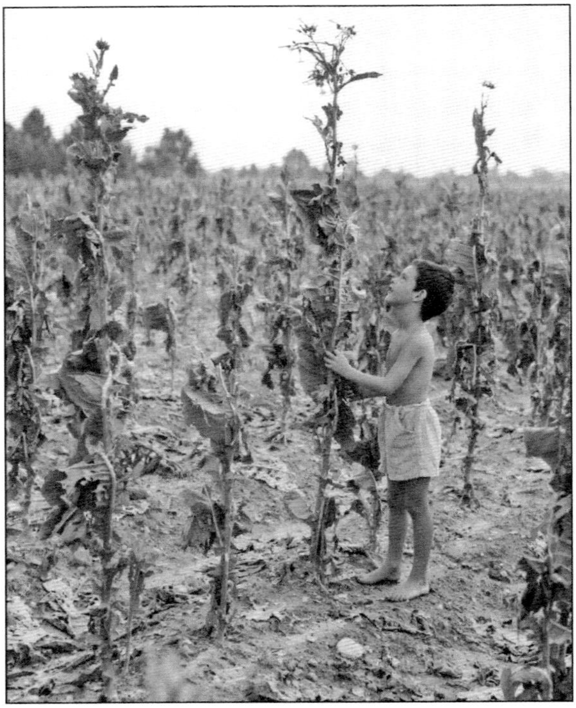

INSPECTING TOBACCO. In 1951, a hail and wind storm hit western Wake County. Pictured here is six-year-old Billy Stephens. He is assessing the damage, which ended up being a 100-percent loss. The tobacco was to be harvested in a few days. (Courtesy of Tommy Stephens and Janet Davis.)

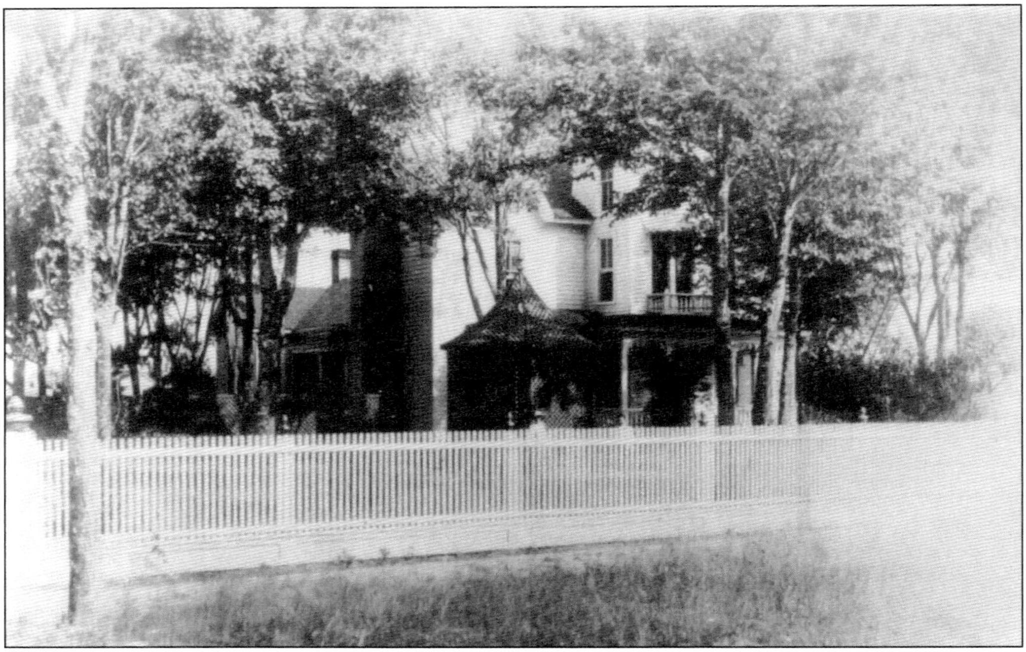

JESSE A. NORRIS HOME. Jesse Norris bought this house from John McC. Ellington in 1880. The home's interior was adorned with oil paintings in gilt and walnut frames. The house had tall slender windows, which reached from ceiling to floor. Jesse's daughter Maude recalled, "In those days, there were no screens, so people just walked in and out of the windows as they would through doors." (Courtesy Ann Grebing.)

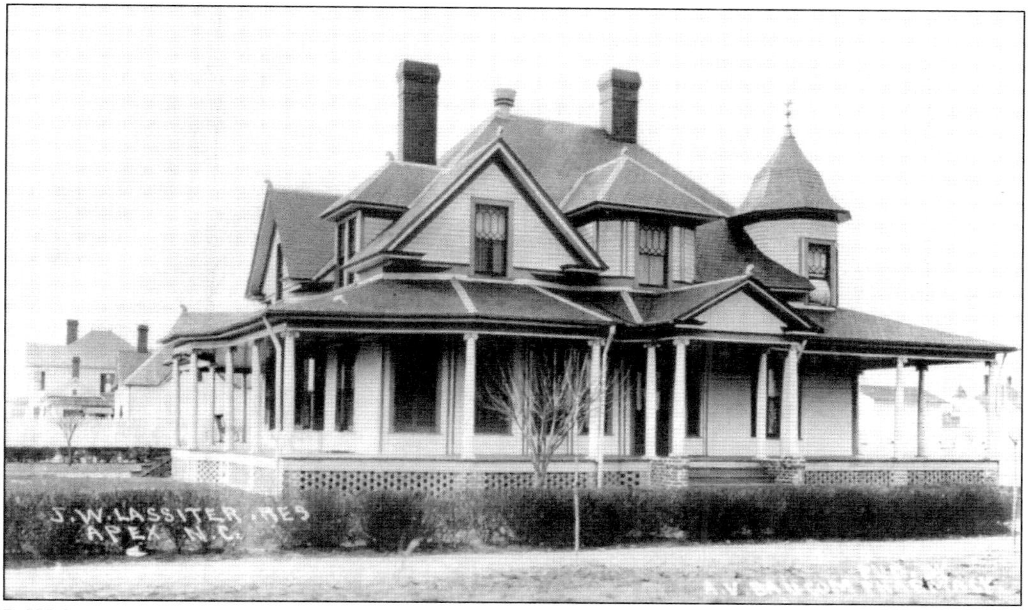

J. W. Lassiter Home. In 1909, J. W. "June" Lassiter opened the Apex Mule and Supply Company. He was the general manager in charge of procuring and selling mules and horses for the store. This home was built in 1905 and is situated on 303 East Moore Street. (Courtesy of Ann Grebing.)

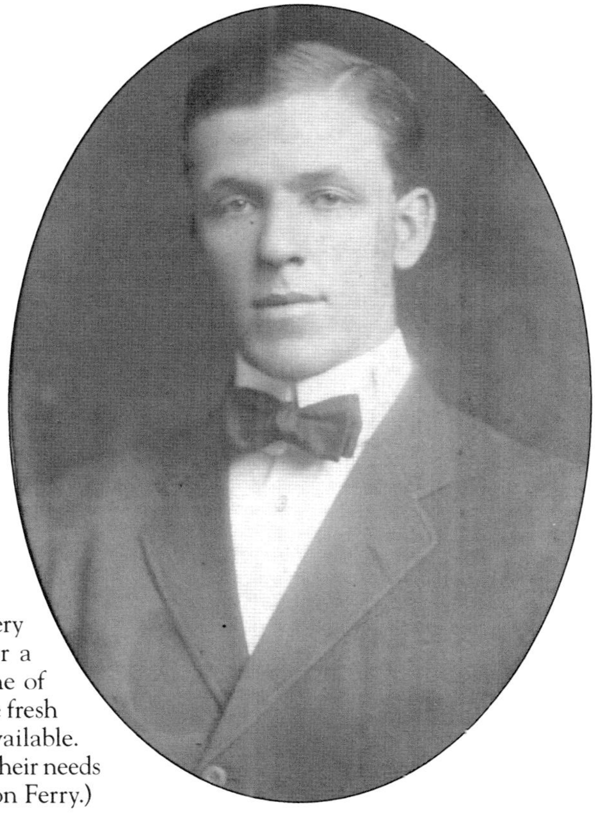

Howard C. Benton. H. C. owned a grocery store in Apex and was in business for a number of years. His store carried a line of general groceries and had a market where fresh meats, frozen foods, and seafood were available. Patrons could also have them prepared as their needs warranted. (Courtesy of Margaret Benton Ferry.)

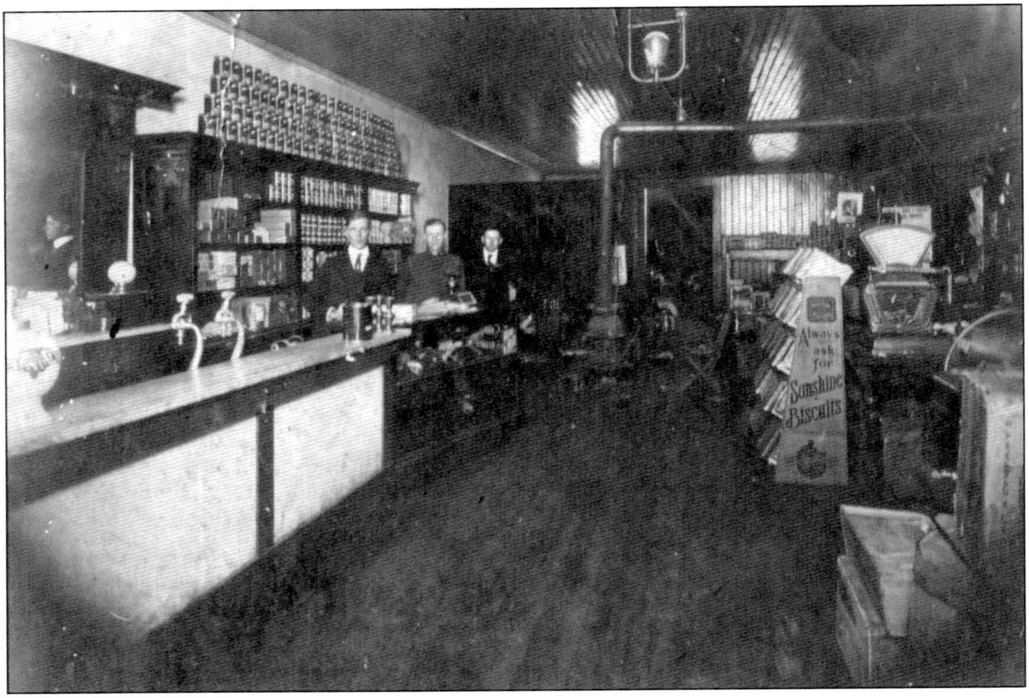

H. C. Benton's Store. In addition to his retail business, Benton also ran a wholesale sausage business. Benton found time to participate in social activities in Apex. Howard Benton was the master of the Apex Masonic Lodge and was a president of the Apex Lions' Club. The men in the photograph above are, from left to right, H. C. Benton, Whit Benton, and Burtis Benton. (Both, courtesy of Margaret Benton Ferry.)

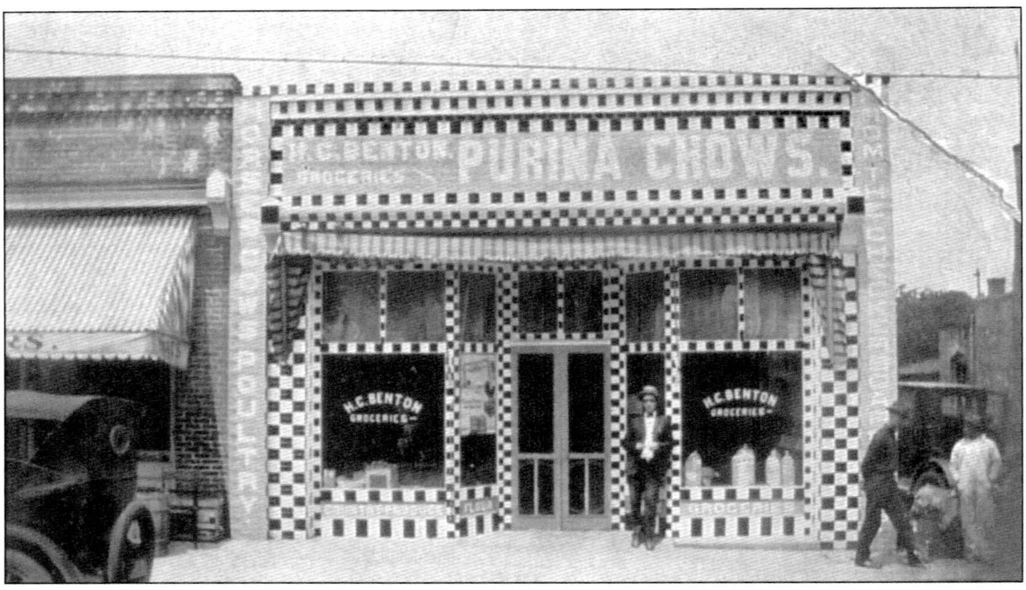

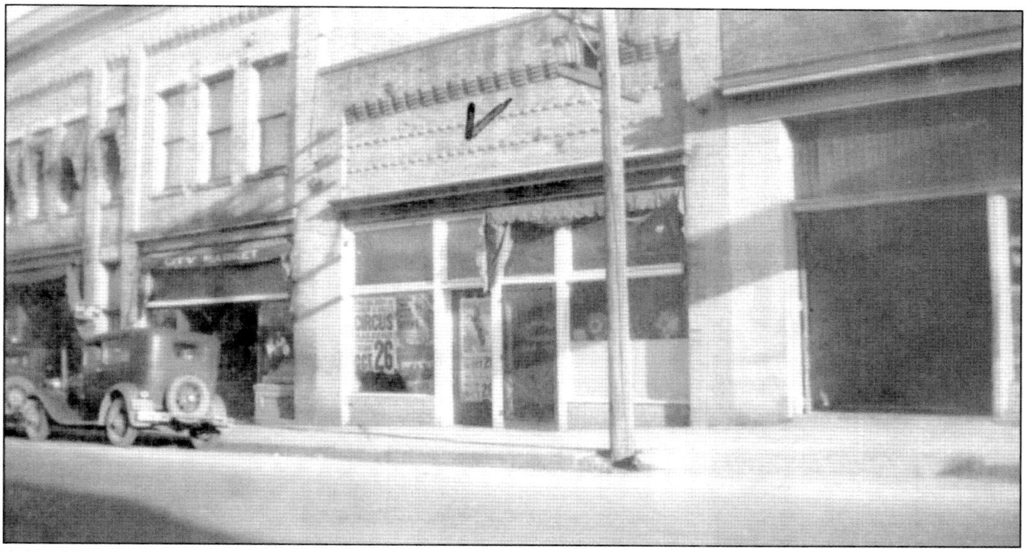

J. R. Harward Store. John was the son of W. H. and eventually joined his father's business. He kept the family tradition of selling the finest goods and kept the Harward name in the good graces within the community. (Courtesy of Ann Grebing.)

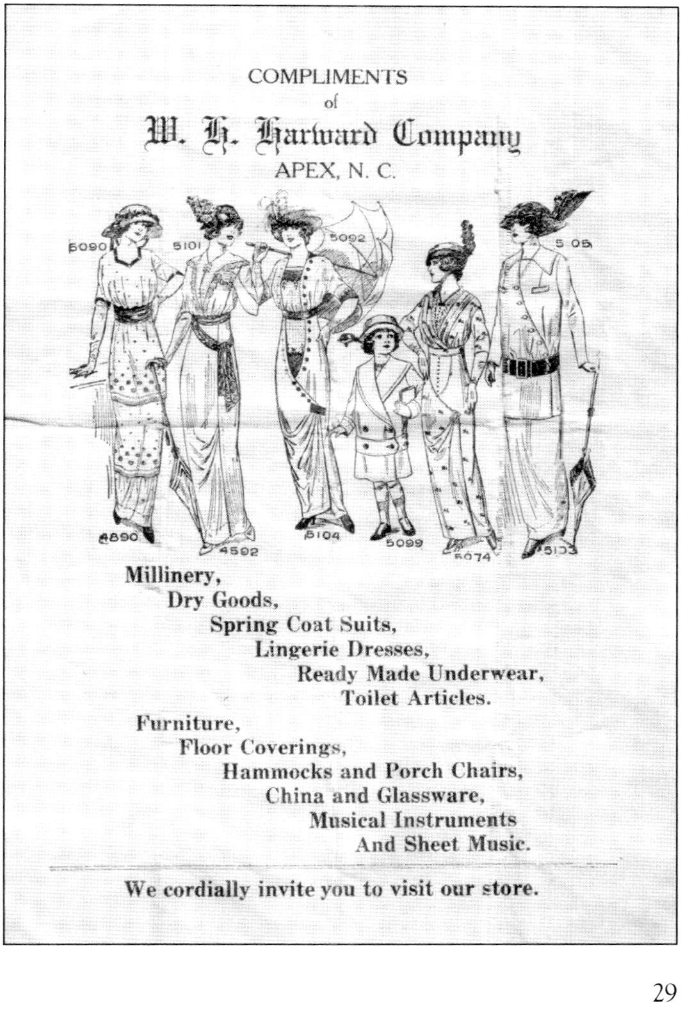

W. H. Harward Advertisement. Harward was a business partner for about 23 years with A. B. Hunter. He eventually opened his own store, where he catered to the town's needs and stylish trends. The W. H. Harward Company offered clothing, furniture, kitchen and dinner wares, and musical instruments. (Courtesy of the Wake County Public Library.)

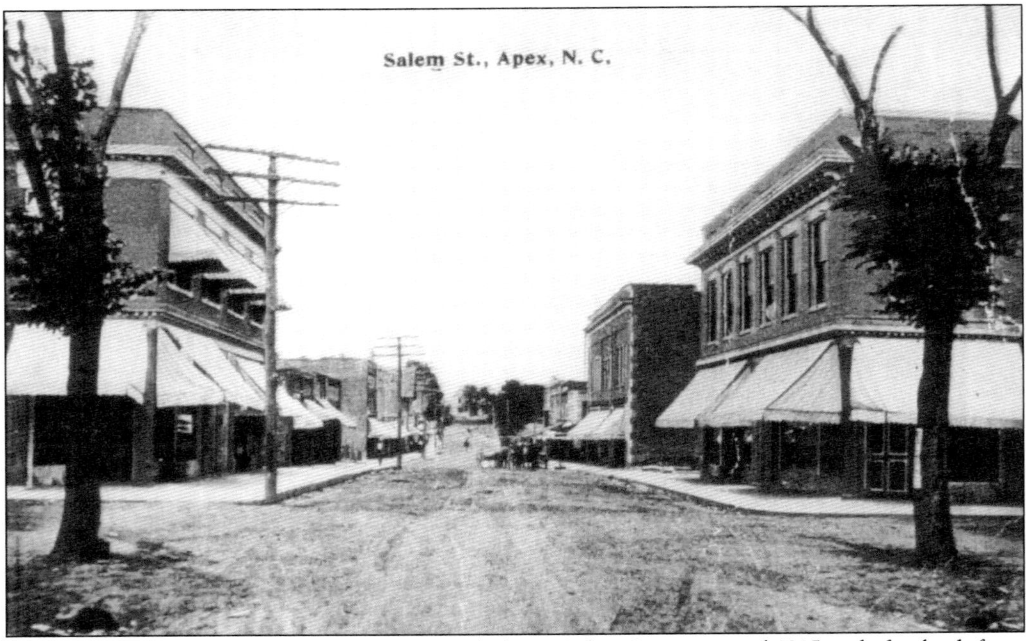

SALEM STREET, AROUND 1915. This photograph shows Salem Street around 1915 and after both fires. Notice the lack of trees, which were seen in pre-fire photographs. (Courtesy of Ann Grebing.)

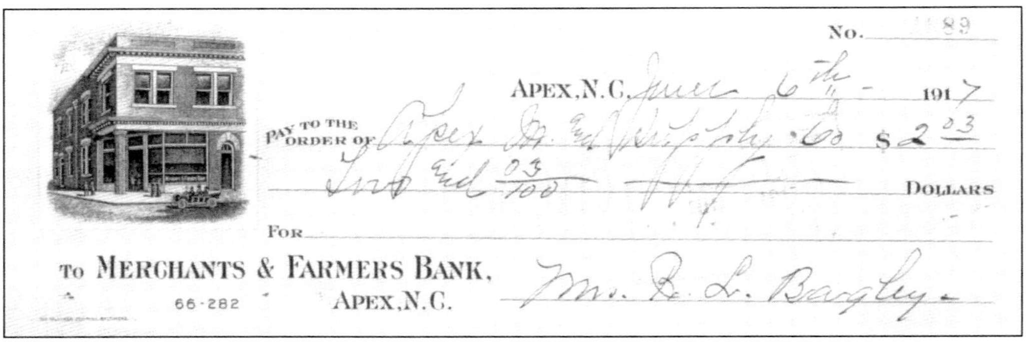

MERCHANTS AND FARMERS BANK OF APEX. J. B. Mason of Durham established the bank in 1905. He secured the cooperation of Lindsay and Percy Olive, and they enlisted support from prominent townsmen, who then established the bank. (Courtesy of the Wake County Library.)

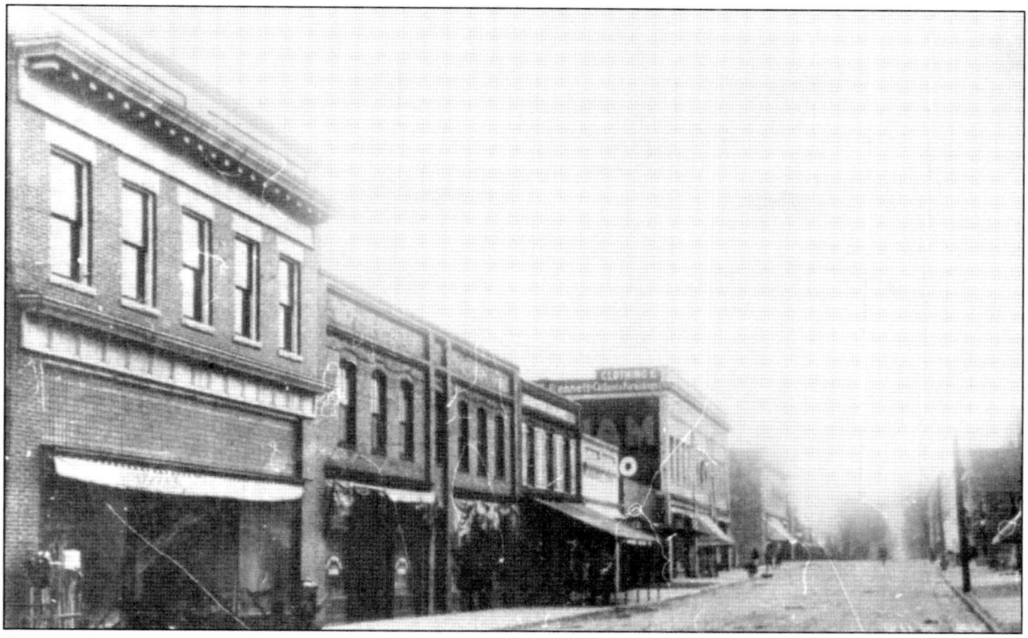

Salem Street Views. These street scenes represent two different eras in Apex's history. The photograph above is from the late 1800s or early 1900s and shows both brick and frame buildings. The first building on the left is the Watkins-Seymour Company hardware store, and farther down the street was the Bennett Company, which furnished gentlemen's clothing. The photograph below is from the 1920s and shows how Apex progressed with its buildings and businesses. After the 1905 fire, all buildings in town were required to be made of brick. (Both, courtesy of Ann Grebing.)

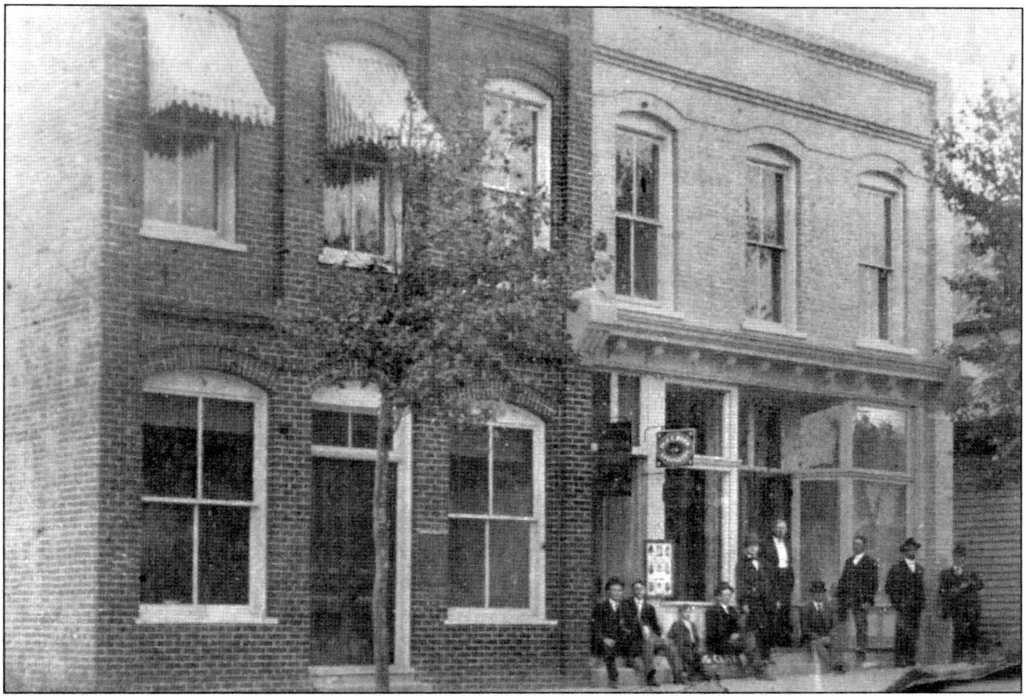

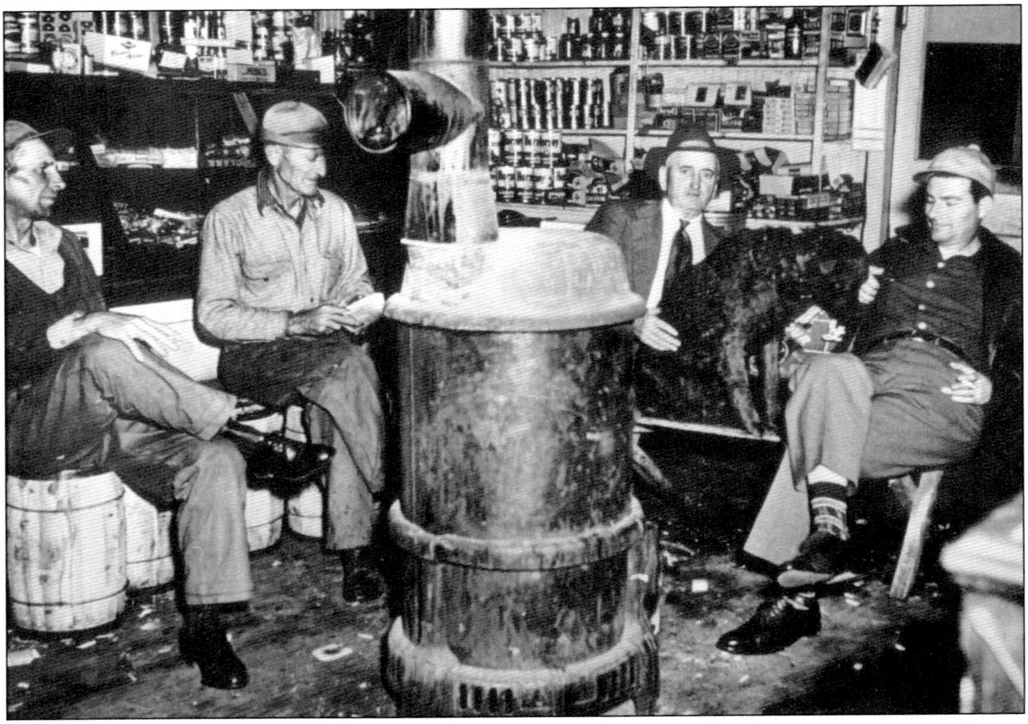

Apex Store, 1940s. This photograph shows men sitting around a downtown store in Apex. From left to right are unidentified, Clee Scott, Ted Seawell and his dog, and Glen Goodwin. (Courtesy of Ann Grebing.)

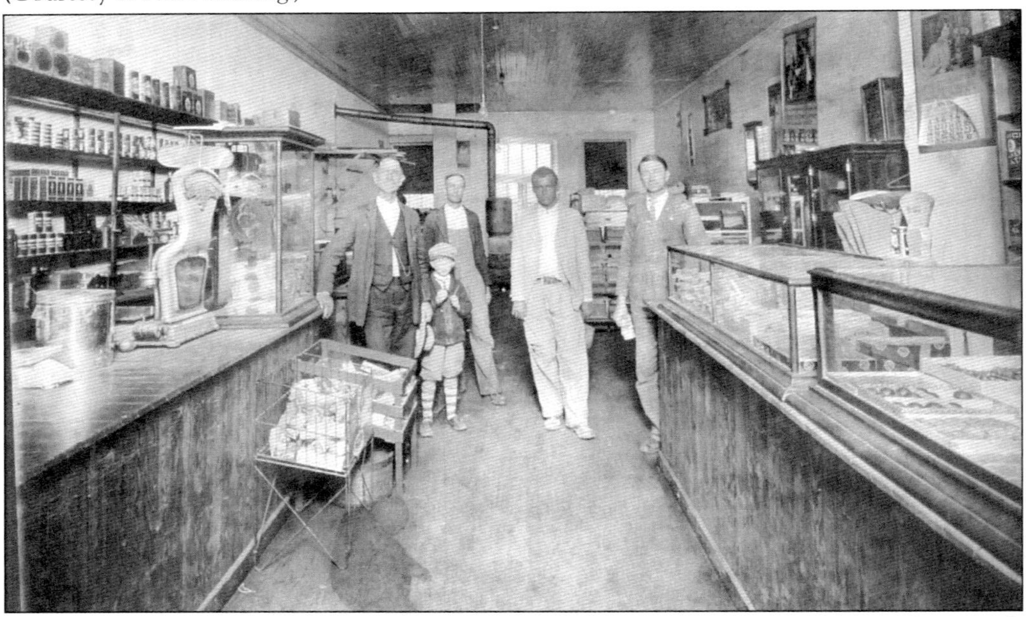

Apex Store, around 1923. This is the interior of an Apex store. The men in the photograph are, from left to right, Hugh Campbell, an unidentified boy, Bobby Maynard, "John," and Cyrus Maynard. (Courtesy of Ann Grebing.)

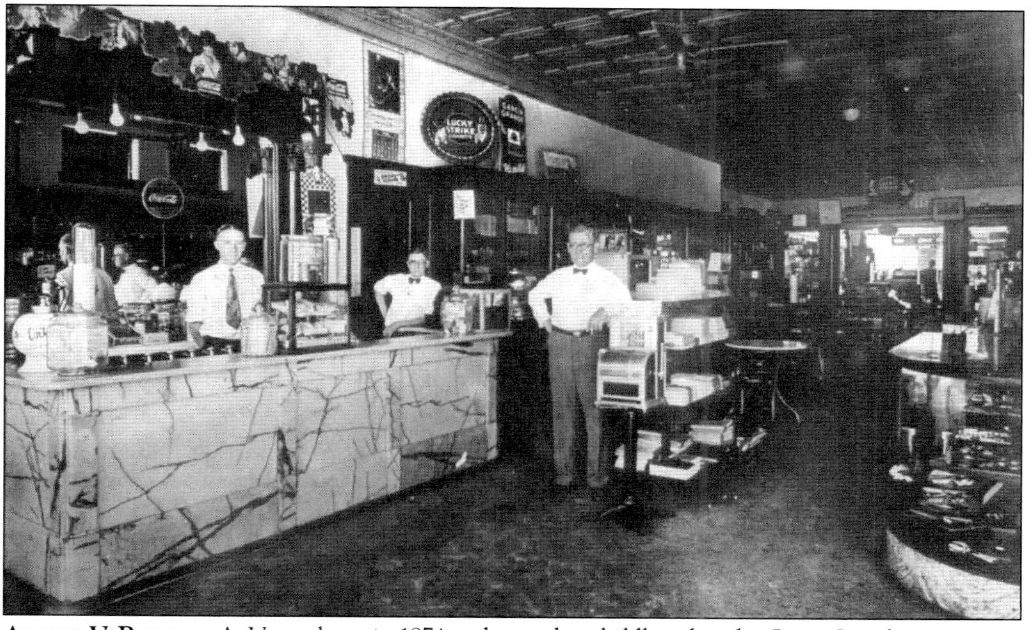

Alfred V. Baucom. A. V. was born in 1874 and spent his childhood in the Green Level community. He attended the pharmaceutical department at the University of North Carolina. In 1900, he opened a drug business with W. H. Harward and A. B. Hunter. In 1910, he purchased the entire interest in the company and called it the A. V. Baucom Pharmacy. He lost his business to the 1911 fire and soon rebuilt it on W. H. Harward's old location. The new brick edifice included a soda fountain and solid onyx counters. He sold jewelry, cut glass, and silverware, which were displayed in a mirror case opposite the fountain. A. V. is pictured above on the far right. (Above, courtesy of Apex Volunteer Fire Department; below, courtesy of the North Carolina State Archives.)

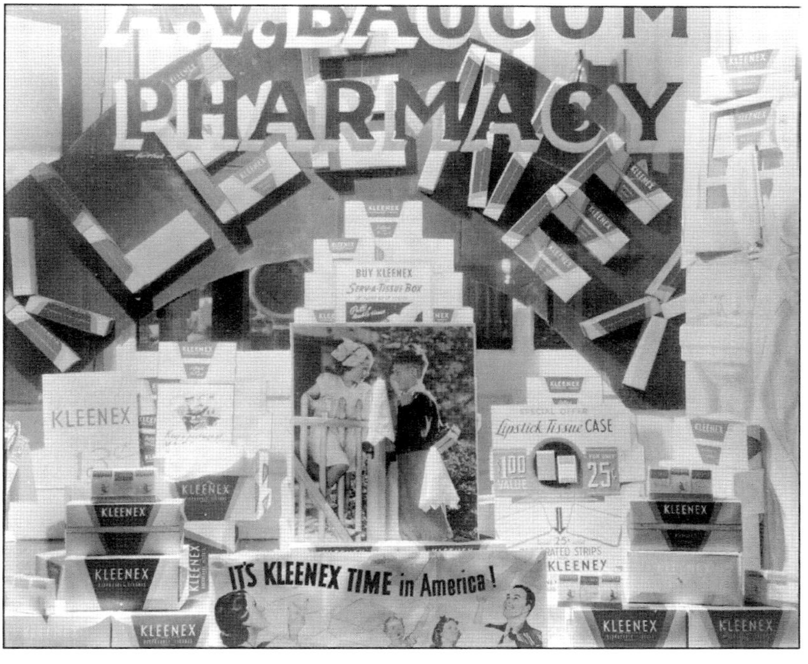

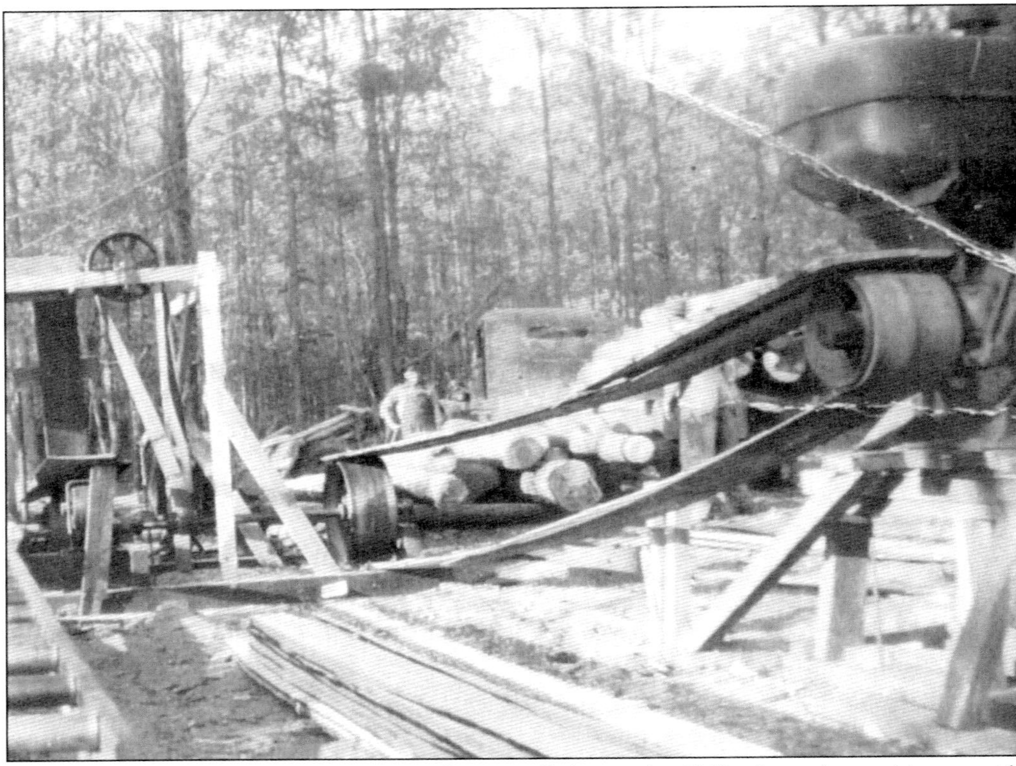

Penny Sawmill. Larry B. Penny operated a sawmill during the 1940s. It was located just outside the Apex city limits. (Both, courtesy of Ann Grebing.)

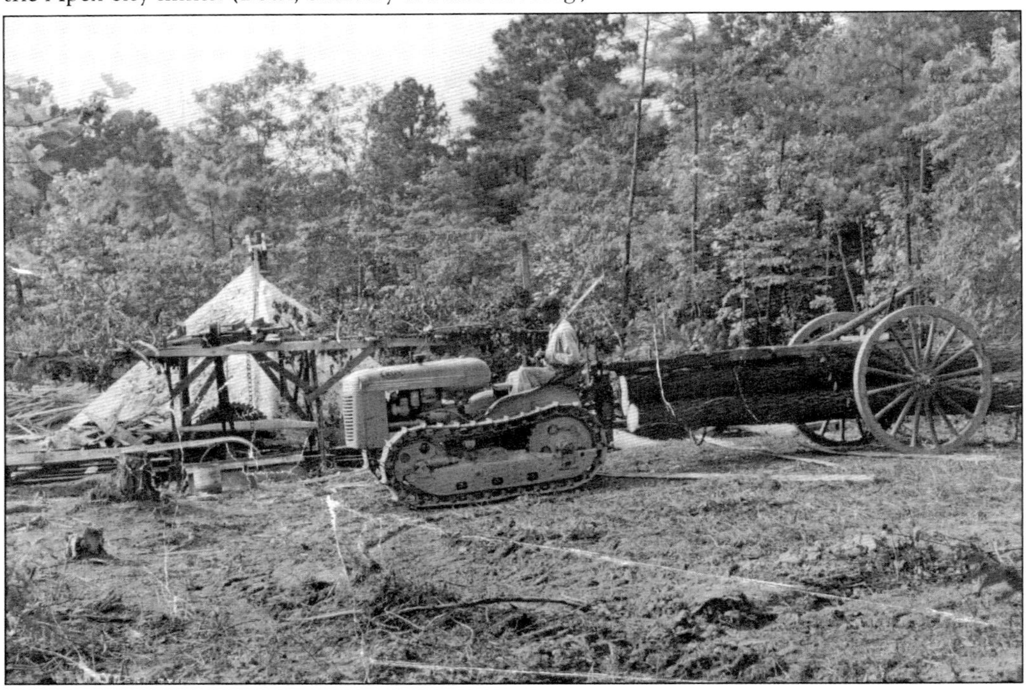

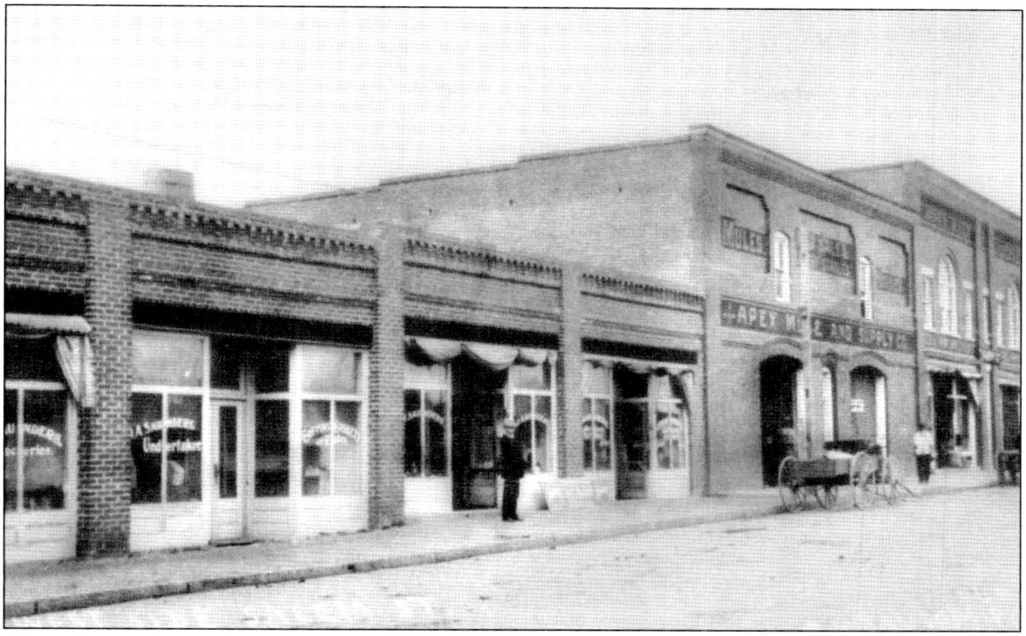

West Side of Salem Street, 1920s. This photograph shows the Apex Mule and Supply Company. The one-story section housed the offices of D. A. Saunders, who was Apex's first undertaker. (Courtesy of the Apex Volunteer Fire Department.)

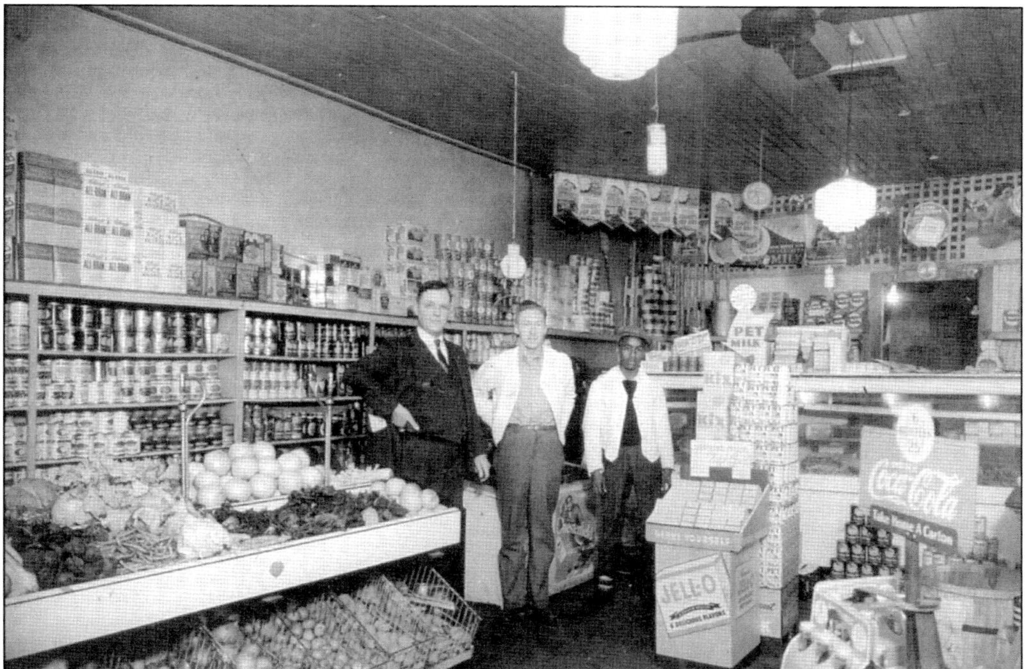

H. C. Benton Store, around 1939. This picture shows the inside of H. C. Benton's store in 1939. From left to right are H. C. Benton, Bruce Benton, and John Terry. (Courtesy of Margaret Benton Ferry.)

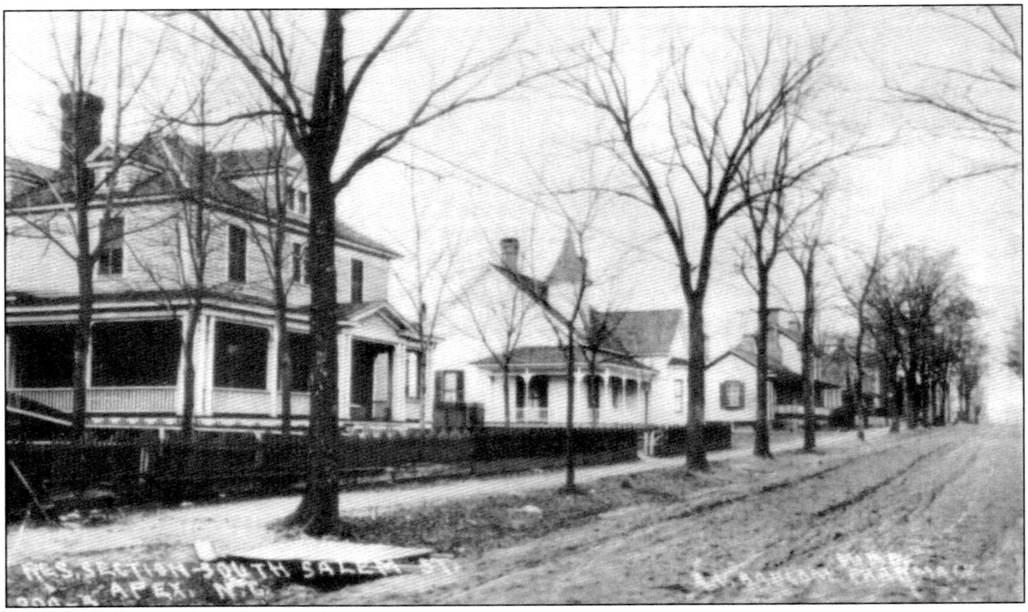

South Salem Street, 1910s. South Salem Street is the section where many stately residential homes and churches were located. (Both, courtesy of Ann Grebing.)

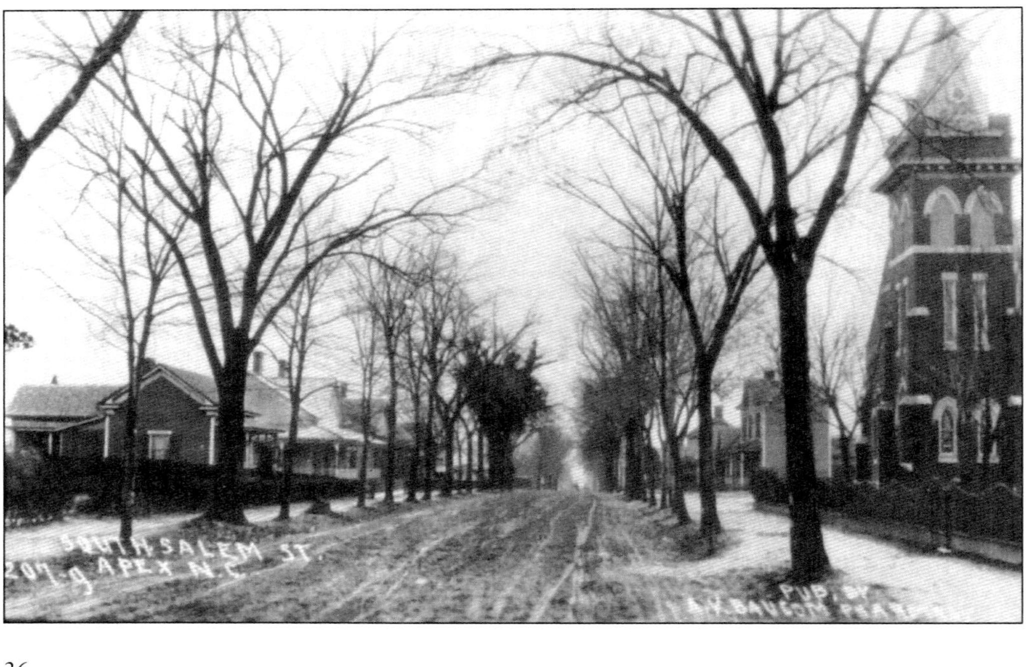

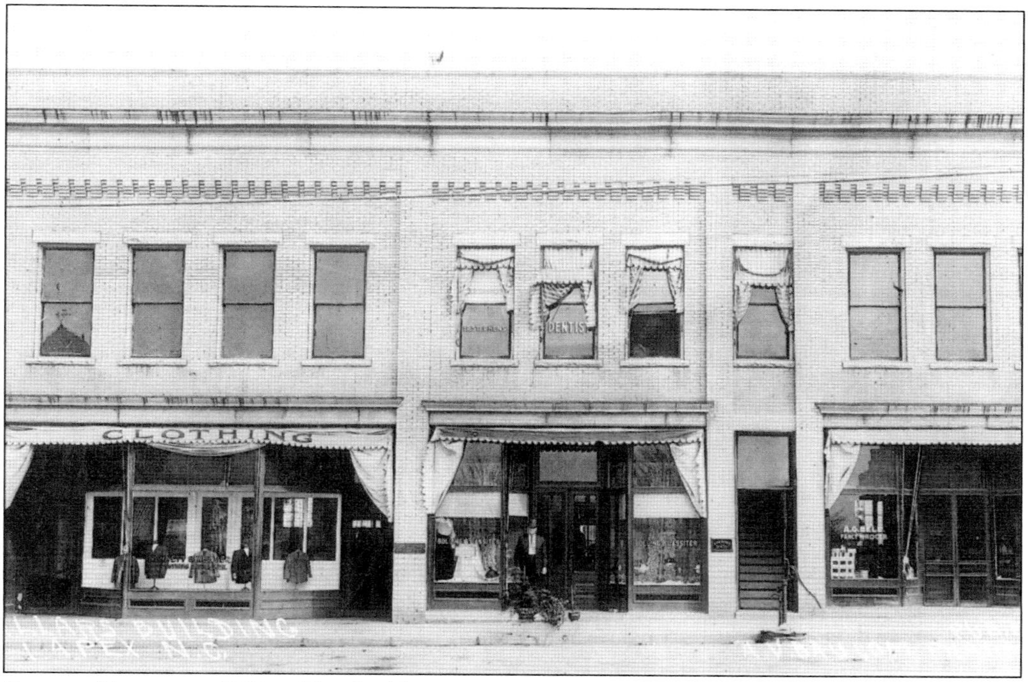

SELLARS BUILDING, 1920S. This building housed many businesses, including Watkins-Seymour, Bennett and Weaver, Dr. Romulus Stephens, Bolling and Lassiter, and A. G. Bell. Dr. Stephens is visible in the open upstairs window. Charles Sellars served as mayor, president of the Dixie Land Company, director of the Merchants and Farmers Bank, and director of the Apex Land and Improvement Company. (Courtesy of Ann Grebing.)

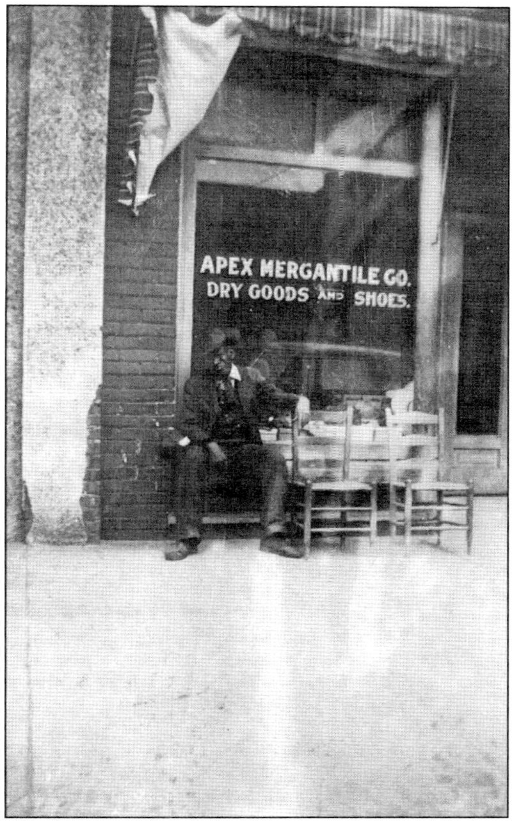

APEX MERCANTILE COMPANY. It began operating in 1910 and was run by George Upchurch. W. B. Upchurch was president. The store offered dry goods, millinery, shoes, furniture, and groceries. It also carried caskets and coffins. The man in the photograph is a Mr. Booker, who could not speak. (Courtesy of Ann Grebing.)

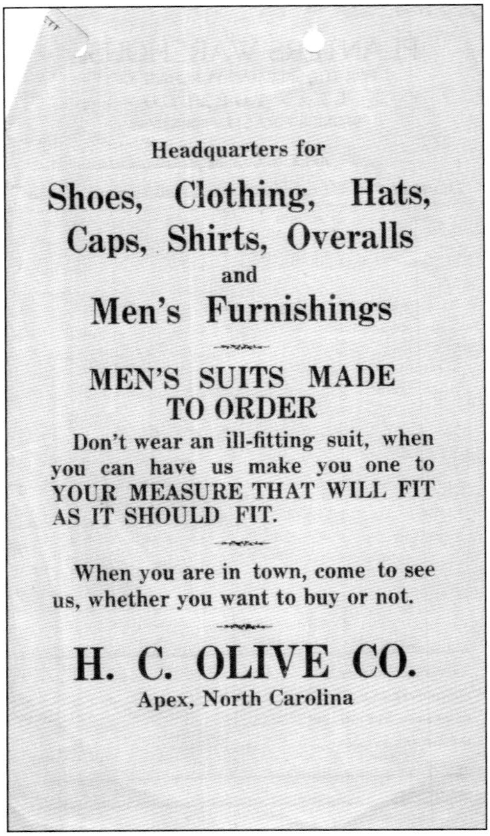

H. C. Olive Store Advertisement. Although Henry Calvin Olive was no longer alive, his sons kept the family tradition of offering nothing but the finest to Apex's citizens. In this advertisement, they are claiming that no one should have to wear an ill-fitting suit when all they had to do was visit their store. (Courtesy of the Wake County Public Library.)

Seaboard Air Line Railroad. One of Apex's citizens poses in front of the caboose for the Seaboard Air Line in the 1950s. (Courtesy of North Carolina State Archives.)

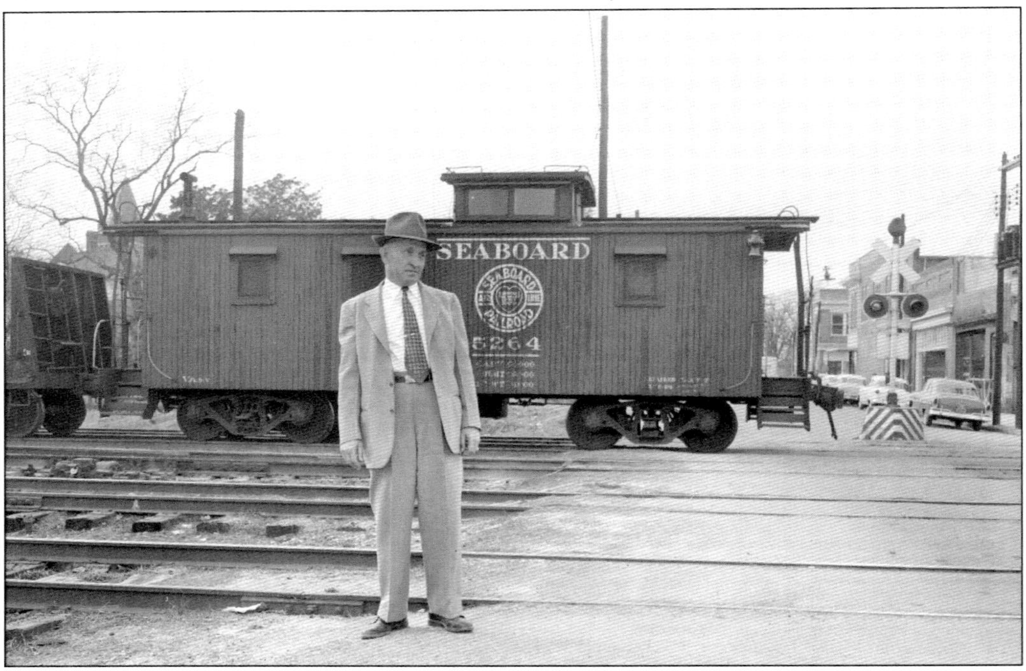

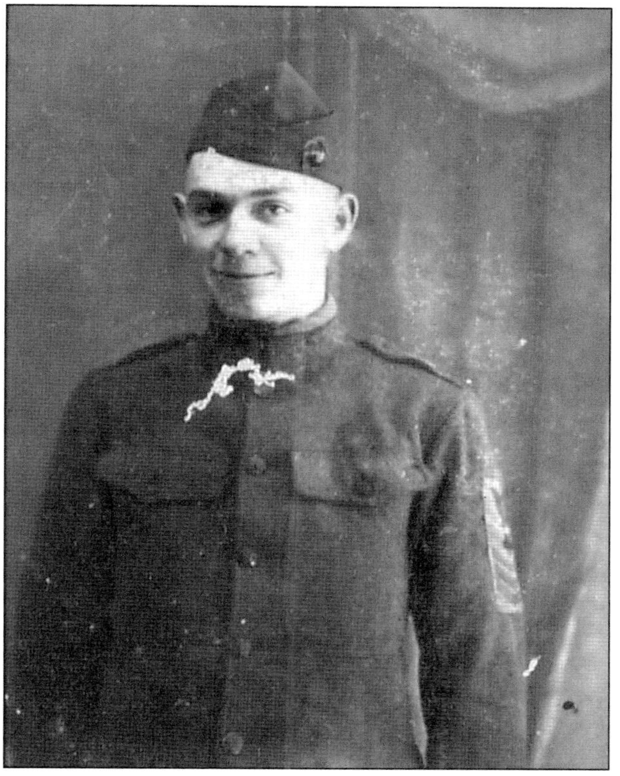

Dr. Oscar Goodwin. Dr. Oscar Sexton Goodwin was a physician in Apex for a number of years. He was born in 1894 and served as a corpsman in the U.S. Navy in World War I, where he earned the Navy Cross. Dr. Goodwin had a family practice on Salem Street above A. V. Baucom's store. His daughter, Jacque Goodwin Burgess, recalls, "His office was on the second floor, which his heart patients probably didn't appreciate." He took care of Apex's residents from 1924 until a few days before he passed away in 1976. During the Depression and even later, he often accepted hams, chickens, vegetables, and other items as payment for his services. (Both, courtesy of Jacque Goodwin Burgess.)

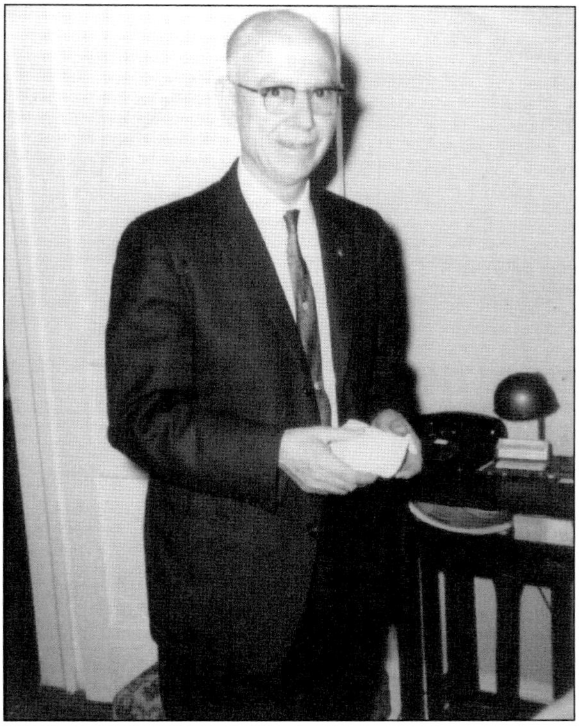

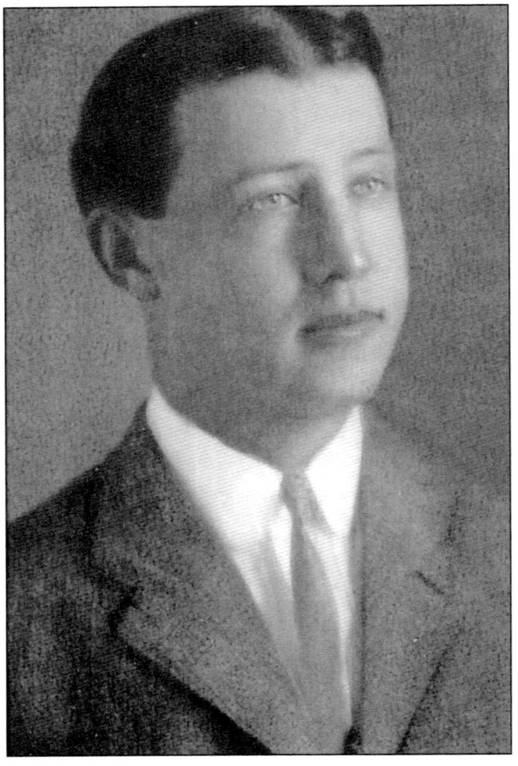

Dr. Romulus and Dovie Stephens. Romulus Stephens was born in 1877 and passed away in 1938. He became a dentist in Apex in 1901 and served as the vice president of the Peoples Bank of Apex in 1911. It was also during this time that he suffered a loss in the 1911 fire. In 1938, likely prompted by his experience with the lack of Apex's ability to fight fires, Dr. Stephens and 18 other men met to address concerns about the lack of sufficient fire protection in town. Just prior to his death, he became a charter member of the Apex Volunteer Fire Department. His wife, Dovie Suggs-Stephens, affectionately called "Granny Stephens," was born in 1890 and passed away in 1962. (Both, courtesy of Tommy Stephens and Janet Davis.)

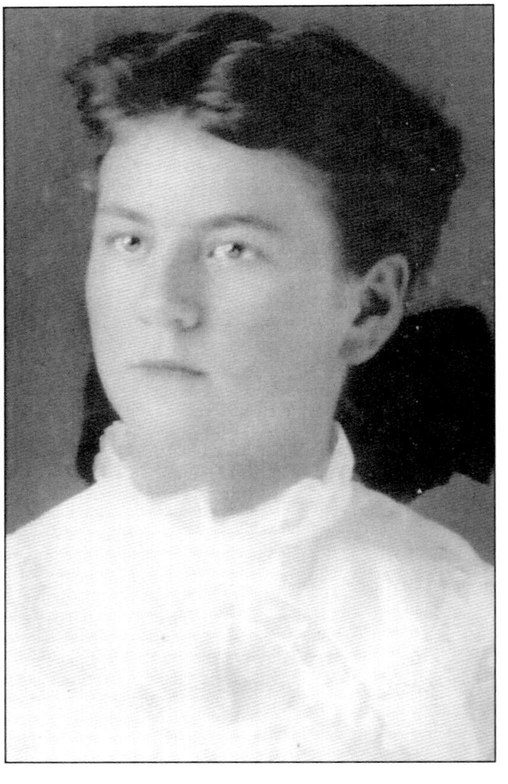

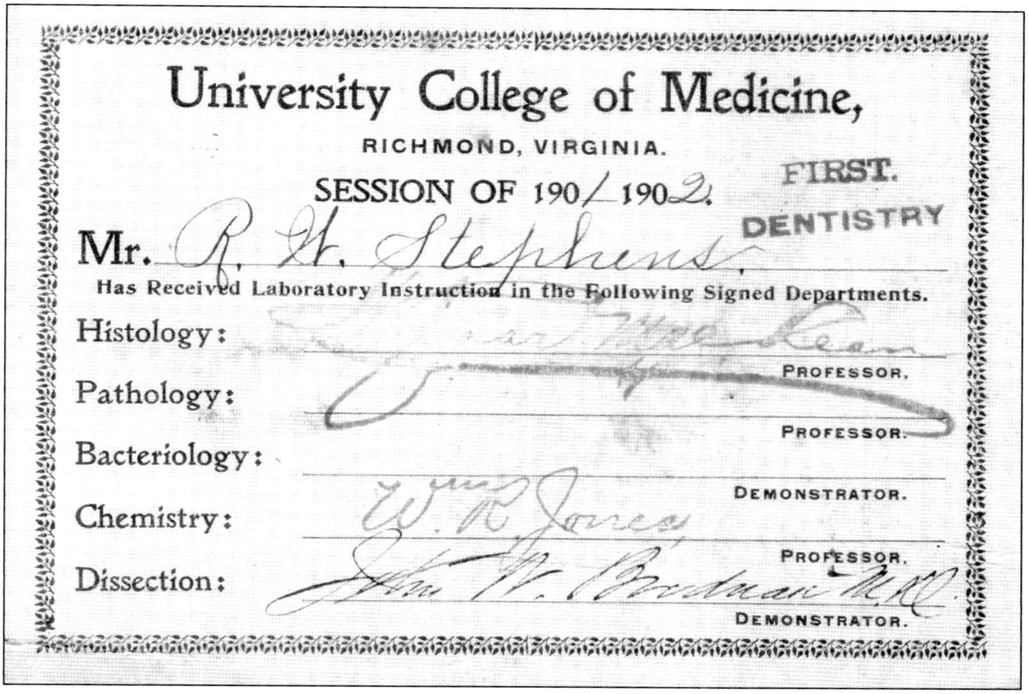

University College of Medicine,

RICHMOND, VIRGINIA.

SESSION OF 190*1*–190*2*. FIRST. DENTISTRY

Mr. *R. H. Stephens*,

Has Received Laboratory Instruction in the Following Signed Departments.

Histology: PROFESSOR.

Pathology: PROFESSOR.

Bacteriology: DEMONSTRATOR.

Chemistry: *W. R. Jones* PROFESSOR.

Dissection: *John W. Brodnax M.D.* DEMONSTRATOR.

Dr. Romulus Stephens Medical Record and Tax Bill. Dr. Stephens attended the University College of Medicine in Richmond, Virginia, where he studied dentistry. This card shows his attendance for 1901–1902. The Stephenses had a beautiful home in the residential area of Apex. This tax bill (below) shows that they paid $200 to a Sheriff Page in 1899. (Both, courtesy of Tommy Stephens and Janet Davis.)

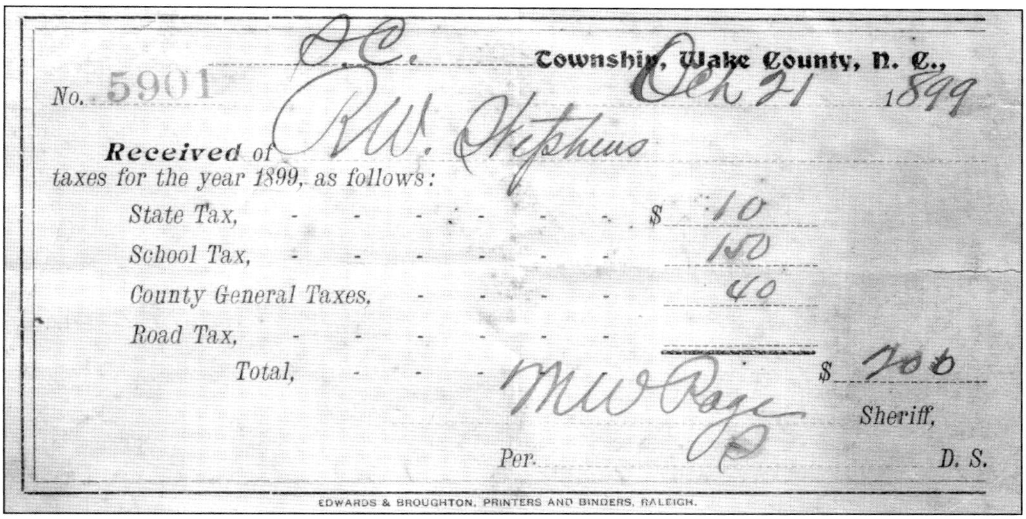

O. C. Township, Wake County, N. C., *Oct 21* 18*99*

No. 5901

Received of *R. W. Stephens*

taxes for the year 1899, as follows:

State Tax,	$ *10*
School Tax,	*150*
County General Taxes,	*40*
Road Tax,	
Total,	$ *200*

M W Page Sheriff,

Per. *P* D. S.

EDWARDS & BROUGHTON, PRINTERS AND BINDERS, RALEIGH.

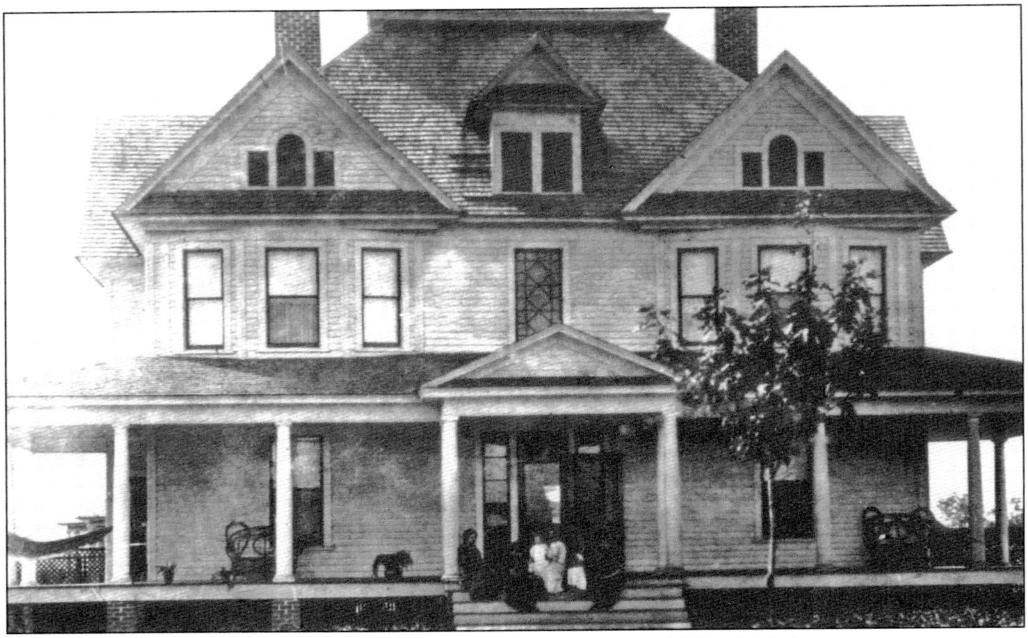

THE HOME OF DR. ROMULUS AND DOVIE STEPHENS, AROUND 1900. This house sat on a quarter of one block on South Mason Street. Another building on this block was a teacherage. When it overfilled, the Stephenses' home was used. The home's kitchen was 18 feet long and housed a stove in the corner. They had a smokehouse, a pigeon house (Dr. Stephens sold squab), a carriage house, a barn, a chicken house, a pump house, and a garden. Family members recall that only Dr. Stephens was allowed to plant and prune the tomato plants, and if there was an open patch of dirt, he planted something in it. (Courtesy of Tommy Stephens and Janet Davis.)

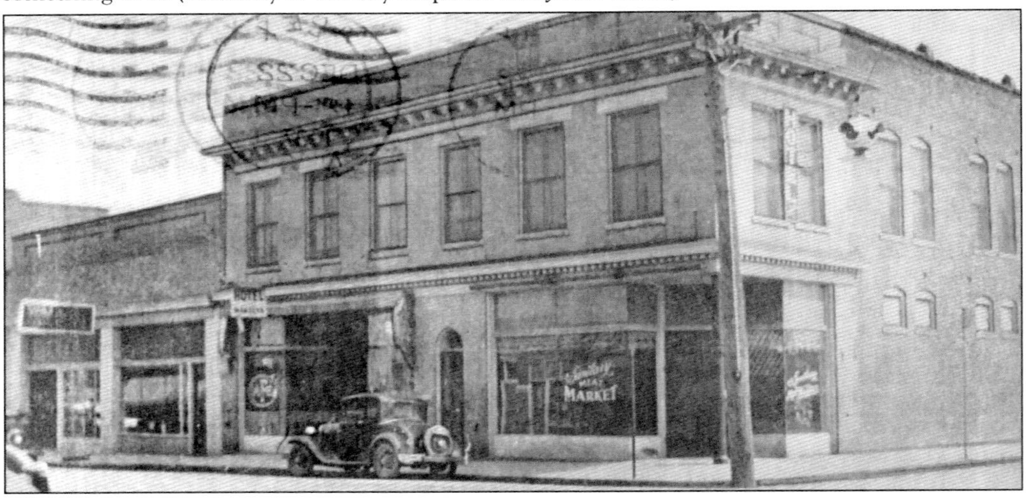

HOTEL WAKELYN, 1930S. This postcard is from the Hotel Wakelyn. Mrs. S. M. Finch, the proprietor, advertised, "Hot and cold water in every room. Café. Garage. Route U.S. 1 and 55." The back of the postcard reads, "Dear Hattie & Frank, Staying here to night (Tues). Nice place. Car run fine so far, only wish you both was with us. Only bought 24 gal gas to day. Went 330 miles. Hope you both keep well. Write me, Daytona Beach Fla., Gen Dely, Love, Eva." (Courtesy of University of North Carolina at Chapel Hill.)

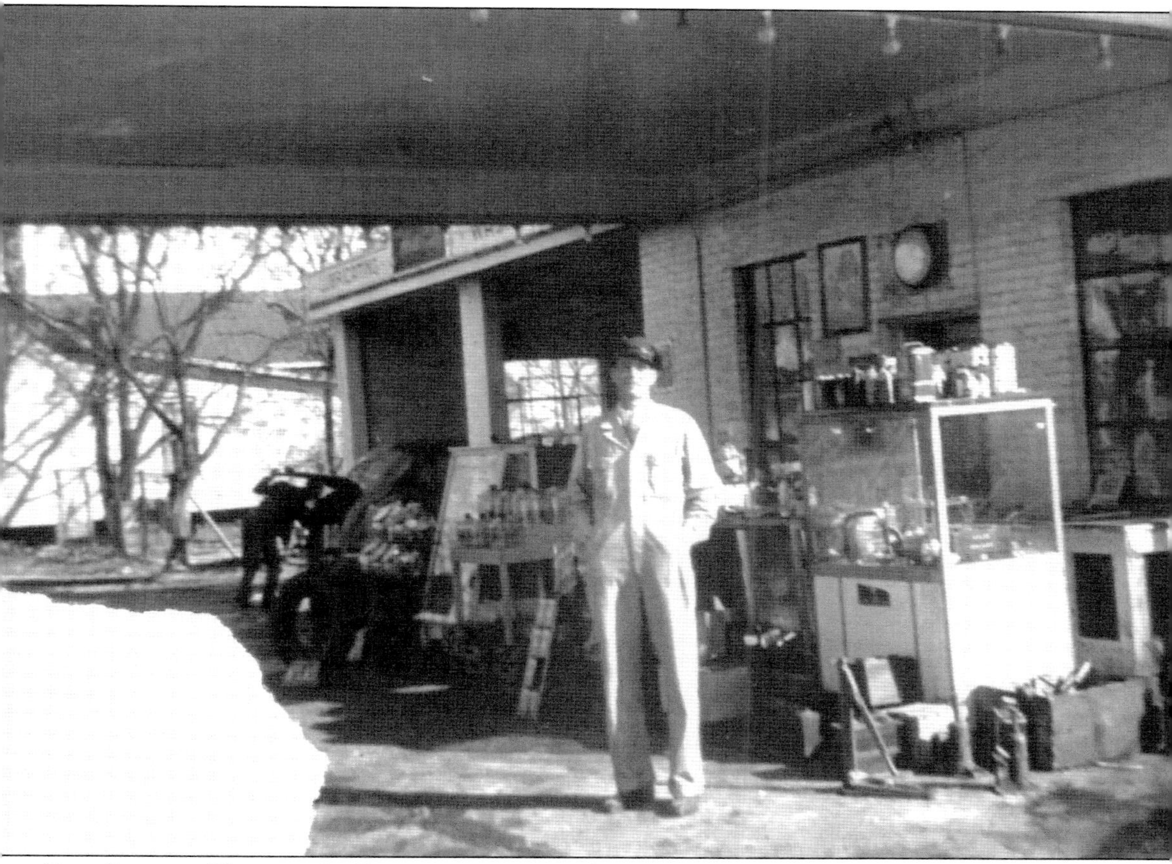

Esso Station. This was the Esso gas station on Salem Street during the 1940s. The gas station attendant is Charles Matthews. The station pumped gas and serviced vehicles 24 hours a day. (Courtesy of Ann Grebing.)

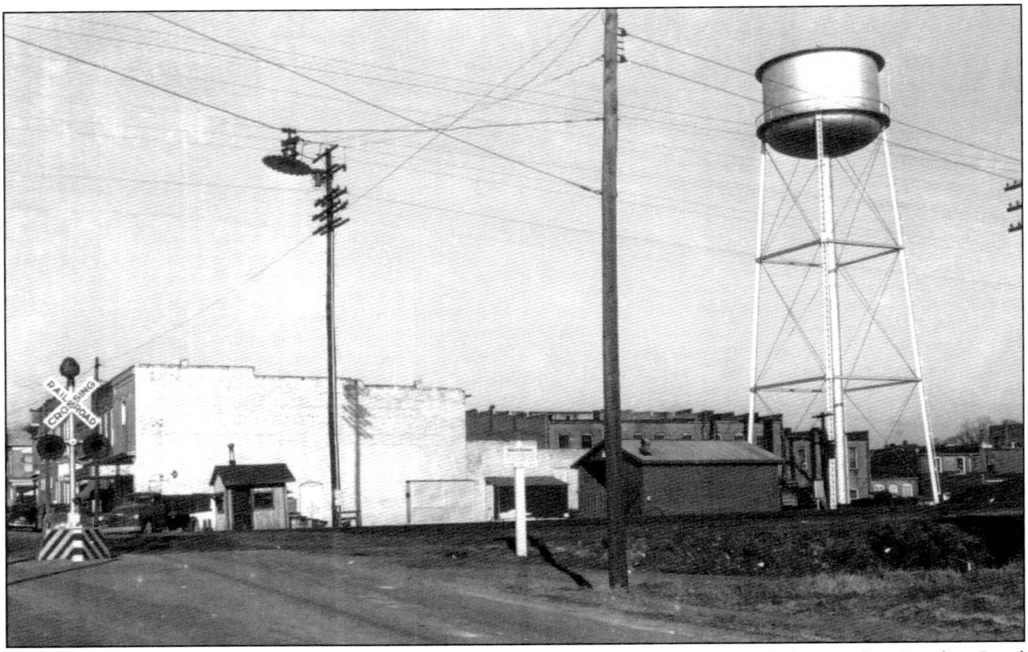

Cooke Coal Company. These photograph was taken in the 1950s and shows the Cooke Coal Company, the water tower, the train depot, and the Poe Brothers' warehouses. Coal was an important commodity to Apex from its early beginnings. By the 1950s, coal had become a major business enterprise. The coal company and warehouses were ideally and strategically situated right next to the train tracks. (Both, courtesy of Ann Grebing.)

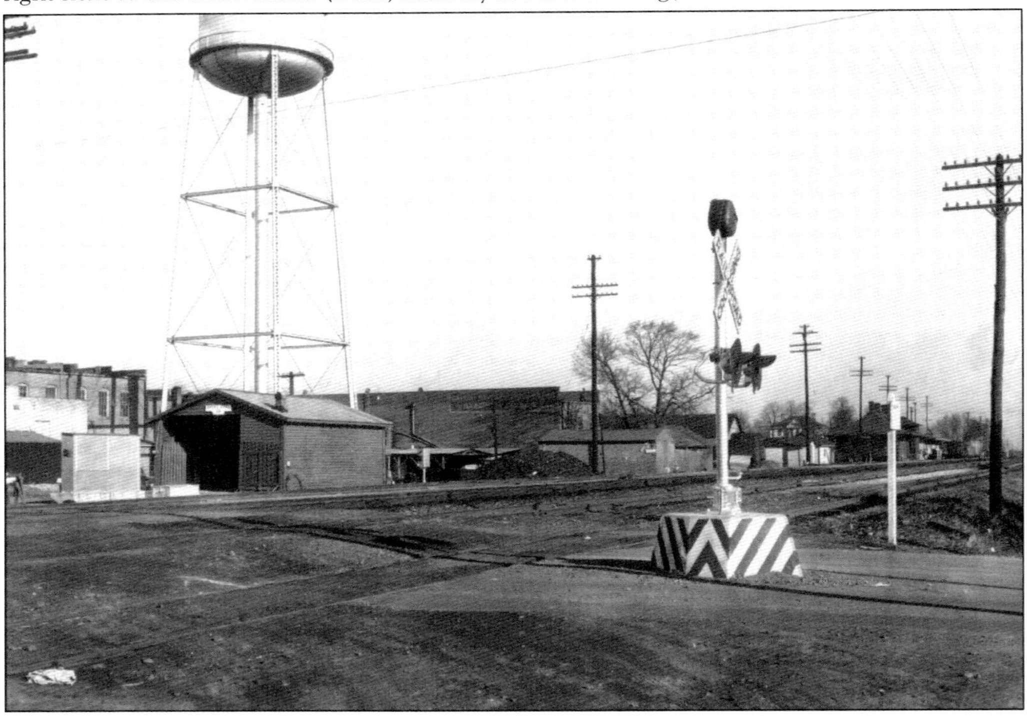

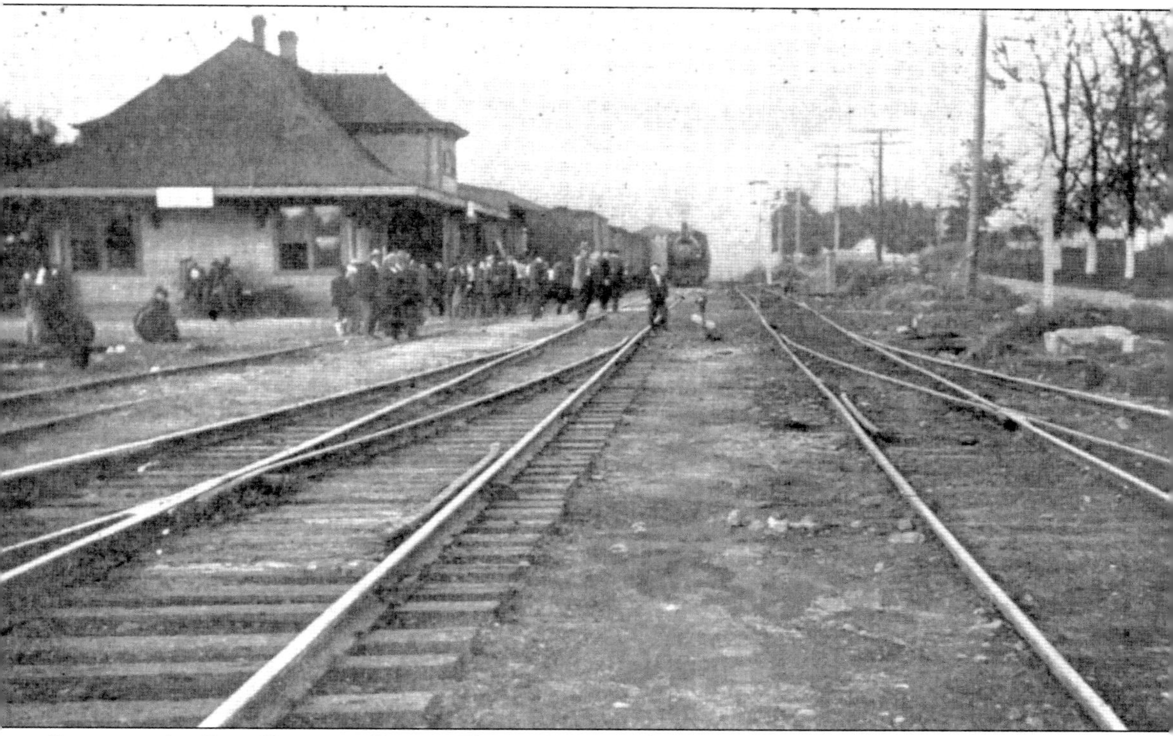

Seaboard Air Line Railroad Depot. This 1907 picture shows people waiting for the approaching train, which carried both passengers and freight. Freight trains not only brought goods, they also brought hobos. Apex residents often had to deal with men who hopped off the train to look for handouts. Dr. Goodwin's daughter, Jacque Goodwin Burgess, recalls, "Papa often had dealings with the bums who wanted cash, but he refused to give them money saying handouts only made a man lazy. Instead, he offered them odd jobs, like grass cutting so they could earn their money." She also stated that Apex residents provided them with food. (Courtesy of the North Carolina State Archives.)

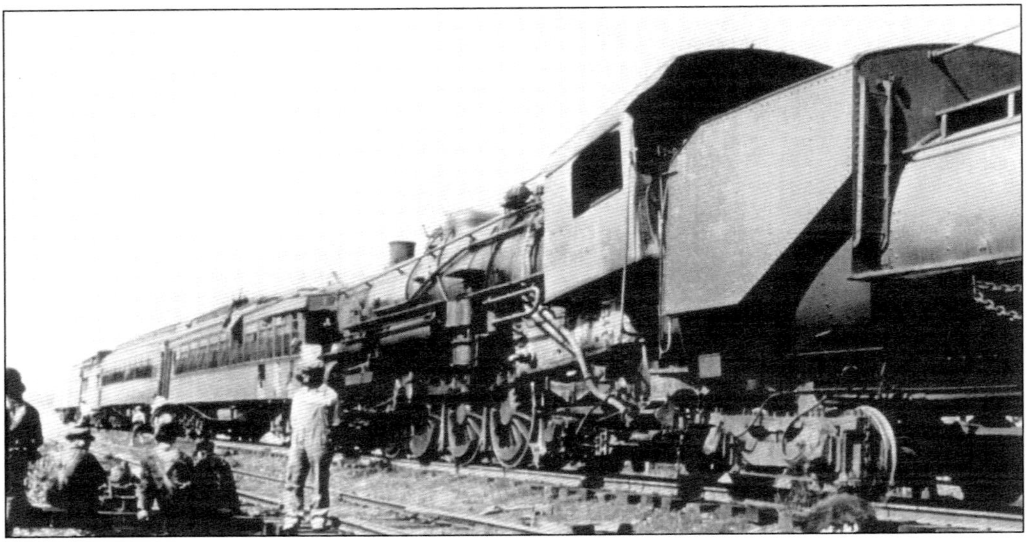

Seaboard Air Line Railroad Shoe Fly Wreck. Around 1922, the Shoe Fly train wreck took place. A shoe fly is a temporary track built around a train wreck or washout. It is likely this wreck happened on a shoe fly track, thus giving the wreck its name. The train made short runs between Apex and New Hill. This accident occurred just short of a mile from the Apex depot as people were returning from New Hill. Apex resident Ann Snell wrote about the wreck, "My grandmother and grandfather, Dixon and Dora Maynard, were sitting with relatives when this accident happened right before their eyes." Below, Dixon Maynard is the man in the dark suit and hat in the lower right-hand corner. (Both, courtesy of Ann Grebing.)

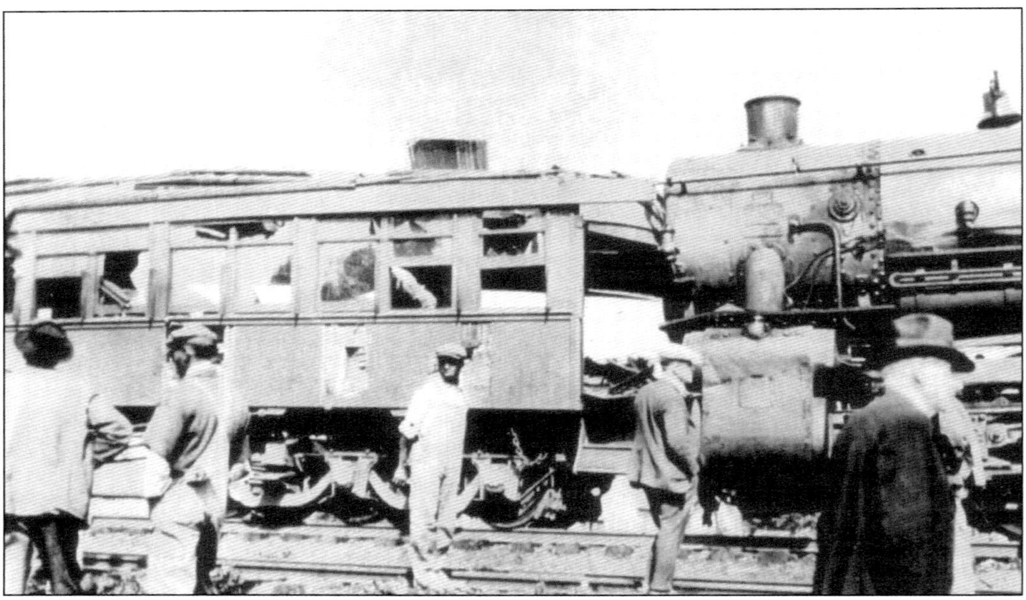

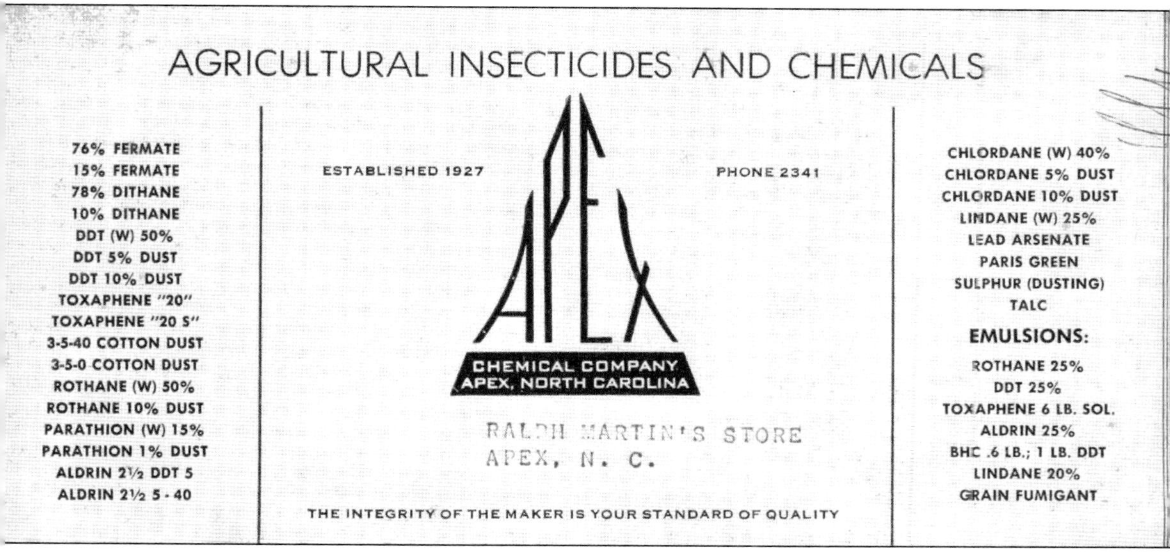

APEX CHEMICAL COMPANY. The company was established in 1927 and manufactured soap and agricultural insecticides. Its goods could be purchased at Ralph Martin's store in downtown Apex. The plant was located on North Salem Street, near Grove and Pate. (Courtesy of Bob Crowley.)

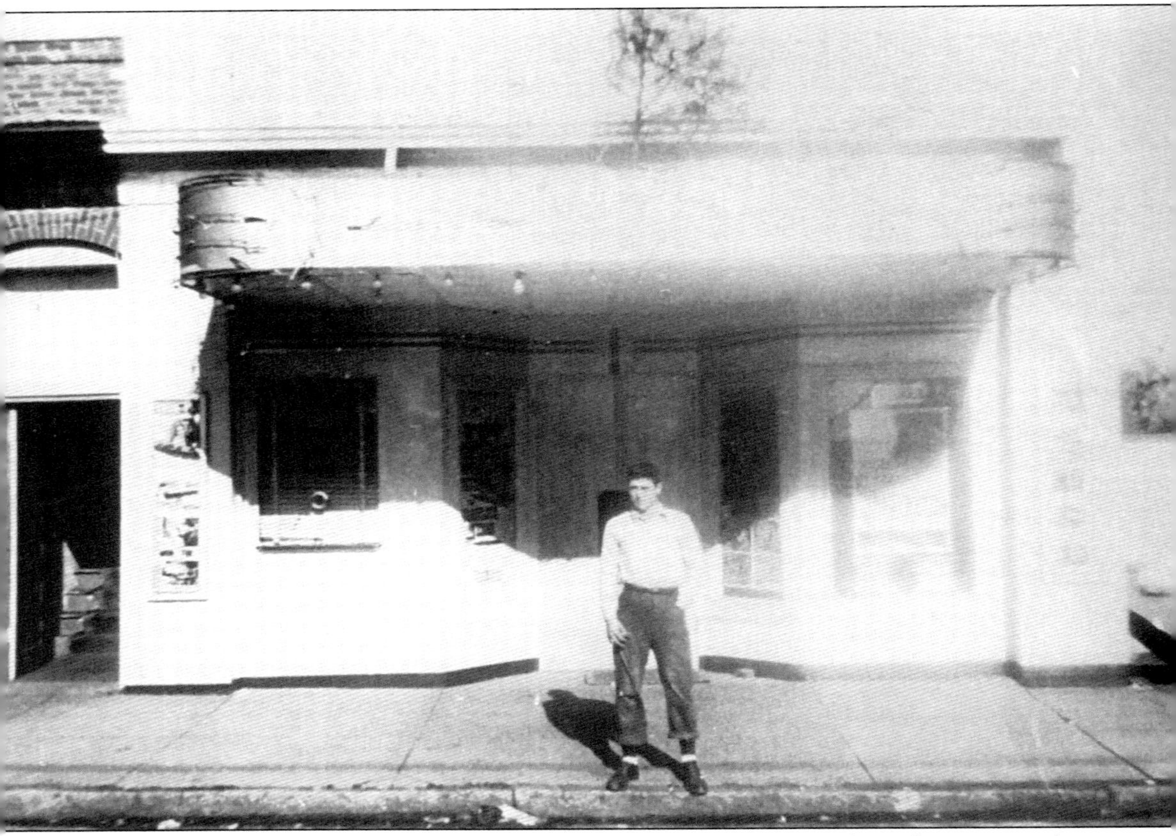

Apex Movie House. This is the Apex movie house before the 1954 fire. The man standing in the picture is Harry Beasley. The door on the left was for non-whites who wanted to go in and watch a movie. (Courtesy of Ann Grebing.)

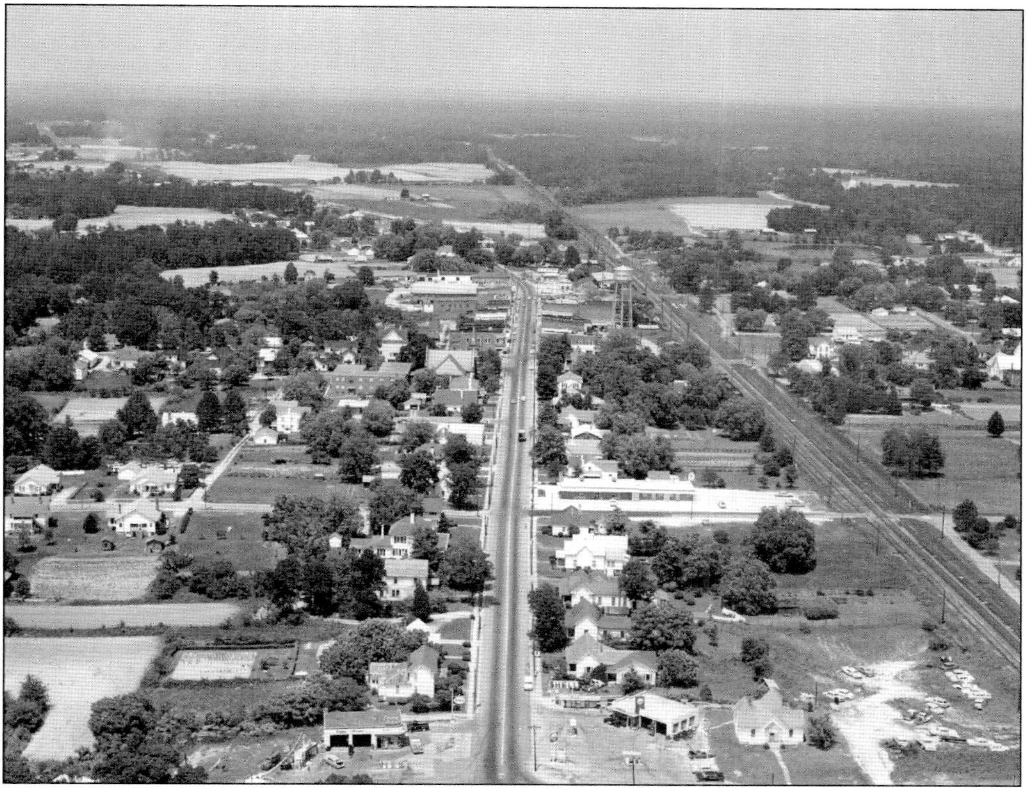

Aerial Apex and Brochure. The photograph above was taken in the 1950s or 1960s and truly shows Apex's sprawling progress. While the population had nearly doubled from 1910 to 1950, it had been a slow climb. In the summer of 1957, economic development recruiters from North Carolina traveled the East Coast and parts of the Midwest to get research-oriented companies interested in moving operations to what would become Research Triangle Park. In 1958, the town of Apex produced a brochure showing how close it was to the newly formed Research Triangle Park. (Above, courtesy of Diane Long; right, courtesy of Wake County Library.)

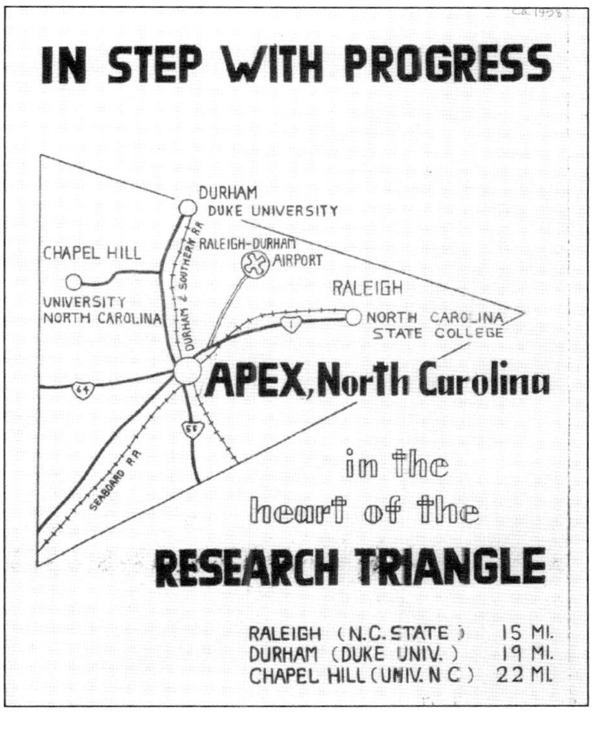

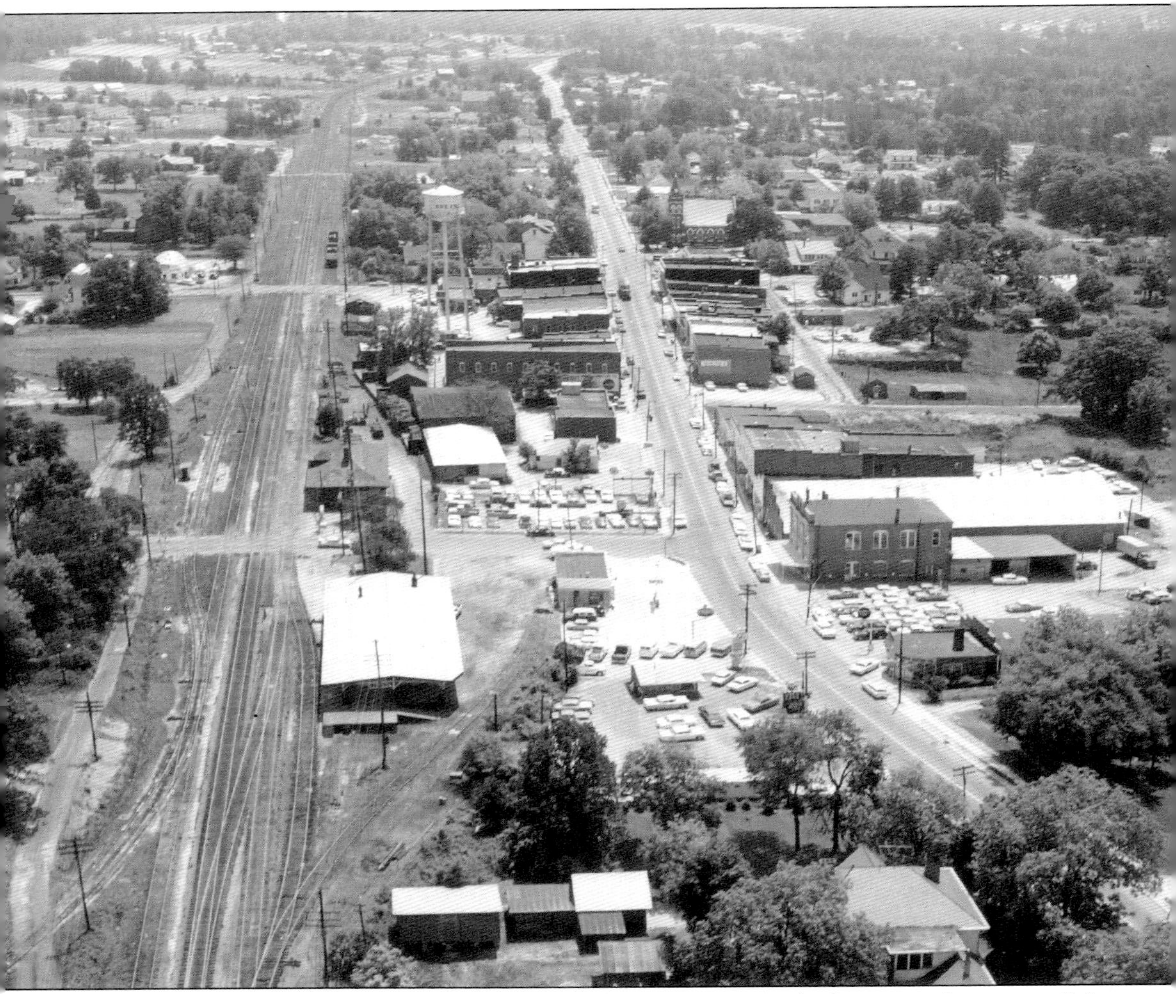

Aerial Apex. This photograph was taken in the 1950s or 1960s looking over downtown Salem Street in Apex. The town hall is the two-story brick building on the right. Farther down the block on the same side is the Apex Baptist Church. The railroad tracks and train depot are on the left side of Salem Street. Seymour Watkins's two-story brick building is on the left side of Salem Street, and the old water tower is just beyond that. (Photograph by Moody Long, courtesy of Diane Long.)

Three

School Memories

Mamie Bolling, 1904 Class. This is a 1904 class photograph that included student Mamie Bolling. She was born in 1889 and was five feet, four inches tall and had brown eyes. She voted in her first election in 1908. Mamie was the daughter of Robert J. and Louisa Bolling. Robert Bolling worked at A. B. Hunter's store, was on the board of directors of the Merchants and Farmers Bank, and was the mayor in 1914. Mamie married George T. Cunningham, who was a tobacconist, but they never had children. They remained devoted to one another until the day he died. Mamie chose to be called "Mamie-George" to honor her husband. Their original home sat at the southwest ramp of U.S. 64 and North Salem Street until it was purchased by the North Carolina Department of Transportation. Mamie had a brick home built at the southwest corner of South Hughes and Moore Streets. (Courtesy of the Wake County Public Library.)

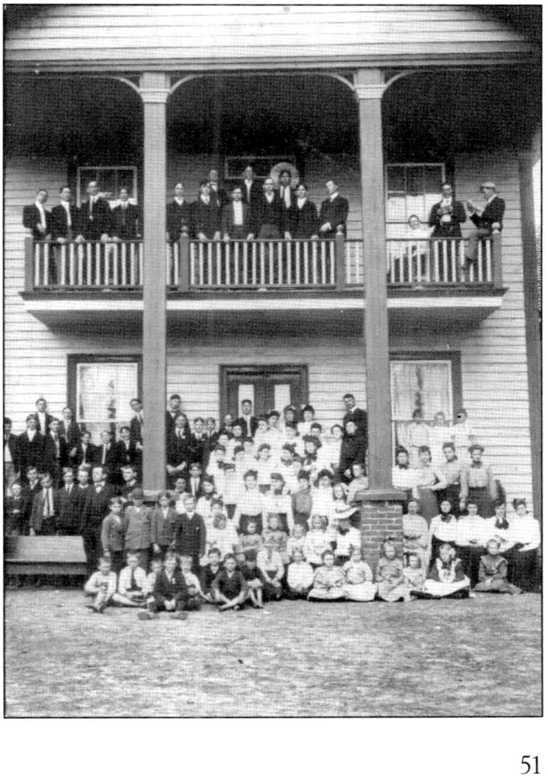

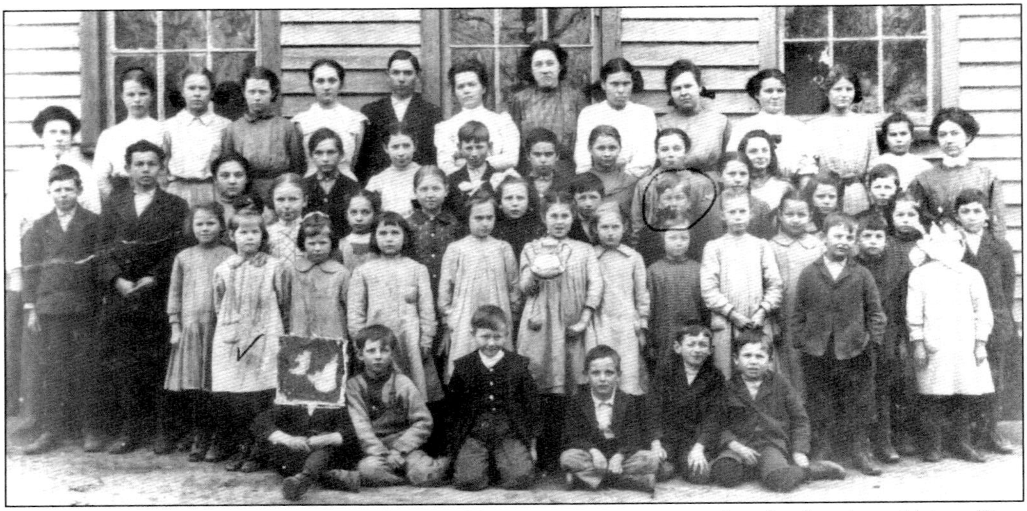

OLIVE'S CHAPEL PUBLIC SCHOOL. Johnson Olive was a young man when he first heard his calling after attending a sermon delivered by Rev. Patrick W. Dowd. He was so moved that he studied and eventually became a minister himself. He settled in an area just north of the New Ruin community, which had a tavern and was notorious for leading men to ruin. There was constant drinking, gambling, and other vices available to men. Fed up with sinners and not having a church close at hand, Johnson Olive and his nearby brethren began preaching the gospel around 1853 in Olive's Chapel, which is now known as Olive Chapel. Schooling was also near and dear to his heart, so he set up a school. This photograph was taken in the early 1900s. (Courtesy of the North Carolina State Archives.)

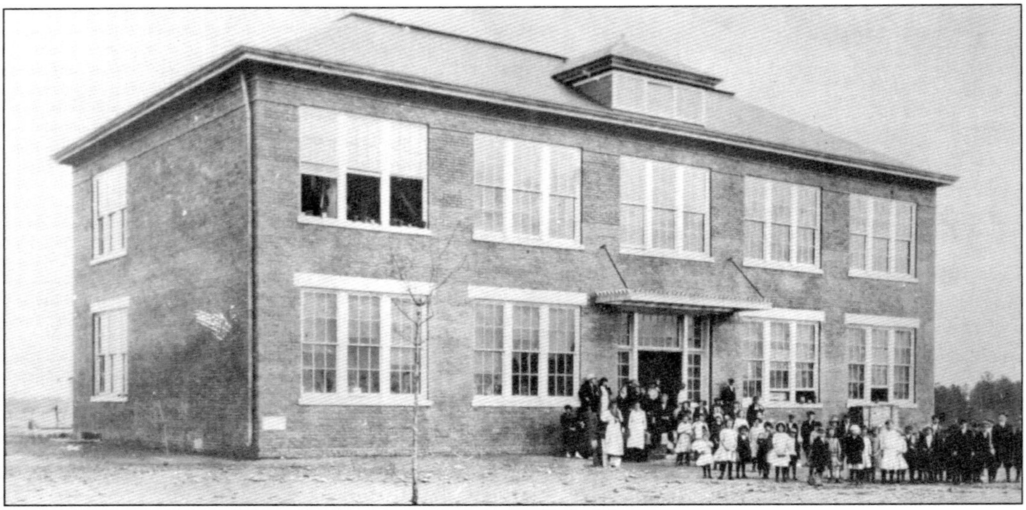

GRADED SCHOOL, 1906 TO 1915. This photograph was taken of the students at the Apex Graded School. The children are standing outside of the school building facing an empty field. The school was built in 1906 at a cost of $7,000 and had 125 students its first year. By 1911, there were more than 100 students in attendance. Prof. M. S. Giles was the principal. His assistants were Meda Rollins, Valinda Hamilton, and Eula Baucom. Kate Furman was the music director. The school itself was well equipped with modern furniture, a piano, a ventilated auditorium, commodious, well-lit classrooms, and a large playground. (Courtesy of the Durwood Barbour collection at the University of North Carolina at Chapel Hill.)

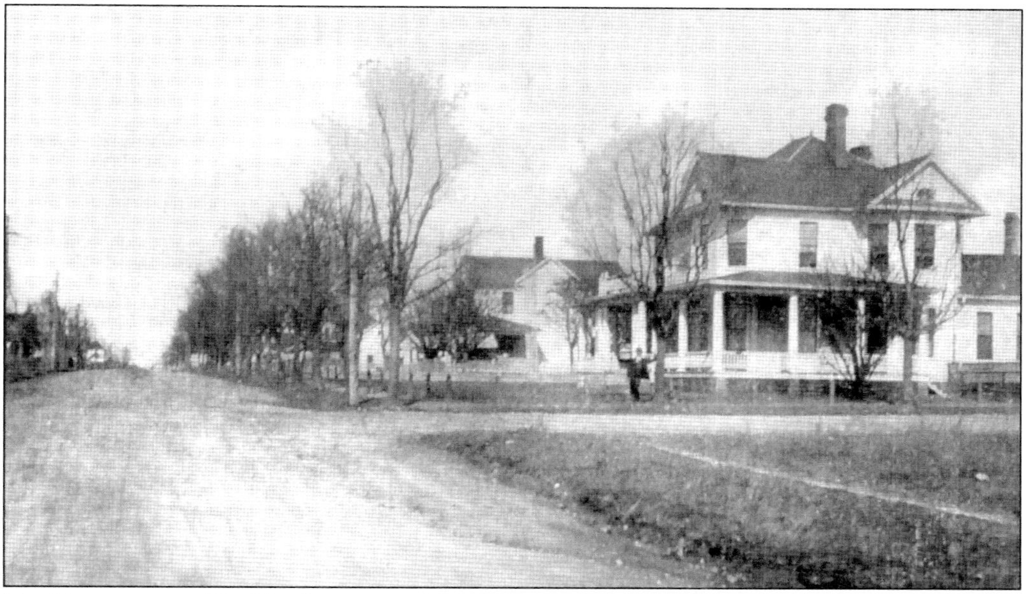

THE TEACHERAGE. The Teacherage was located at 209 South Hughes Street and was built around 1910. It served as the home to single female teachers while they taught at the local school. It was owned by Wake County and normally accommodated four teachers, the principal, and his wife. (Courtesy of Ann Grebing.)

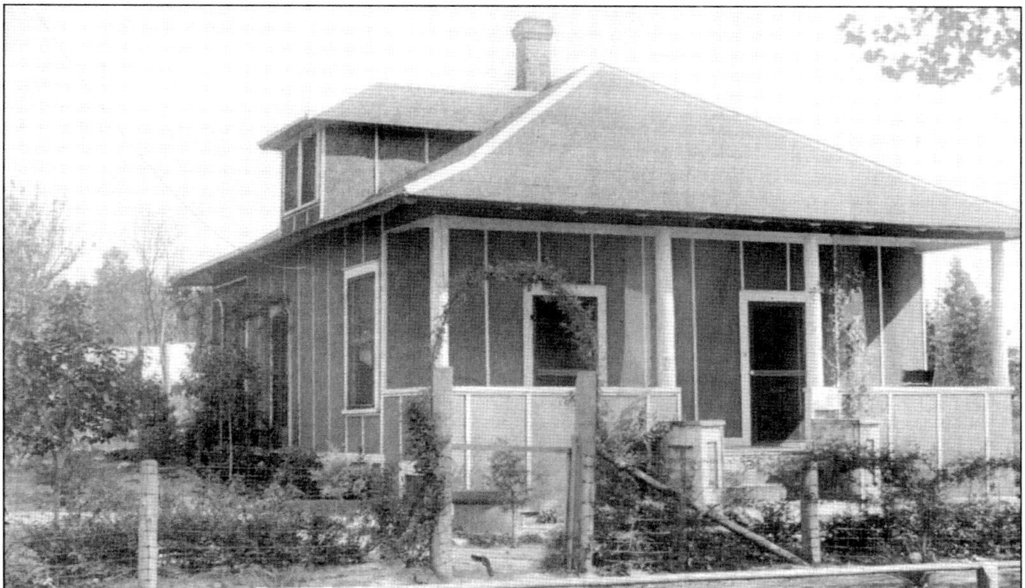

J. P. PEARSON HOME. Little is known about J. P. Pearson. J. P. was listed in the 1889 edition of *Branson's North Carolina Business Directory* as a teacher. The back of the postcard reads, "Home JP Pearson, Public School Teacher, Apex, NC, 1910–18." (Courtesy of the University of North Carolina at Chapel Hill.)

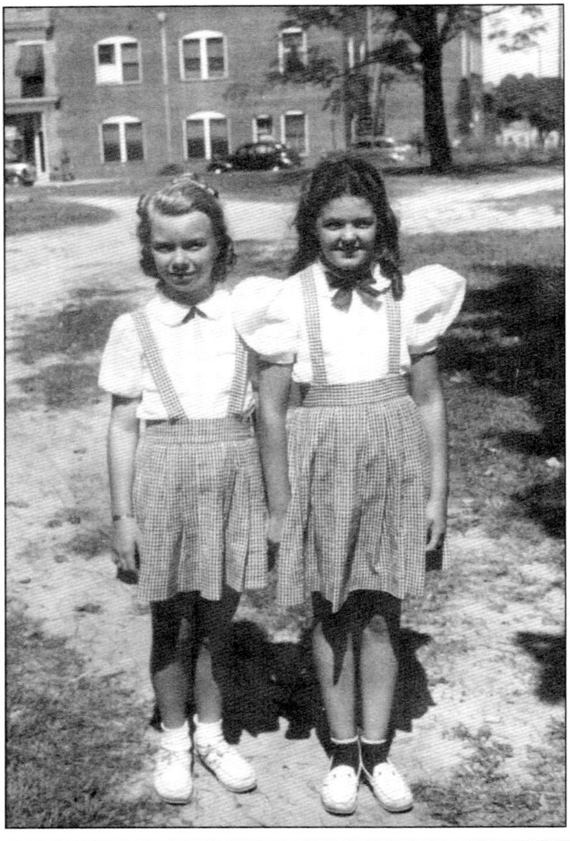

SCHOOLMATES. Jacque Goodwin (left) and her best friend, Marie-Grace Blades, posed for this picture in front of their school. The picture was taken in 1939. (Courtesy of Jacque Goodwin Burgess.)

CLASS PICTURE. This photograph (below) includes Walter and Esther Seagroves, who were the children of John and Pearl Seagroves. Walter was born in 1906, and Esther was born in 1908. (Courtesy of Diane Long.)

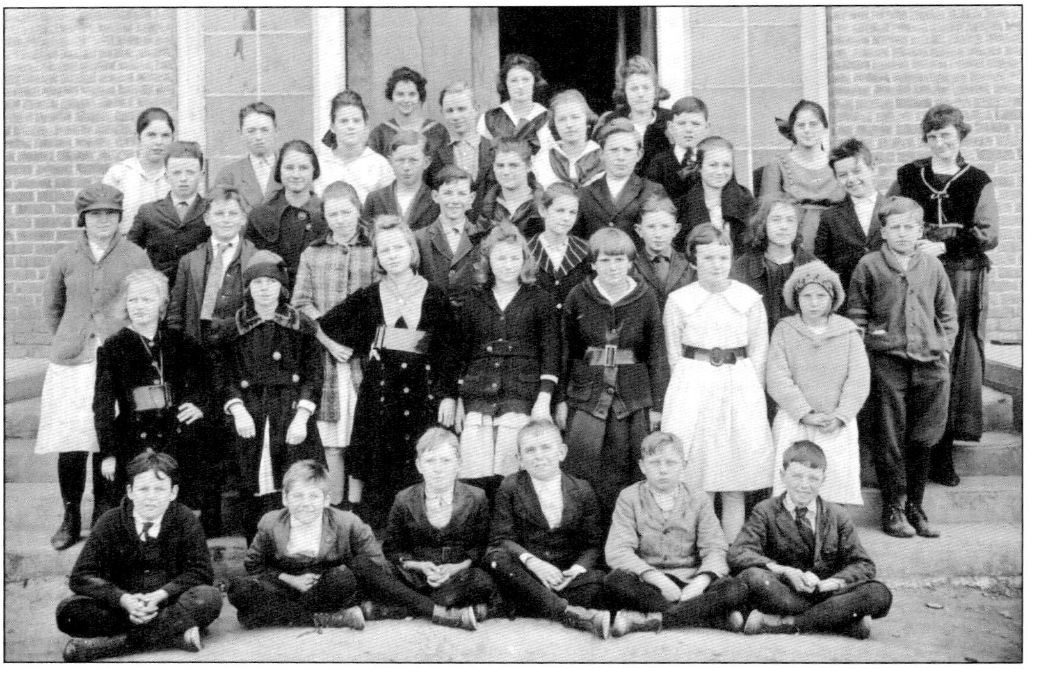

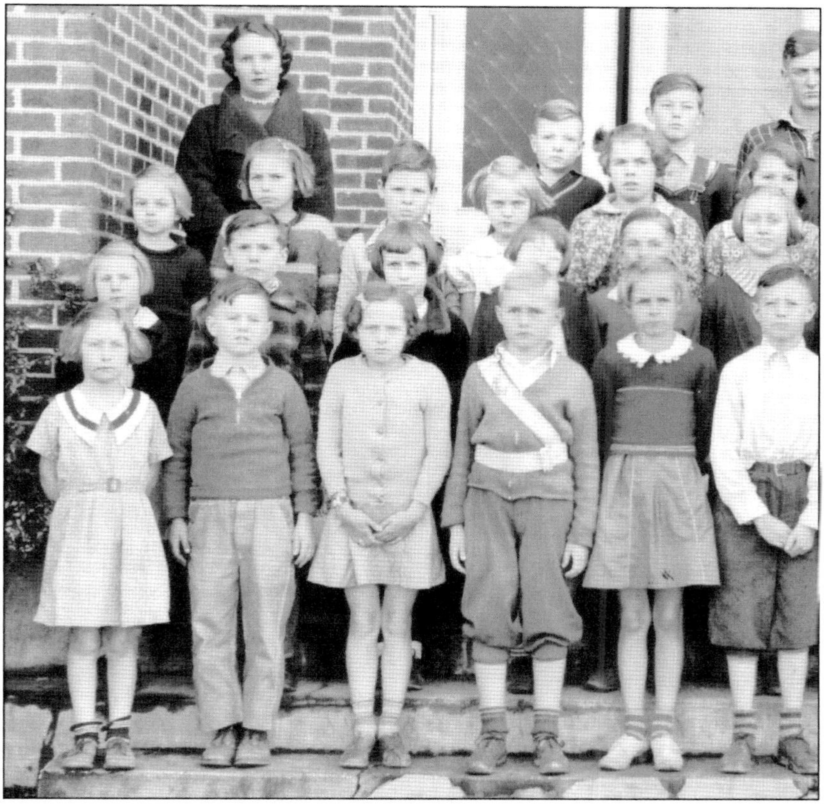

Jessie Ruth Cunningham. Jessie Ruth (above, fourth row, far left) was born in 1909 to James Reives and Lizzie Cunningham. Her family home is located at 202 South Hughes Street and was built in 1906. Jessie lived in this house until 2002, when she passed away at age 94. She was well known in Apex because she taught school here for 39 years. Jessie (below, second row, far right) also played the organ at the Apex United Methodist Church for 47 years. (Both, courtesy of Ann Grebing.)

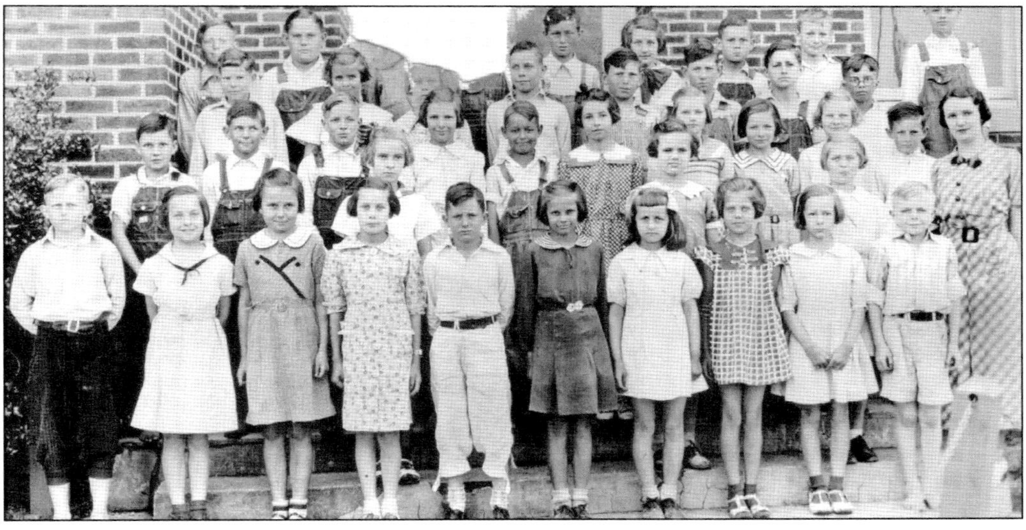

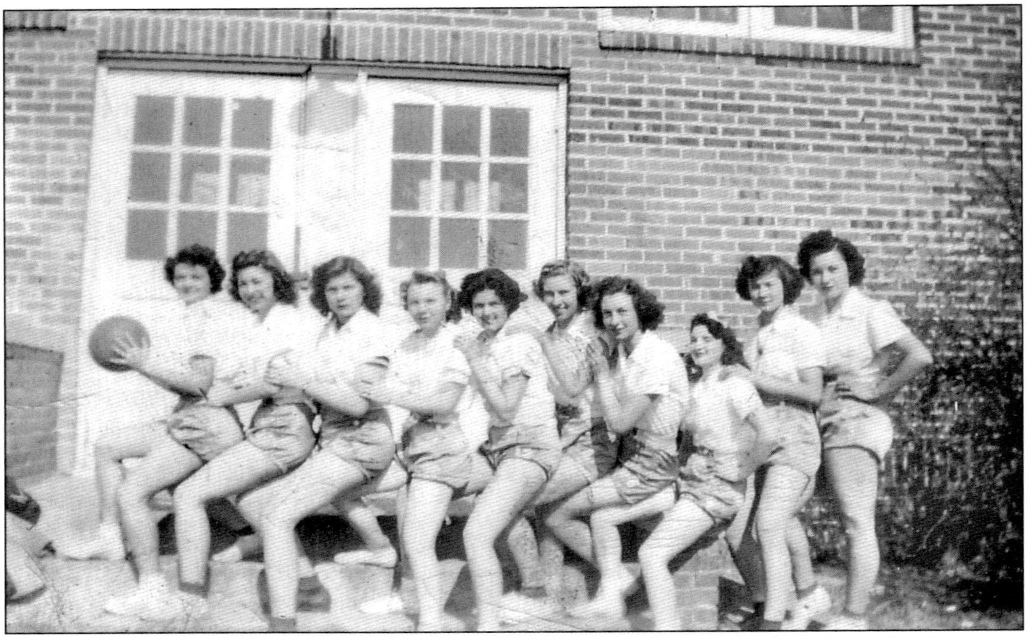

Girls Basketball Team, 1943. Jacque Goodwin was one of the girls that played for the Apex High School basketball team in 1943. She is the fourth from the left. (Courtesy of Jacque Goodwin Burgess.)

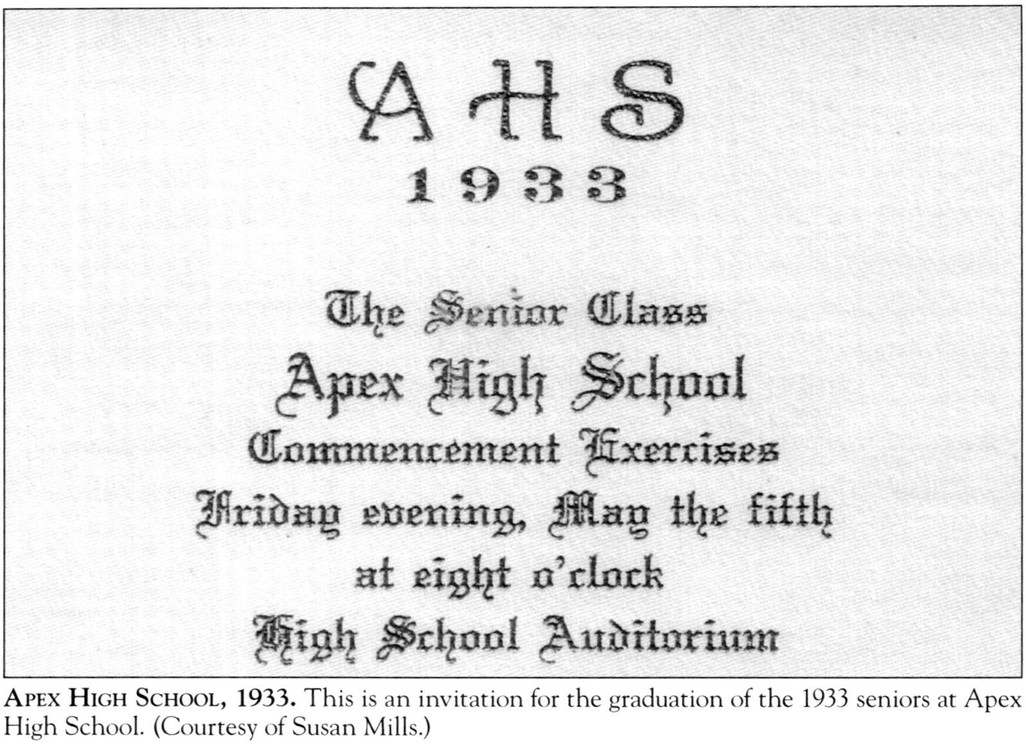

AHS
1933

The Senior Class
Apex High School
Commencement Exercises
Friday evening, May the fifth
at eight o'clock
High School Auditorium

Apex High School, 1933. This is an invitation for the graduation of the 1933 seniors at Apex High School. (Courtesy of Susan Mills.)

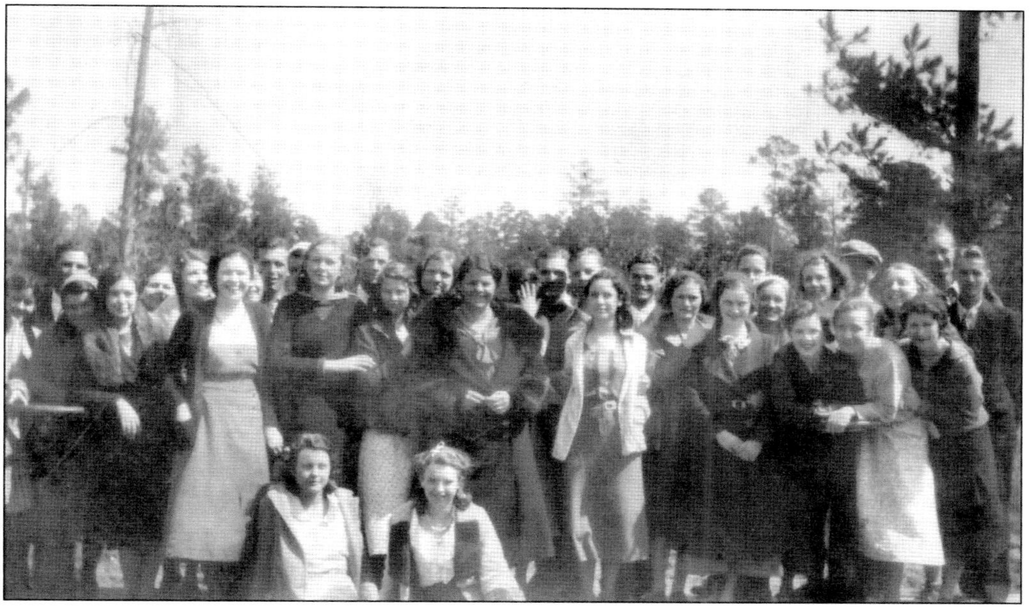

MARGARET BENTON'S SENIOR CLASS PICTURE. Margaret (first row, second from right) was the daughter of Howard C. Benton and was born in 1915. She grew up in Apex and graduated from Apex High School in 1932. (Courtesy of Margaret Benton Ferry.)

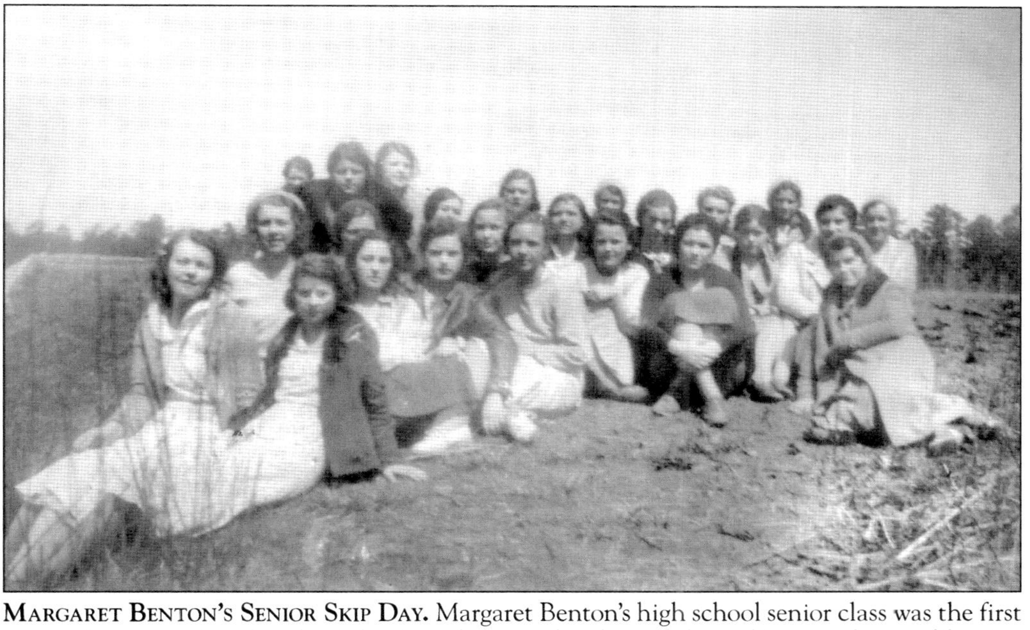

MARGARET BENTON'S SENIOR SKIP DAY. Margaret Benton's high school senior class was the first to ever have a senior skip day. This is a photograph taken of them skipping class and having fun at the nearby pond. Margaret is in the first row, fifth from the left. (Courtesy of Margaret Benton Ferry.)

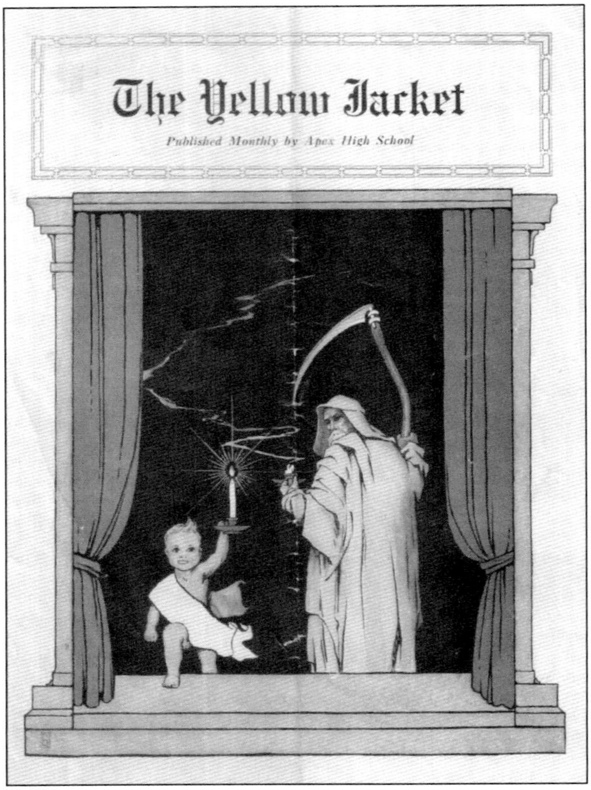

School Newspaper, 1929. The *Yellow Jacket* was published monthly by the Apex High School. There were numerous local stories inside about business, school, and personal items. (Both, courtesy of Diane Long.)

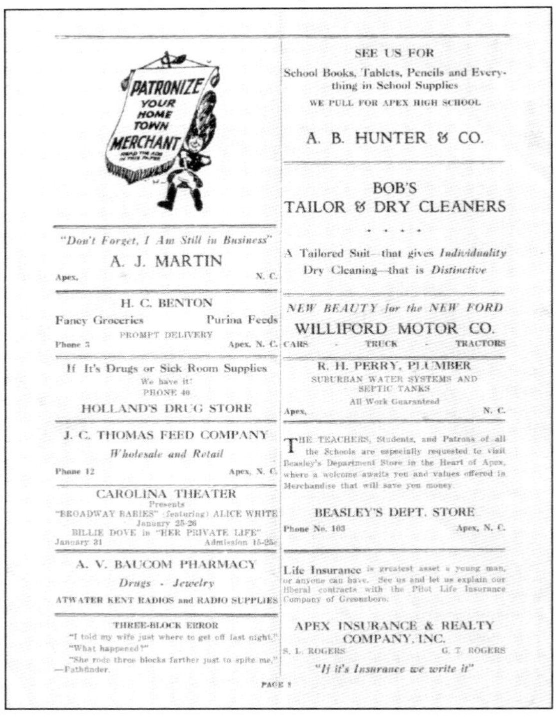

PATRONIZE YOUR HOME TOWN MERCHANT

"Don't Forget, I Am Still in Business"
A. J. MARTIN
Apex, N. C.

H. C. BENTON
Fancy Groceries — Purina Feeds
PROMPT DELIVERY
Phone 3 — Apex, N. C.

If It's Drugs or Sick Room Supplies
We have it!
PHONE 40
HOLLAND'S DRUG STORE

J. C. THOMAS FEED COMPANY
Wholesale and Retail
Phone 12 — Apex, N. C.

CAROLINA THEATER
Presents
"BROADWAY BABIES" (featuring) ALICE WHITE
January 25-26
BILLIE DOVE in "HER PRIVATE LIFE"
January 31 — Admission 15-25c

A. V. BAUCOM PHARMACY
Drugs - Jewelry
ATWATER KENT RADIOS and RADIO SUPPLIES

THREE-BLOCK ERROR
"I told my wife just where to get off last night."
"What happened?"
"She rode three blocks farther just to spite me."
—Pathfinder.

SEE US FOR
School Books, Tablets, Pencils and Everything in School Supplies
WE PULL FOR APEX HIGH SCHOOL
A. B. HUNTER & CO.

BOB'S
TAILOR & DRY CLEANERS
* * * *
A Tailored Suit—that gives *Individuality*
Dry Cleaning—that is *Distinctive*

NEW BEAUTY for the NEW FORD
WILLIFORD MOTOR CO.
CARS - TRUCK - TRACTORS

R. H. PERRY, PLUMBER
SUBURBAN WATER SYSTEMS AND SEPTIC TANKS
All Work Guaranteed
Apex, N. C.

THE TEACHERS, Students, and Patrons of all the Schools are especially requested to visit Beasley's Department Store in the Heart of Apex, where a welcome awaits you and values offered in Merchandise that will save you money.

BEASLEY'S DEPT. STORE
Phone No. 103 — Apex, N. C.

Life Insurance is greatest asset a young man, or anyone can have. See us and let us explain our liberal contracts with the Pilot Life Insurance Company of Greensboro.

APEX INSURANCE & REALTY COMPANY, INC.
S. L. ROGERS — G. T. ROGERS
"If it's Insurance we write it"

PAGE 8

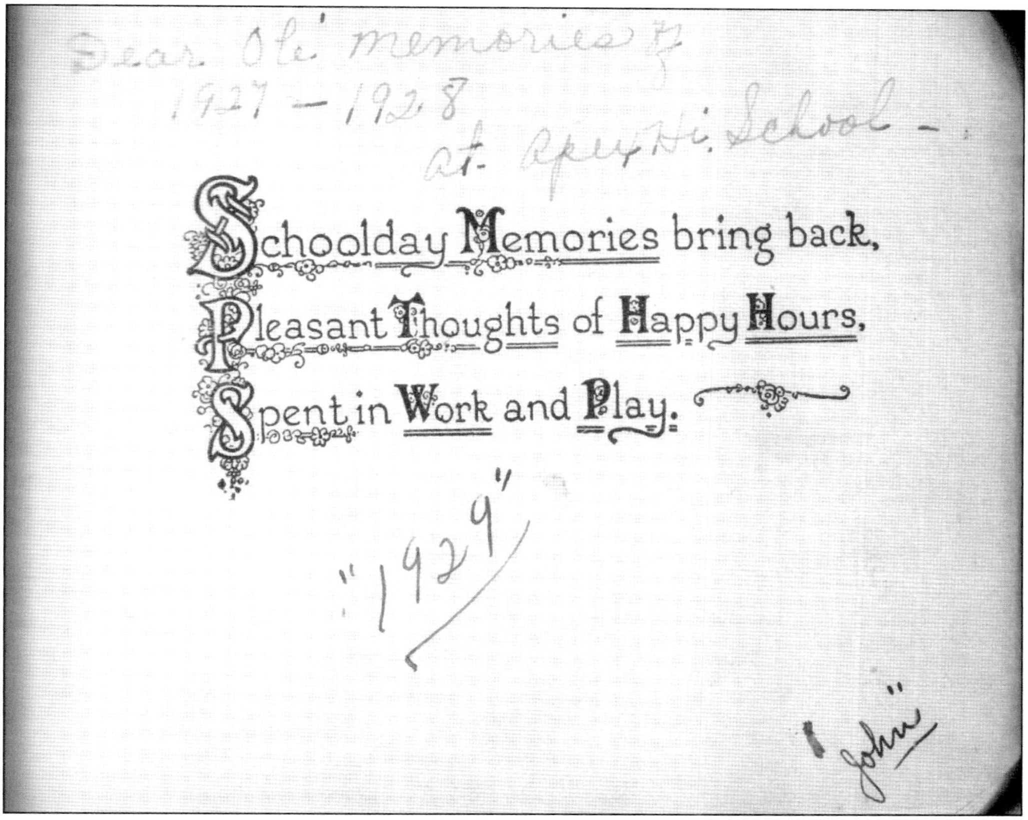

LELIA SEAGROVES'S 1929 SCHOOL MEMORIES BOOK. Lelia is actually pronounced "Leah" according to her family. She is descended from Apex's first postmaster, Daniel Mann. This 1929 booklet reads, "Dear Ole memories on 1927–1928 at Apex High School. School-day memories bring back, Pleasant thoughts of happy hours, Spent in work and play." She wrote 1929 on the bottom along with John, who appears to have been her sweetheart in 1929 and continued into 1930. Lelia's favorite expression in 1930 was, "Isn't he handsome." Her favorite occupation was, "Reading special deliveries from Cary Mann." (Courtesy of Diane Long.)

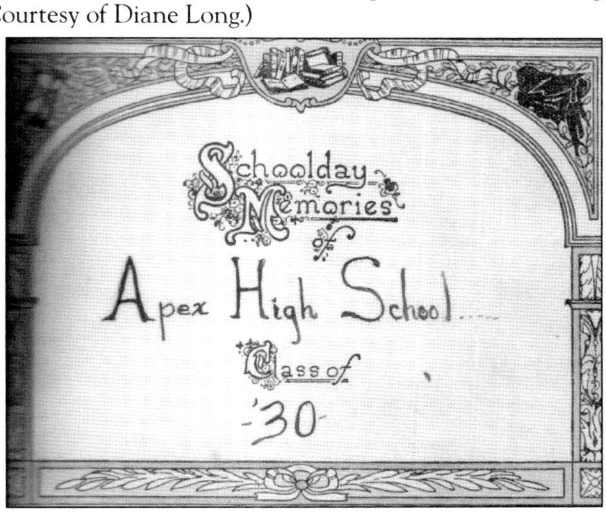

LELIA SEAGROVES'S SCHOOL MEMORIES BOOK 1930. It was common for students in the late 19th and early 20th centuries to have school memory books or autograph books. Lelia not only collected autographs, but she did a little self-reflection as well. (Courtesy of Diane Long.)

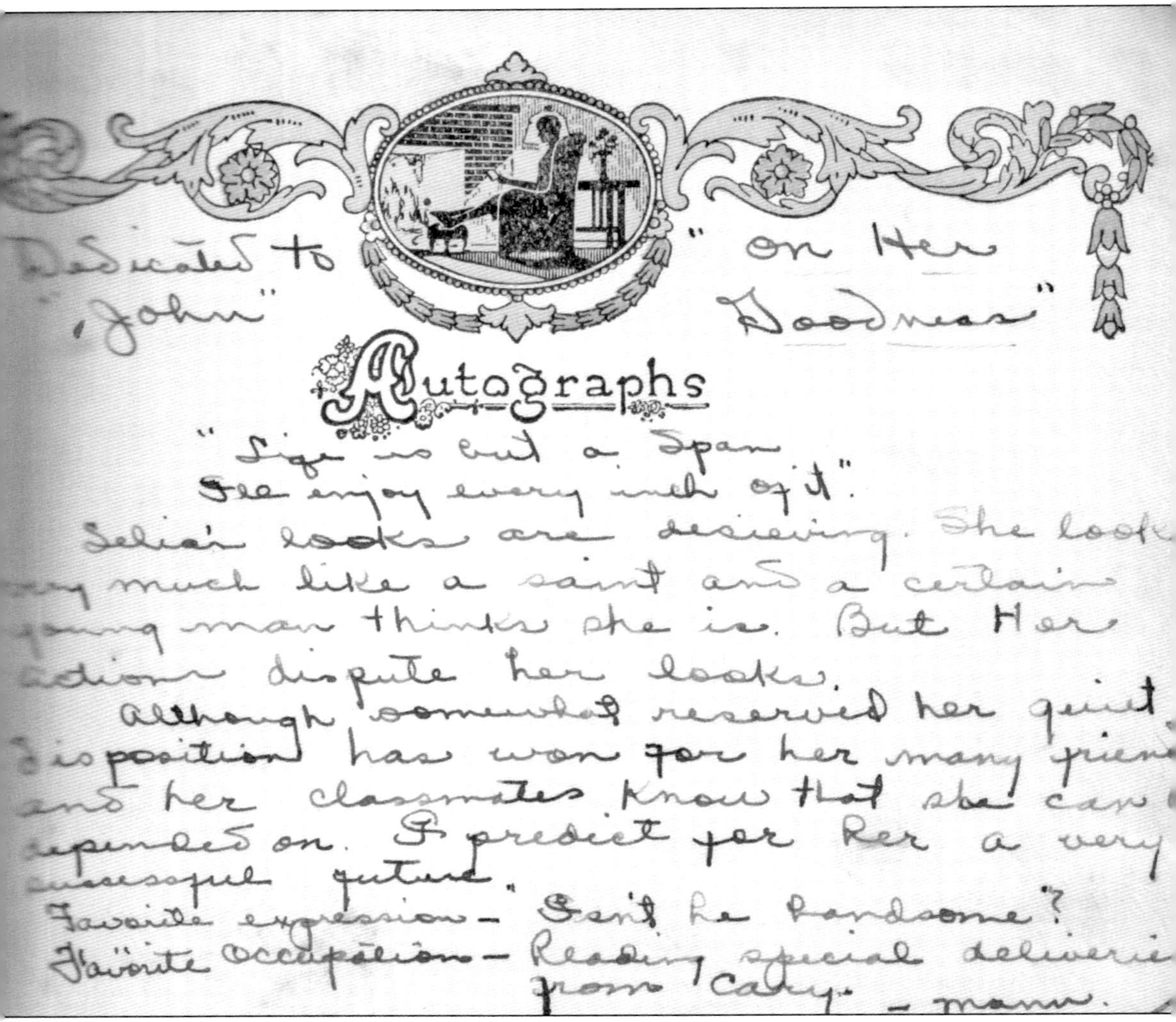

Dedicated to "John" "On Her Goodness"

Autographs

"Life is but a Span
See enjoy every inch of it".
Lelia's looks are deceiving. She looks very much like a saint and a certain young man thinks she is. But Her actions dispute her looks.
Although somewhat reserved her quiet disposition has won for her many friends and her classmates know that she can depended on. I predict for her a very successful future.
Favorite expression – "Isn't he handsome"?
Favorite occupation – Reading special deliveries from Caty. – mann.

Lelia Seagroves's School Memories Book 1930, Inside. This is one of the inside covers, and it reads, "Lelia's looks are deceiving. She looks very much like a saint and a certain young man thinks she is. But her actions dispute her looks. Although somewhat reserved her quiet disposition has won for her many friends and her classmates know that she can depended on. I predict for her a very successful future." (Courtesy of Diane Long.)

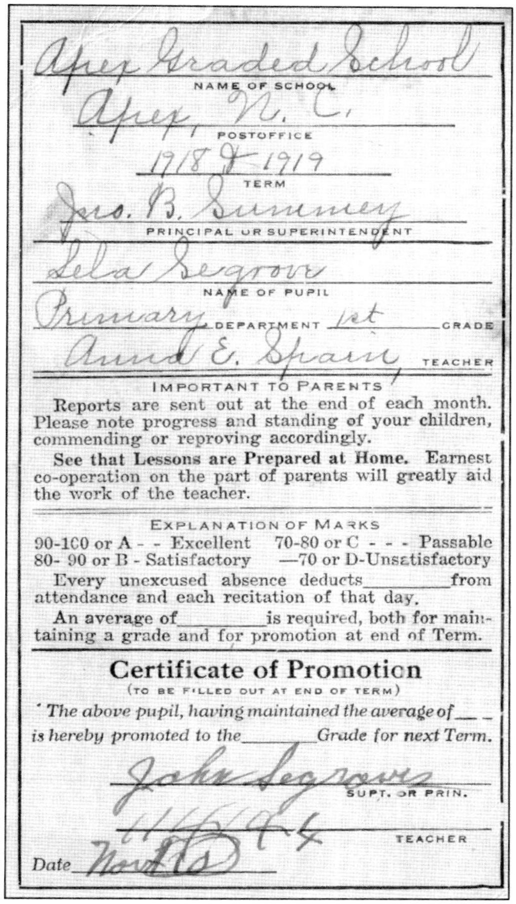
Apex Graded School
NAME OF SCHOOL
Apex, N. C.
POSTOFFICE
1918 & 1919
TERM
Jno. B. Summey
PRINCIPAL OR SUPERINTENDENT
Lela Segrove
NAME OF PUPIL
Primary DEPARTMENT 1st GRADE
Anna E. Spain TEACHER

IMPORTANT TO PARENTS

Reports are sent out at the end of each month. Please note progress and standing of your children, commending or reproving accordingly.

See that Lessons are Prepared at Home. Earnest co-operation on the part of parents will greatly aid the work of the teacher.

EXPLANATION OF MARKS

90-100 or A - - Excellent 70-80 or C - - - Passable
80- 90 or B - Satisfactory —70 or D-Unsatisfactory

Every unexcused absence deducts______ from attendance and each recitation of that day.

An average of______ is required, both for maintaining a grade and for promotion at end of Term.

Certificate of Promotion

(TO BE FILLED OUT AT END OF TERM)

The above pupil, having maintained the average of___ is hereby promoted to the______ Grade for next Term.

John Segroves
SUPT. OR PRIN.
TEACHER

Date Nov 18

LELIA SEAGROVES'S 1918 REPORT CARD. This is five-year-old Lelia's first-grade report card while she attended the newly built Apex Graded School. She received all A and B grades. The cards were signed by her father, John H. Seagroves. (Both, courtesy of Diane Long.)

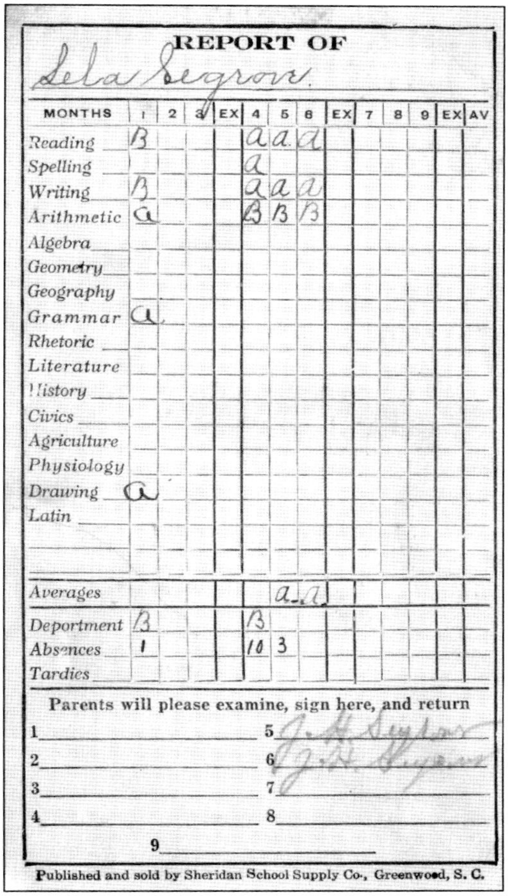
REPORT OF

Lela Segrove

MONTHS	1	2	3	EX	4	5	6	EX	7	8	9	EX	AV
Reading	B				a	a	a						
Spelling					a								
Writing	B				a	a	a						
Arithmetic	a				B	B	B						
Algebra													
Geometry													
Geography													
Grammar	a												
Rhetoric													
Literature													
History													
Civics													
Agriculture													
Physiology													
Drawing	a												
Latin													
Averages						a	a						
Deportment	B				B								
Absences	1				10	3							
Tardies													

Parents will please examine, sign here, and return

1______ 5 J. H. Seagroves
2______ 6 J. H. Seagroves
3______ 7______
4______ 8______
9______

Published and sold by Sheridan School Supply Co., Greenwood, S. C.

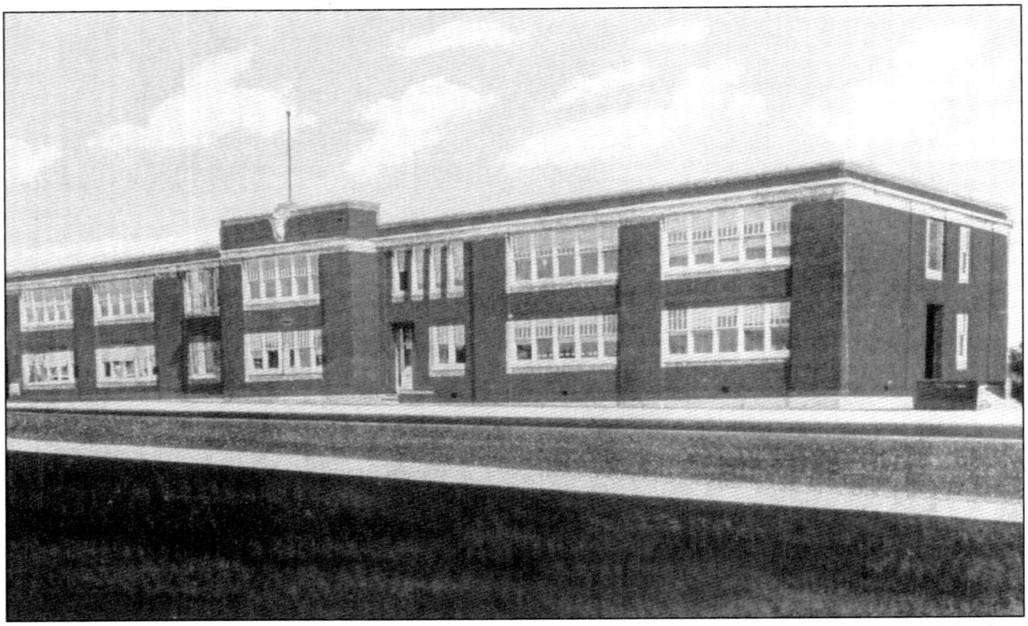

APEX HIGH SCHOOL. This school was built in 1922 after the graded school was destroyed by fire. Apex's student population was quickly growing, so in 1927, the town built an addition. Randolph Benton was the principal from 1921 to 1933. (Courtesy of the University of North Carolina at Chapel Hill.)

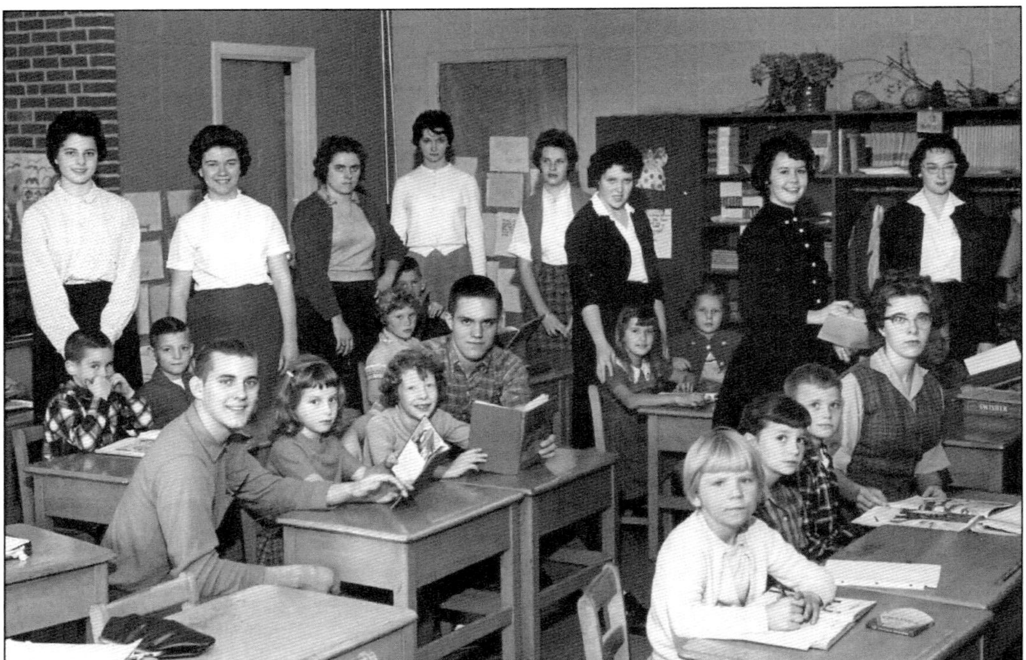

APEX HIGH SCHOOL CLASS. This photograph was taken during the 1950s and shows a few older students helping the younger ones with their studies. (Courtesy of Bob Crowley.)

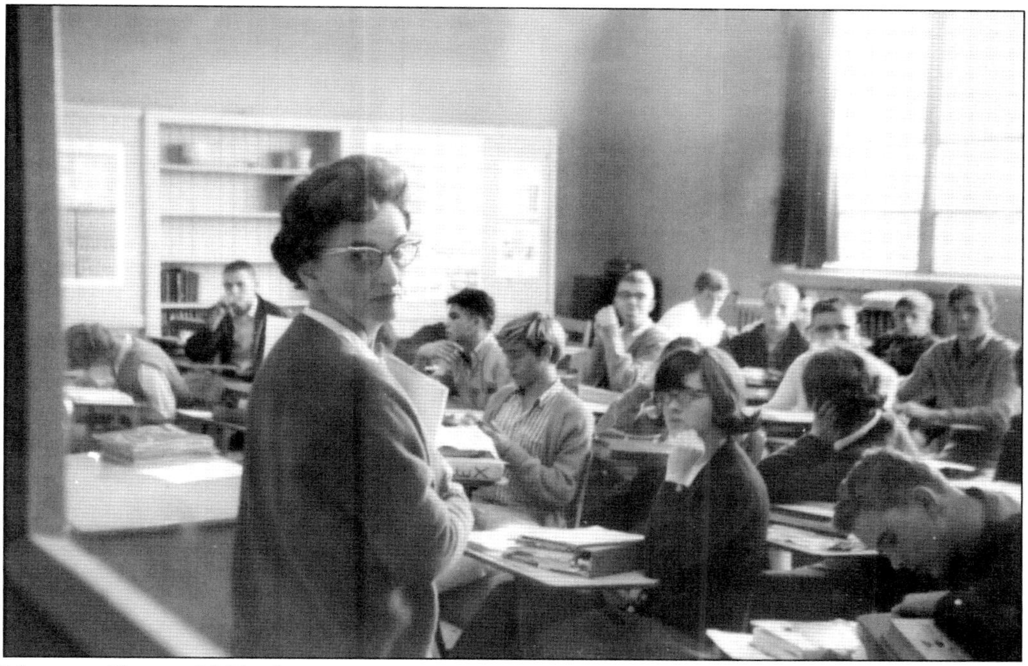

Mildred Cooke. Mildred was regarded as one of the great teachers who educated thousands in Apex. She taught three different classes—chemistry, biology, and physics. Mildred also served as the girls' basketball coach and the driver education teacher. She won the first Wake County Teacher of the Year Award at Apex High School in 1974. (Courtesy of Tommy Stephens and Janet Davis.)

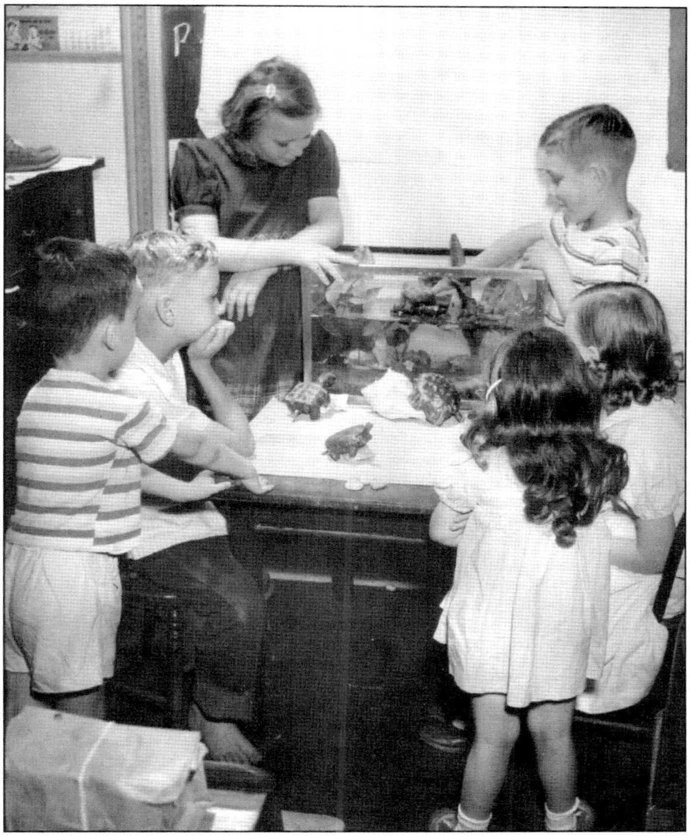

Grade School, 1951. This is a class photograph from 1951 that shows several students infatuated with the aquarium, including Tommy Stephens (front left) and Janet Stephens (front right). (Courtesy of Tommy Stephens and Janet Davis.)

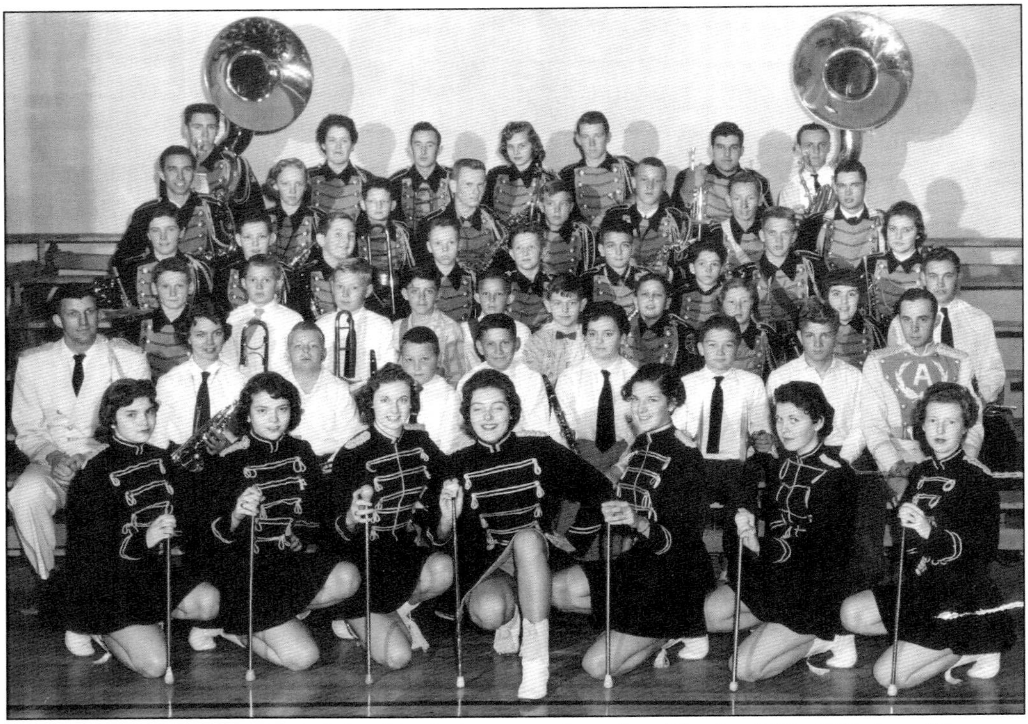

MARCHING BAND. Apex High School had a large marching band for the 1956–1957 class. (Courtesy of Tommy Stephens and Janet Davis.)

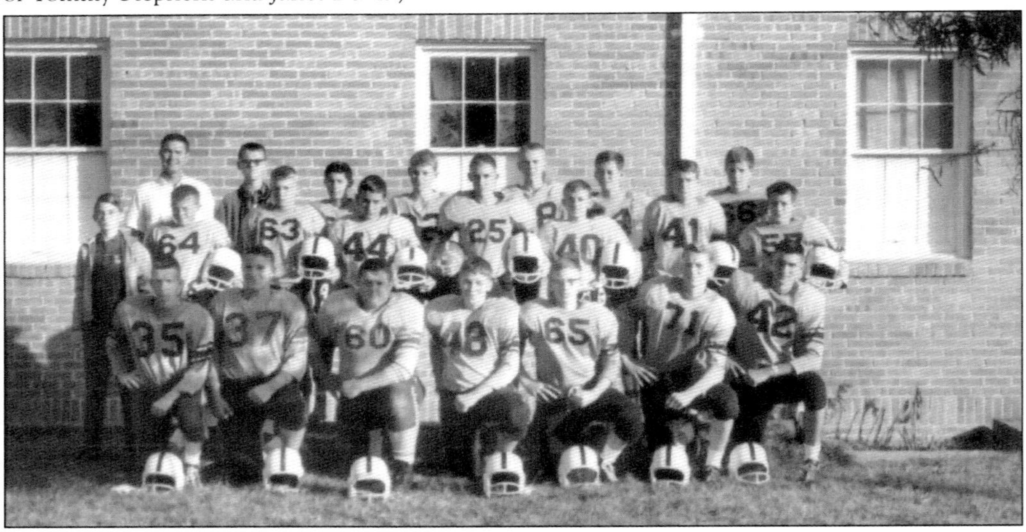

APEX JUNIOR VARSITY FOOTBALL TEAM. This is the group photograph for the 1964 Apex junior varsity football team. Team members were, from left to right, (first row) Carl Goodwin, Mike Obler, Frankie Holland, Ronnie Strickland, Wallace Seagroves, Robert Powell, and Eddie Peagram; (second row) trainer Johnny Maynard, Glenn Pruitt, Mac Walters, Billy Mills, Ronnie Drake, Randy Johnson, Roy Pruitt, and Tommy Stephens; (third row) coach Bob Raynor, manager Donald Edwards, Tim Bell, Bobby Sears, Mike Edwards, Clayborn Yates, and Earl Coggins. (Courtesy of Tommy Stephens and Janet Davis.)

Four

Family Fun and Social Events

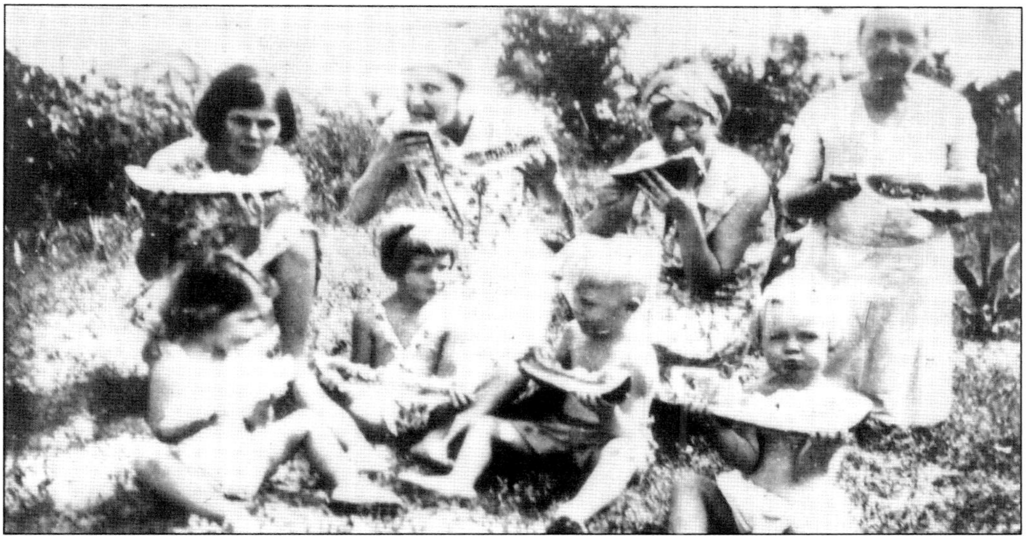

Eating Watermelon. This 1930 photograph captures the Goodwin family enjoying some freshly picked watermelon on the farm. Pictured from left to right are (first row) Grace-Marie Blades, Helen Upchurch, Bill Goodwin, and Jacque Goodwin; (second row) Bebe Blades, Sara Stone, Elizabeth Goodwin, and ? Upchurch. (Courtesy of Jacque Goodwin Burgess.)

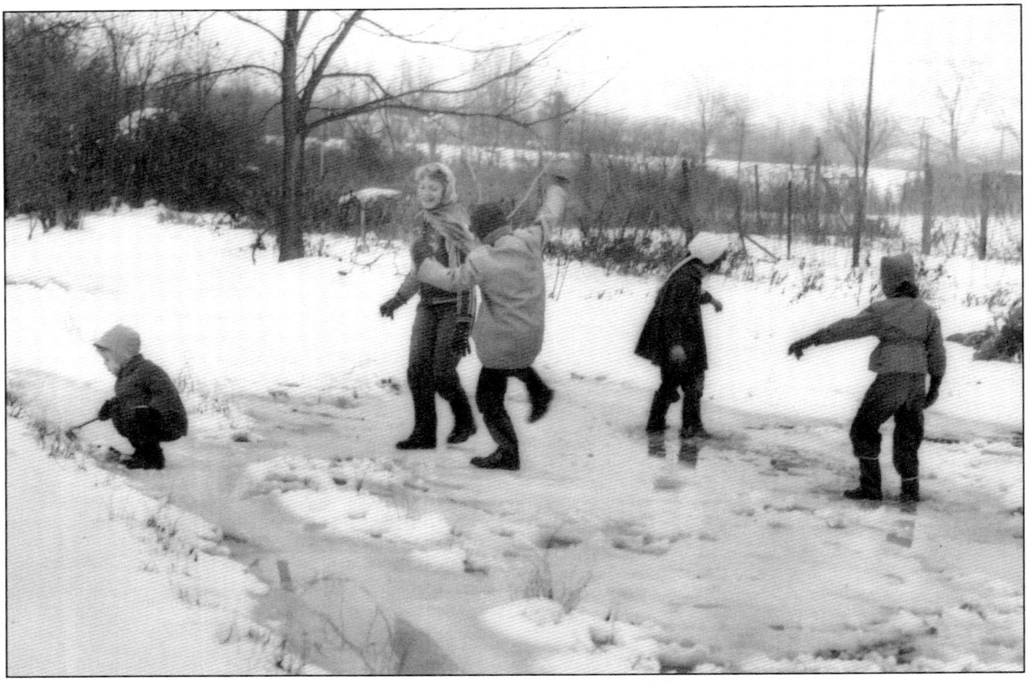

ICE-SKATING. This 1951 photograph shows the Stephens children enjoying a rare winter storm. Pictured from left to right are Tommy Stephens, Linda Stephens, Billy Stephens, Patricia Hart, and Janet Stephens. (Courtesy of Tommy Stephens and Janet Davis.)

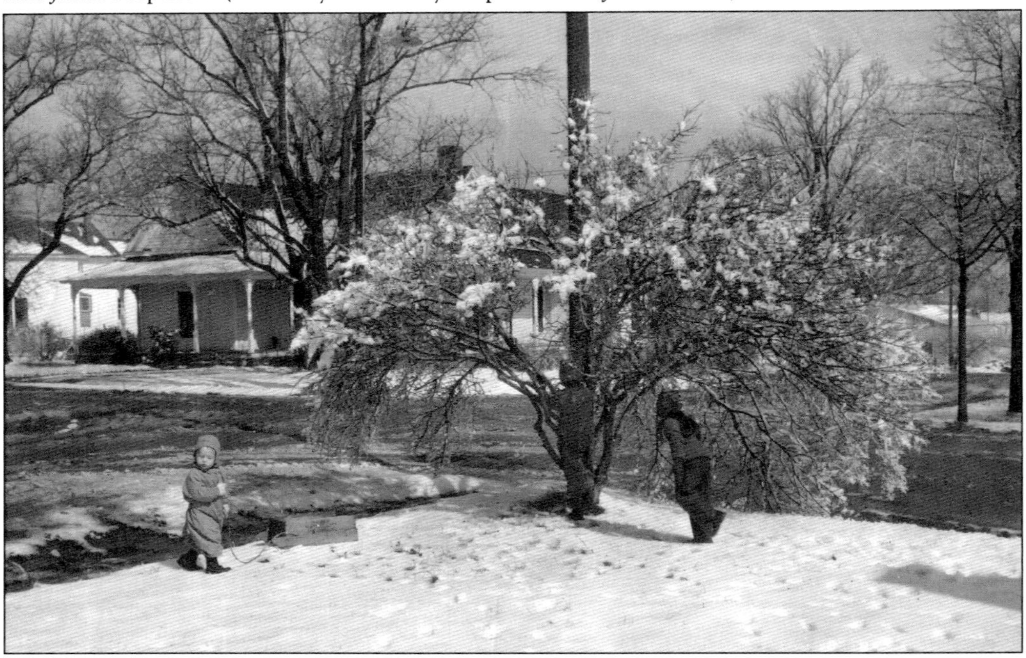

PLAYING IN THE SNOW. Because snow in Apex, North Carolina, happens so infrequently, people loved to photograph it. Tommy Stephens (left) and Billy Stephens enjoy themselves while playing in their yard. This image was taken around 1953. (Courtesy of Tommy Stephens and Janet Davis.)

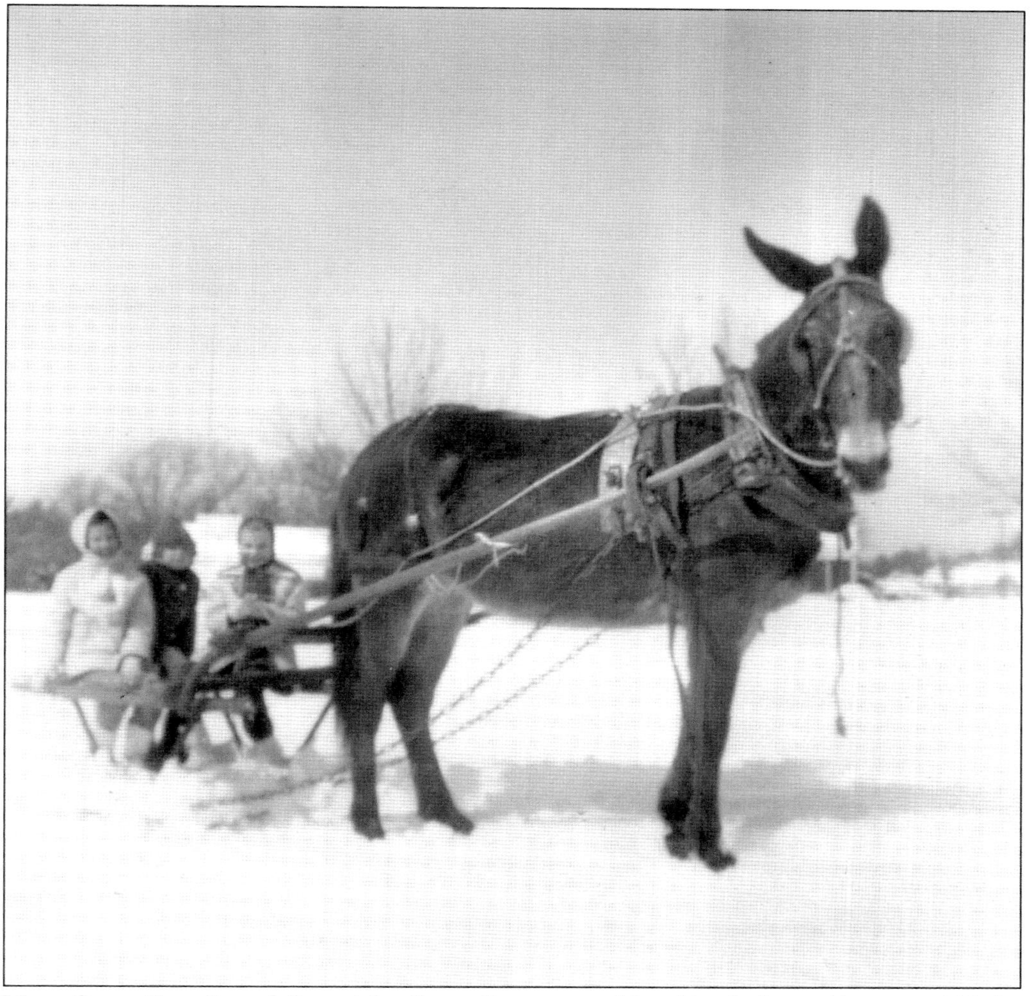

More Snow Fun. From left to right, Susan Seymour and her friends Susan Owens and Kathy Owens take off for a real sleigh ride in 1960 during a snowstorm. Susan is the granddaughter of Alphaeus "Alfred" Seymour, who owned the Seymour-Watkins Hardware store in town. (Courtesy of Susan Mills.)

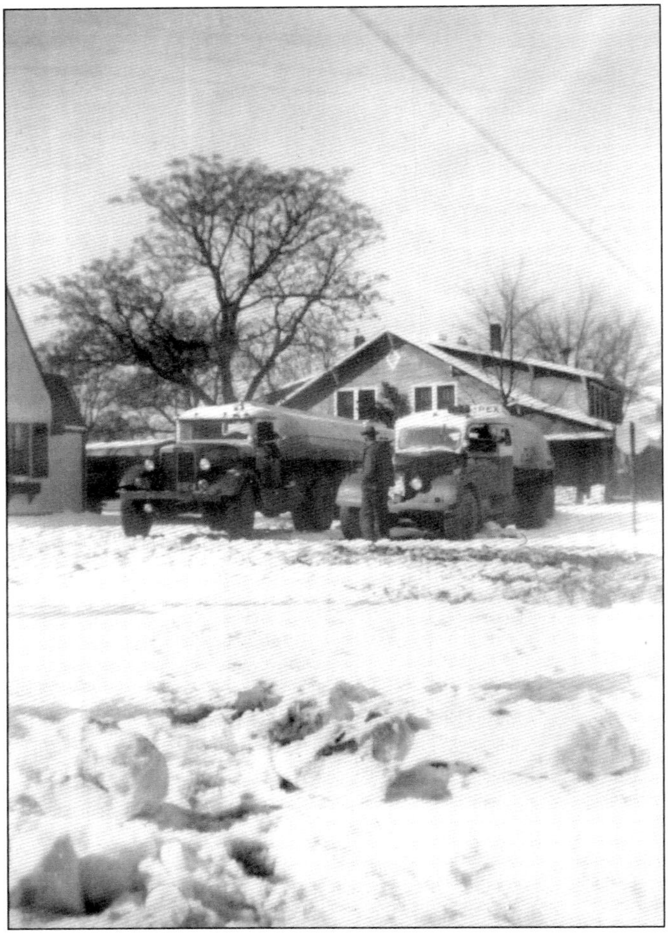

SNOW IN 1946. While this snow is clearly starting to melt, these photographs show the snow's height and trucks that appear to be stuck in it. The image below shows a brave sole venturing out to get gas at the local station. (Both, courtesy of Ann Grebing.)

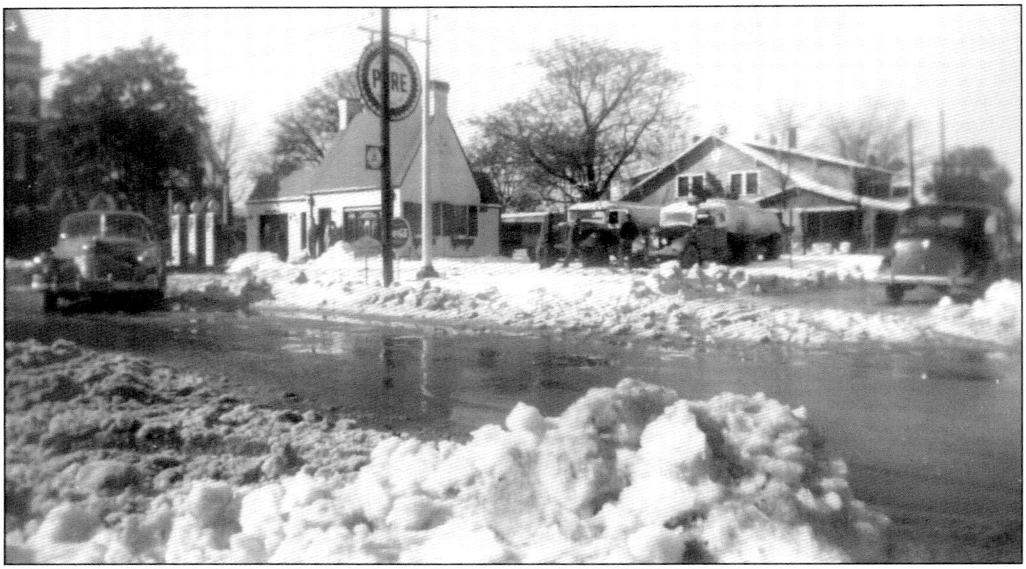

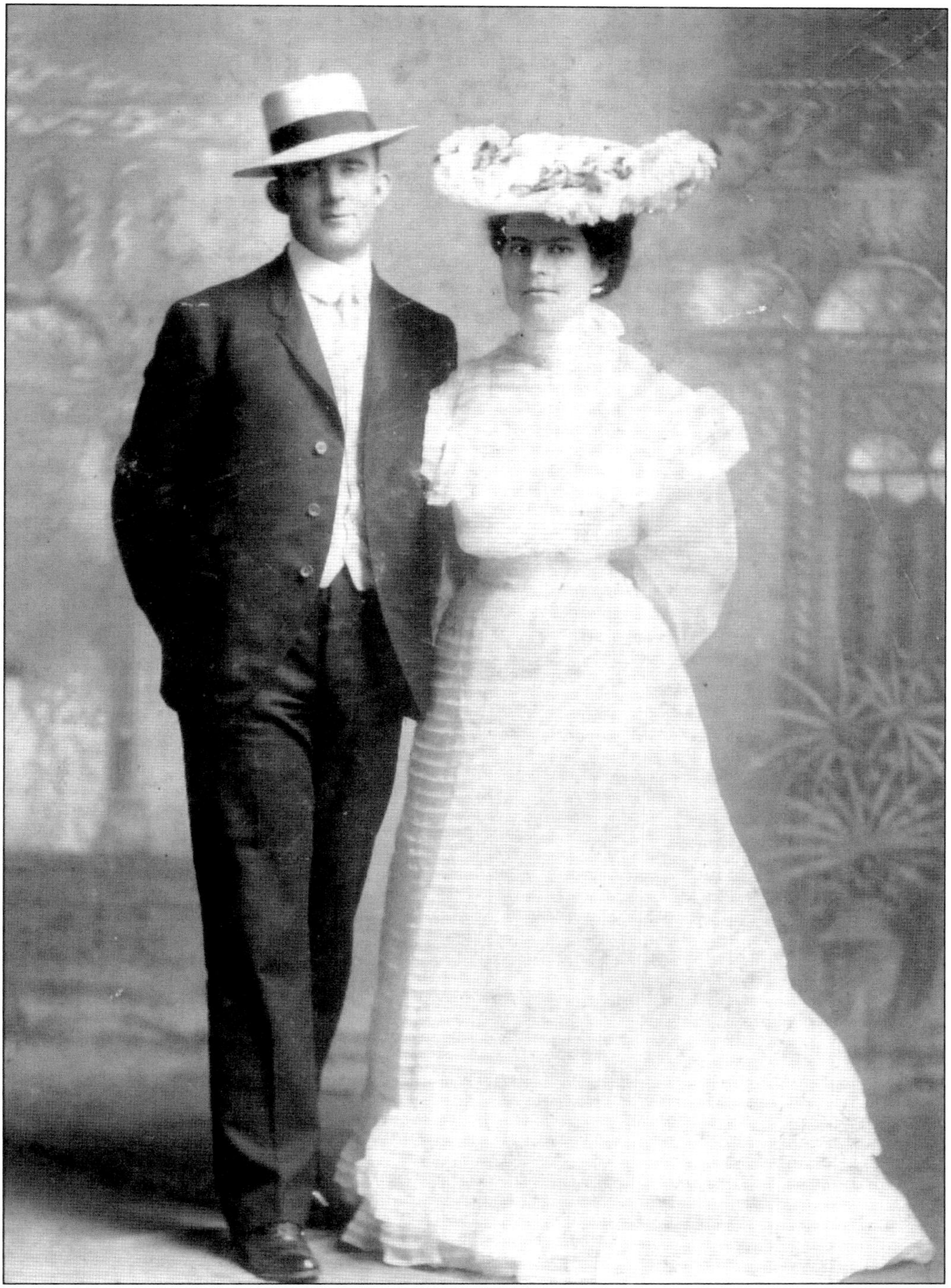

MALPHEUS "MAC" AND LESSIE UPCHURCH. This is Mac and Lessie's 1903 wedding photograph. Lessie was 19 when they were married. They were married for 42 years and were members of the Green Level Baptist Church. Mac was the secretary and treasurer of the Apex Mercantile Company and the cashier at the Apex Peoples Bank. (Courtesy of Gilbert Upchurch.)

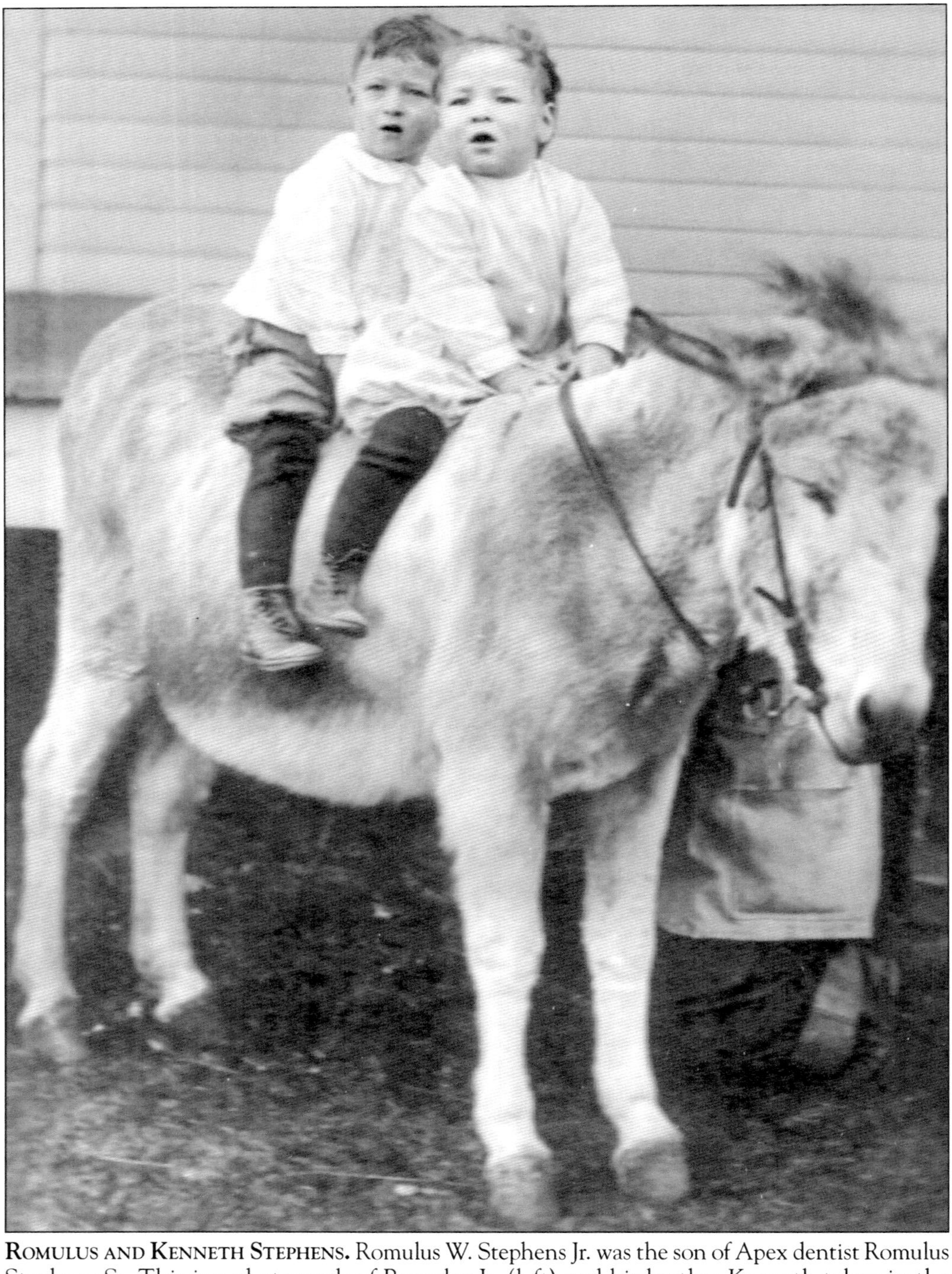

ROMULUS AND KENNETH STEPHENS. Romulus W. Stephens Jr. was the son of Apex dentist Romulus Stephens Sr. This is a photograph of Romulus Jr. (left) and his brother Kenneth taken in the early 1900s. Romulus Jr. was born in 1911, and Kenneth was born about 1914. Romulus went on to be a photographer with the *News and Observer*, while Kenneth attended North Carolina State University, where he boxed. Kenneth even showed Granny Stephens a few boxing moves. (Courtesy of Tommy Stephens and Janet Davis.)

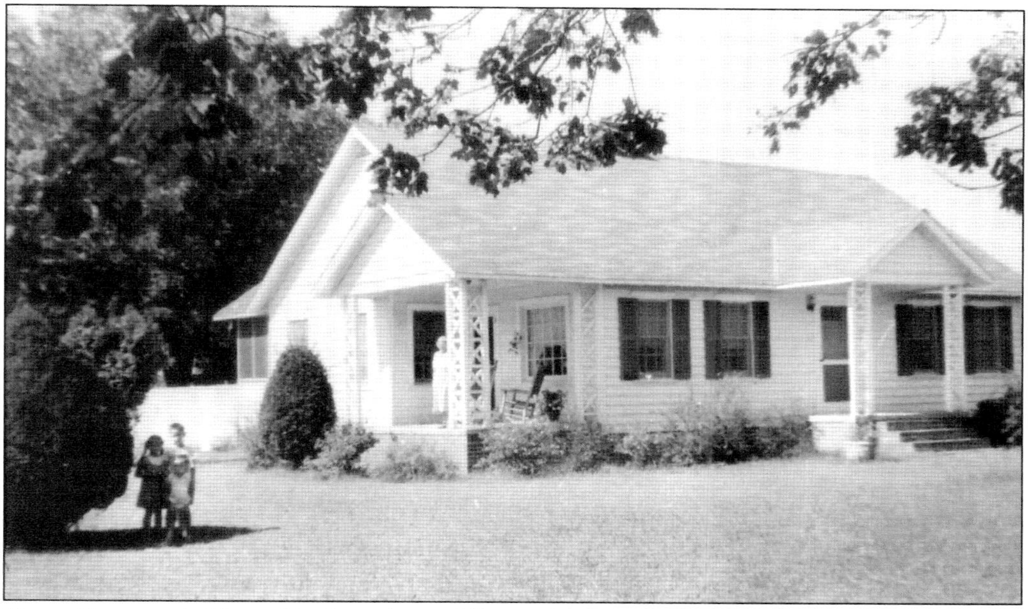

DOVIE STEPHENS'S HOME. Dr. Romulus and Dovie Stephens had a beautiful home that was built in the 1920s. In 1938, Dr. Stephens passed away, and almost 10 years later, the 1920s home burned to the ground. This house was rebuilt for Dovie, who is standing on the porch. Her grandchildren, Janet Stephens (left), Tommy Stephens (front), and Billy Stephens, are on the lawn. (Courtesy of Tommy Stephens and Janet Davis.)

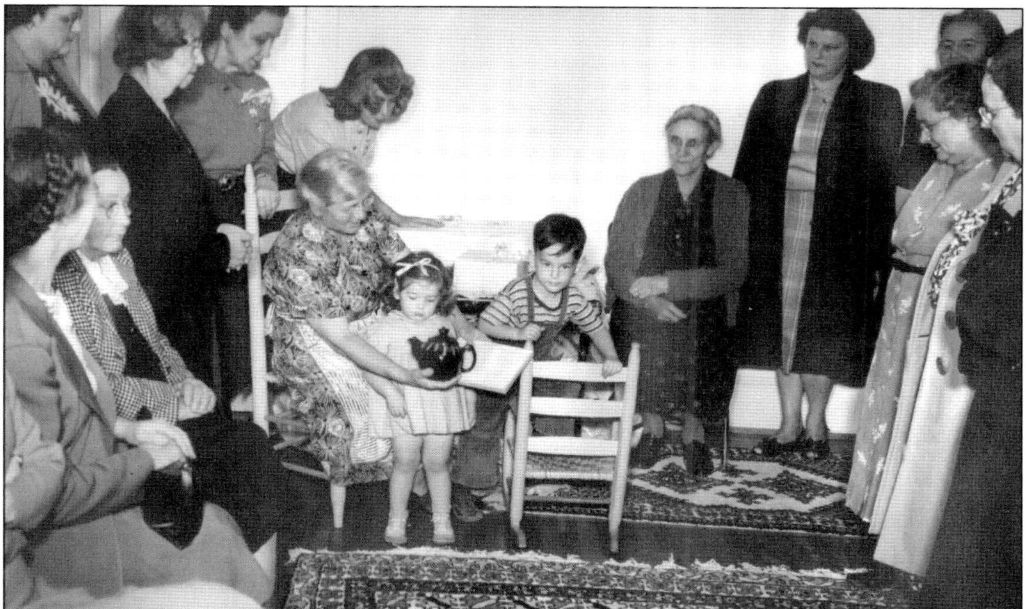

DOVIE STEPHENS'S HOUSEWARMING PARTY. Many Apex residents were invited to Dovie's housewarming party in 1949. Mrs. A. V. Baucom (Anna) is in the far right corner. Dovie is in the center showing Janet and Billy Stephens a teapot. (Courtesy of Tommy Stephens and Janet Davis.)

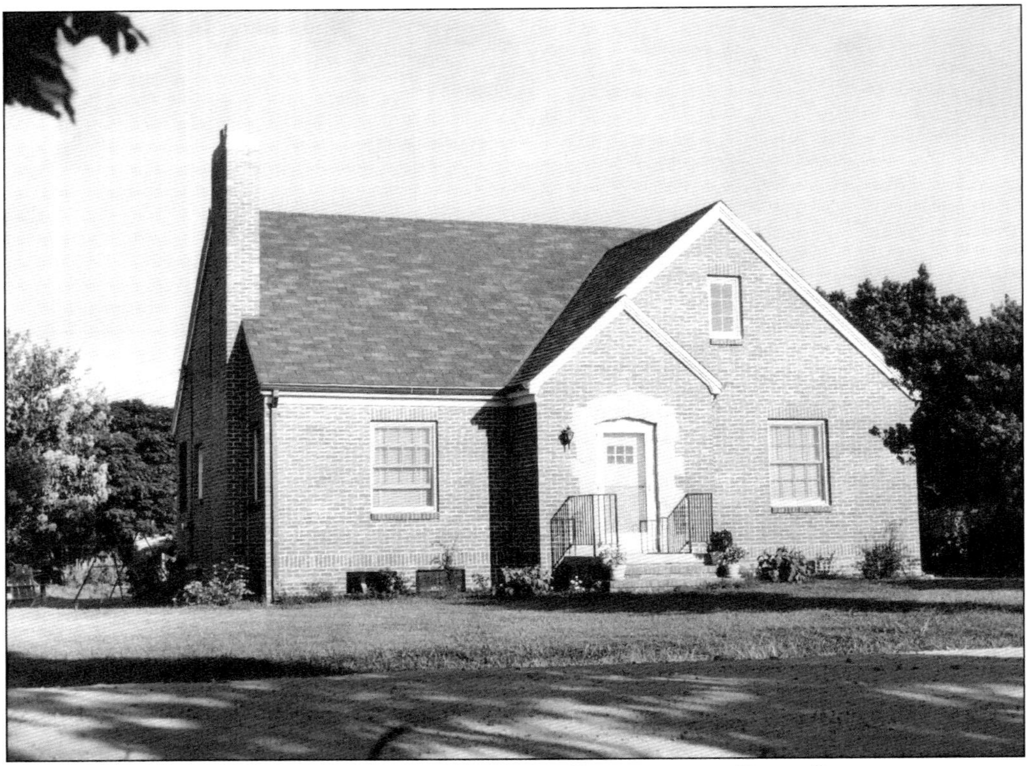

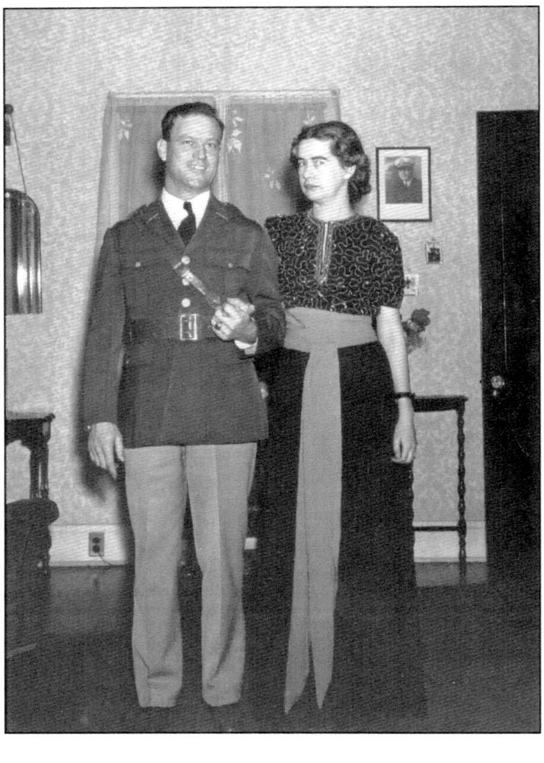

ROMULUS AND EMMA STEPHENS AND THEIR HOME. This was the home of Romulus and Emma Stephens on South Mason Street. Romulus Jr. served in World War II as a captain in the U.S. Army Air Forces. (Both, courtesy of Tommy Stephens and Janet Davis.)

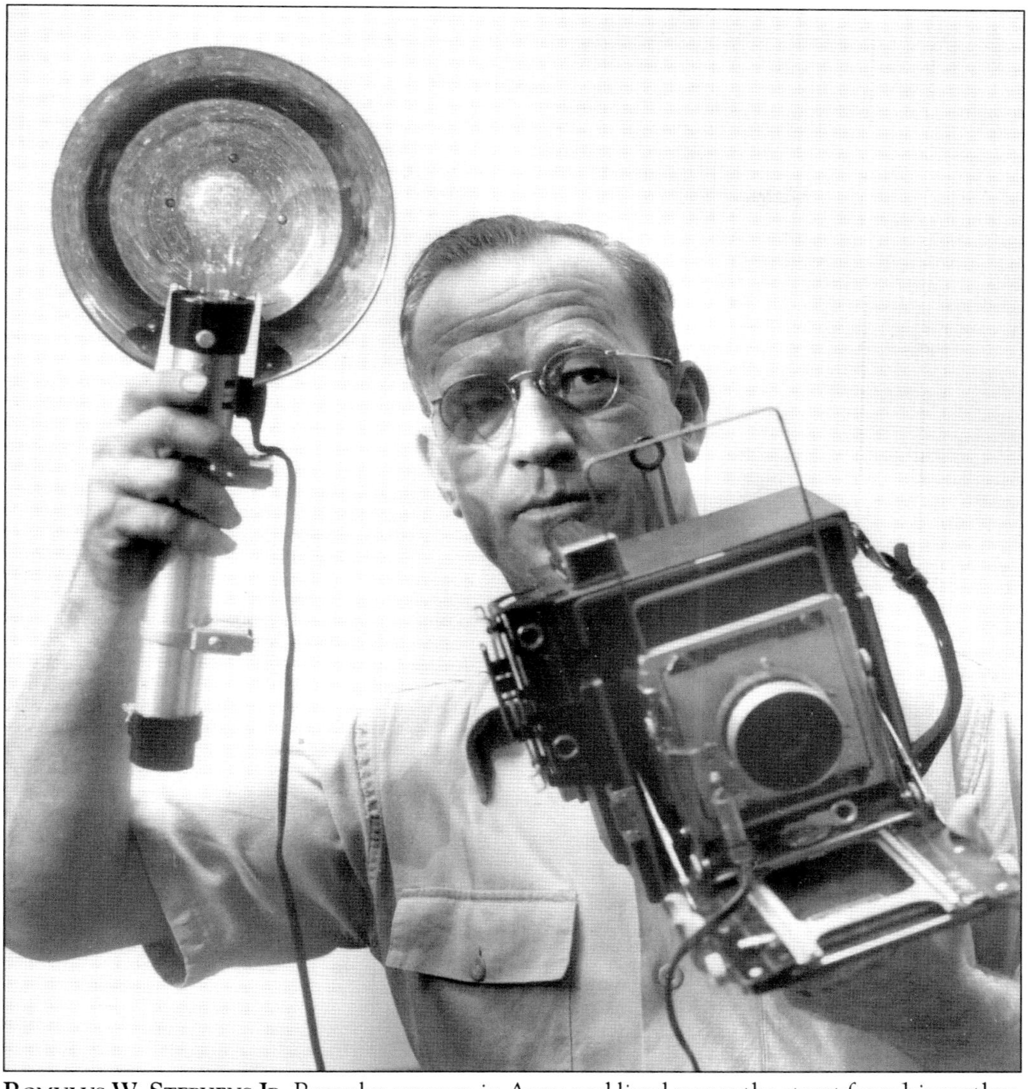

ROMULUS W. STEPHENS JR. Romulus grew up in Apex and lived across the street from his mother, Dovie. He and his wife, Emma, raised their three children, Billy, Janet, and Tommy, in the house shown on the opposite page. He served in World War II, and when he returned home from the war, he took a job with the *News and Observer* as a photographer. He also photographed many local events. His images captured Apex's history from the 1940s through the 1950s. He passed away in 1956 at the age of 45. (Courtesy of Tommy Stephens and Janet Davis.)

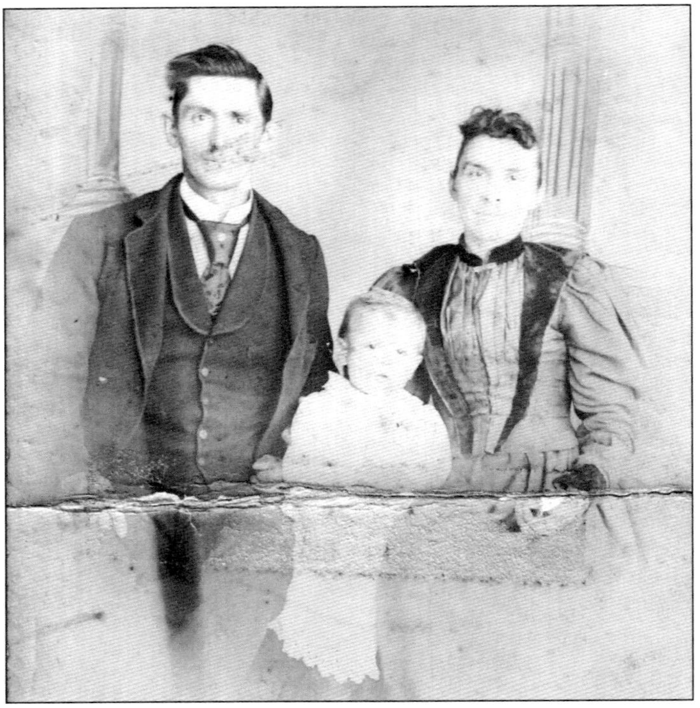

Asa, Rena, and Oscar Goodwin. This photograph was taken when Asa and Rena welcomed their first child. Oscar was born in 1894 in a log cabin. (Courtesy of Jacque Goodwin Burgess.)

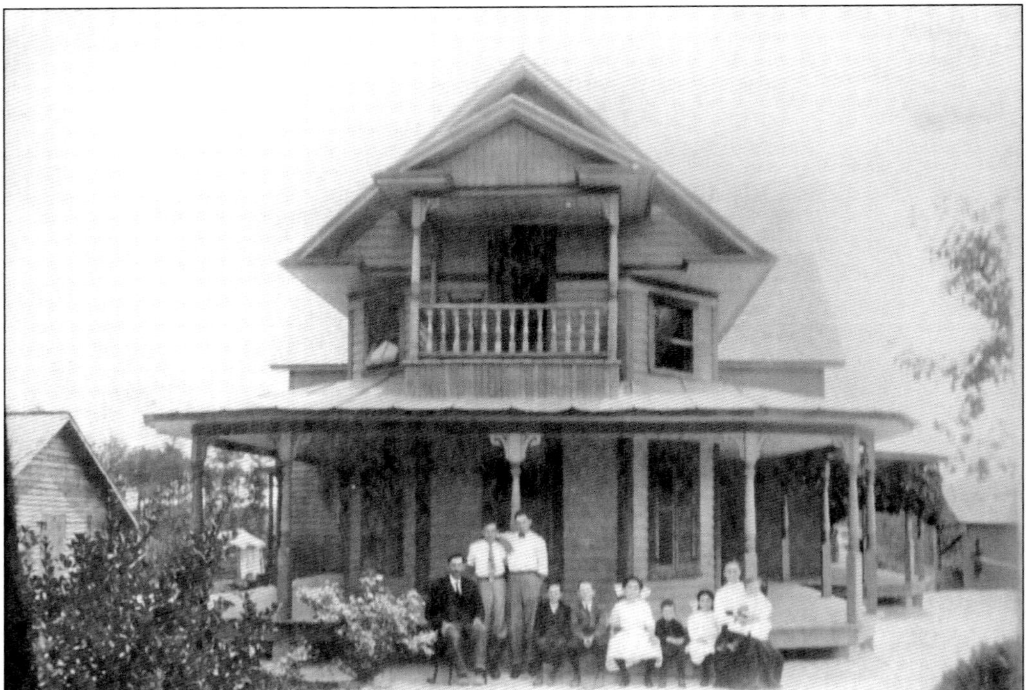

Asa Goodwin Home, around 1910. This house was built in 1903 for the Goodwin clan. Asa and Rena had eight children, who are all pictured here. From left to right are Asa, Omer, Oscar, Clarence, Carl, Bernice, Cary, Annie, Rena, and Frank. (Courtesy of Jacque Goodwin Burgess.)

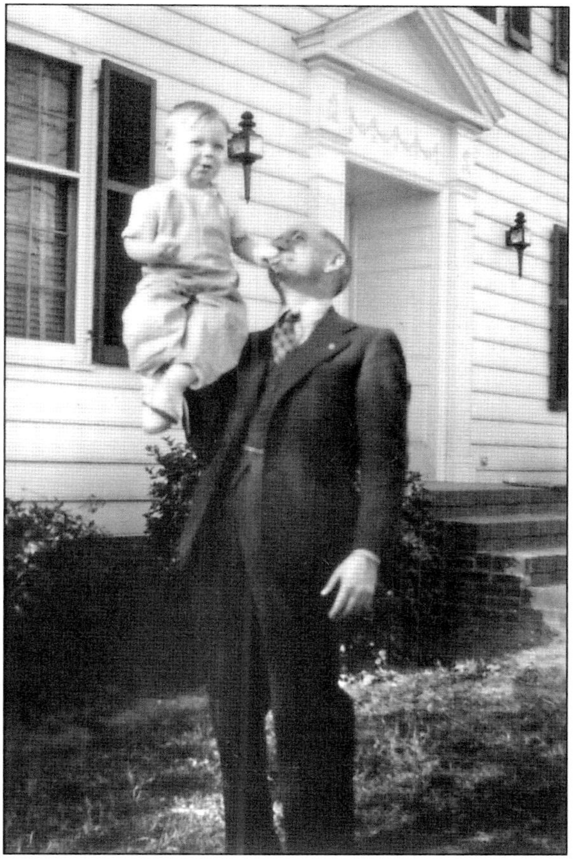

DRS. OSCAR AND JAMES GOODWIN. Dr. Oscar practiced medicine in Apex for a number of years. He attended the University of North Carolina–Chapel Hill in 1924 and then went on to Jefferson Hospital in Philadelphia. His son Jimmy followed in his father's footsteps and became a doctor as well. (Courtesy of Jacque Goodwin Burgess.)

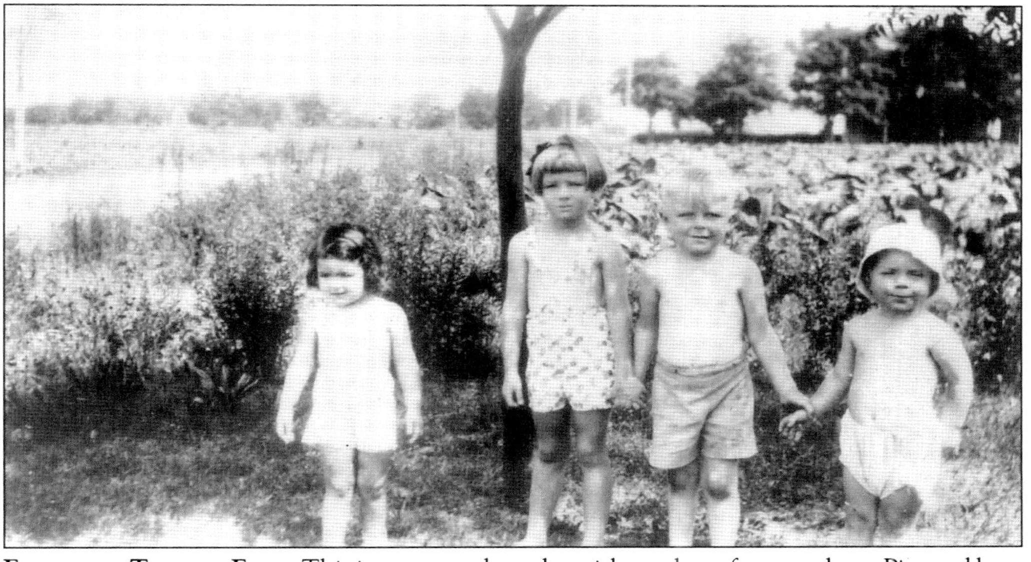

FUN IN THE TOBACCO FIELD. This just goes to show that girls can have fun anywhere. Pictured here from left to right are Grace-Marie Blades, Helen Upchurch, Bill Goodwin, and Jacque Goodwin. (Courtesy of Jacque Goodwin Burgess.)

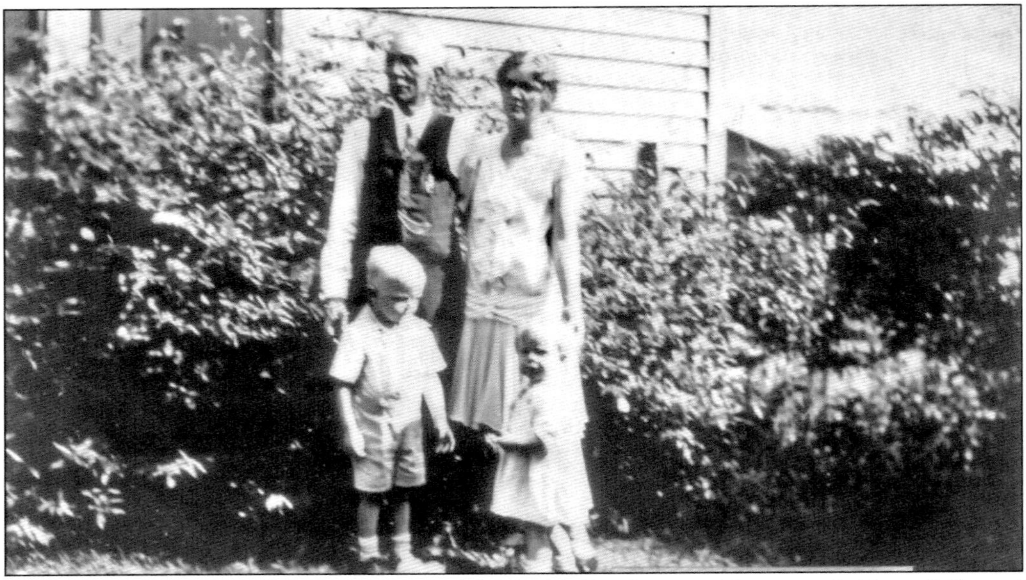

VISITING THE FAMILY. This is Mrs. Oscar (Elizabeth) Goodwin and her two children, Billy and Jacque. They were visiting her family in Philadelphia. The man in the photograph is her father, Isaac Shreve. (Courtesy of Jacque Goodwin Burgess.)

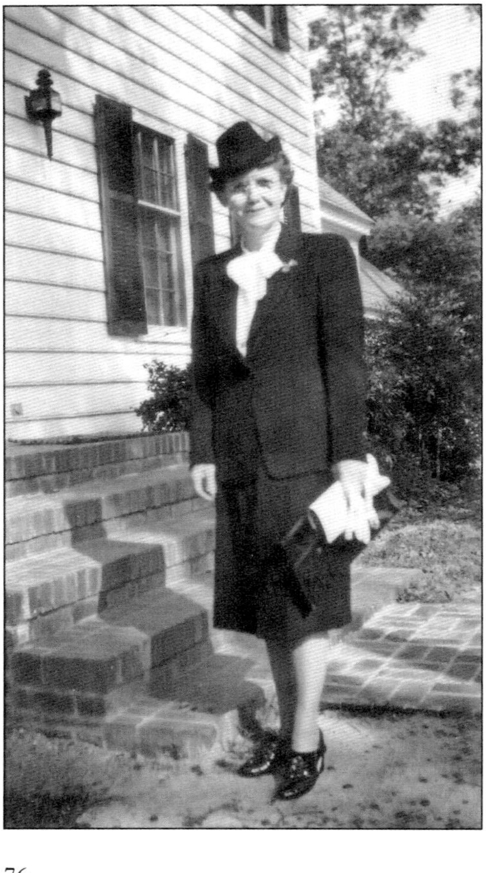

MRS. ELIZABETH GOODWIN. Elizabeth Shreve married Dr. Oscar Goodwin even though his parents did not approve. Her only downfall was that she was a Yankee. Despite that, they were married and lived a very happy life in Apex. (Courtesy of Jacque Goodwin Burgess.)

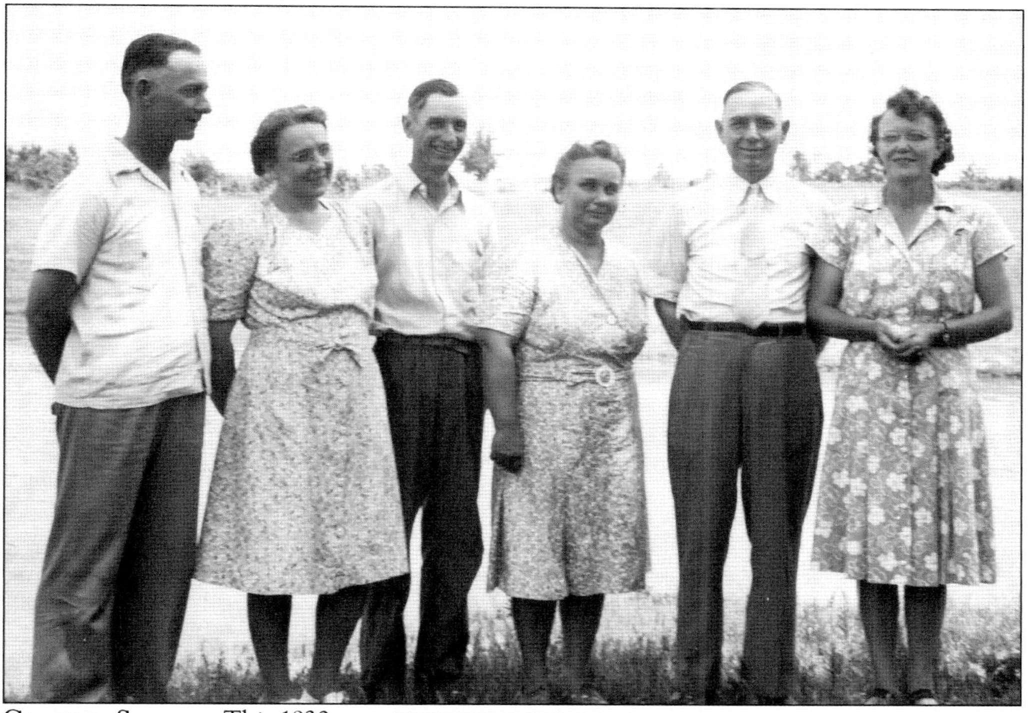

GOODWIN SIBLINGS. This 1930 photograph captures a reunion among some of the Goodwin siblings. From left to right are Carl; his wife, Nellie; Clarence; his wife, Rachel; Oscar; and his wife, Elizabeth. (Courtesy of Jacque Goodwin Burgess.)

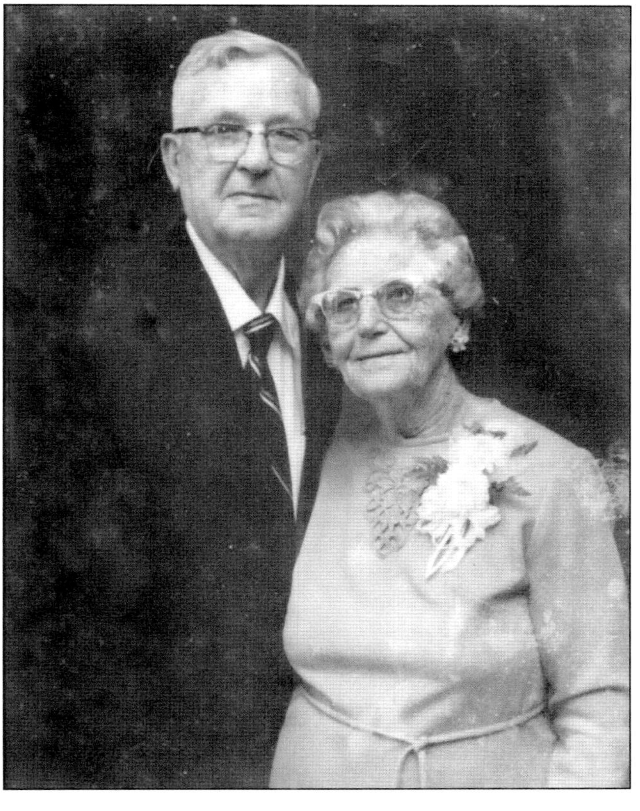

BENTON 50TH ANNIVERSARY. Howard Benton and his wife, Lillian, celebrated their 50th wedding anniversary in 1963. They were married in 1913. Howard was a successful businessman in Apex for a number of years. (Courtesy of Margaret Benton Ferry.)

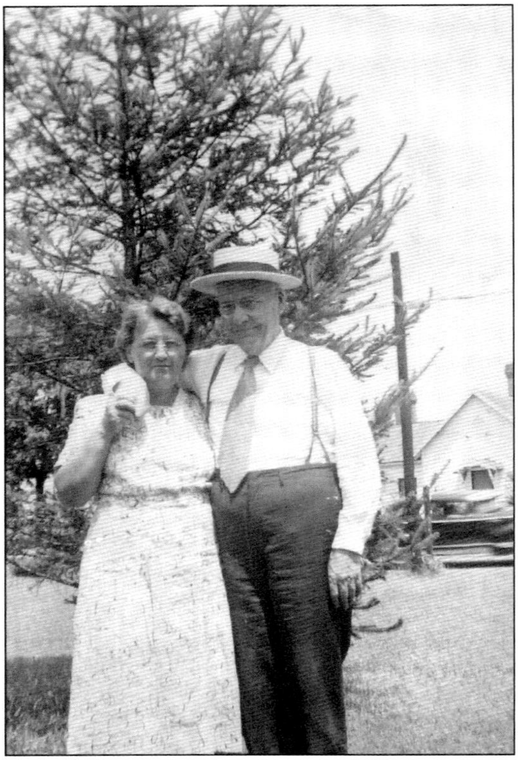

A. T. and Lila Seymour. Alphaeus, or "Alfred," and Lila May Stone-Seymour raised three children in Apex. A. T. had a variety of businesses in Apex. He was a partner in the Watkins-Seymour Company, which operated a hardware store. He was also involved with the Seymour Stockyards and was a real estate agent. (Courtesy of Susan Mills.)

A 25th Wedding Anniversary. In 1938, A. T. and Lila Seymour celebrated their 25th wedding anniversary. (Courtesy of Susan Mills.)

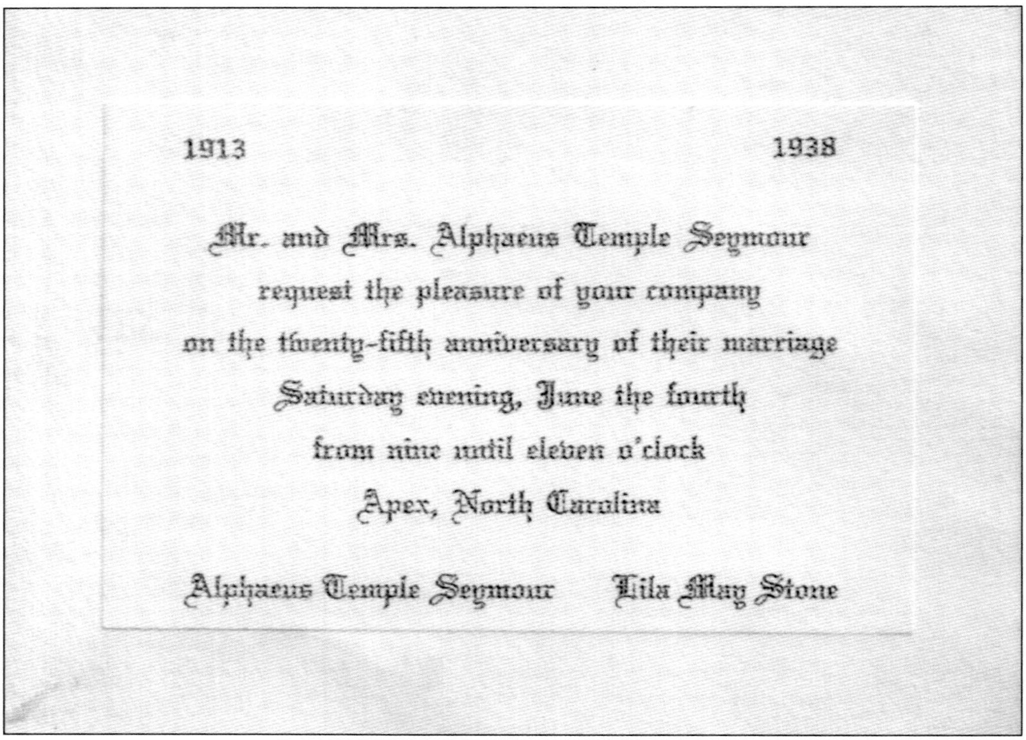

1913 1938

Mr. and Mrs. Alphaeus Temple Seymour
request the pleasure of your company
on the twenty-fifth anniversary of their marriage
Saturday evening, June the fourth
from nine until eleven o'clock
Apex, North Carolina

Alphaeus Temple Seymour Lila May Stone

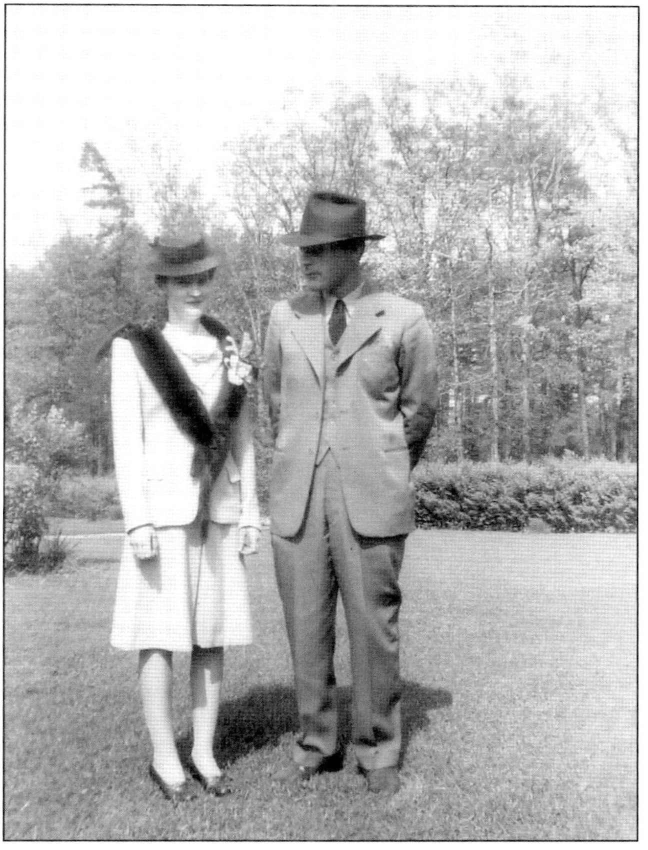

A. T. Jr. and Doris Seymour. The next generation of Seymours began with A. T. Seymour Jr., who was born in 1914. He married Doris Bright in 1934. They raised two daughters, Anne and Susan, and a son, Alphaeus III. (Courtesy of Susan Mills.)

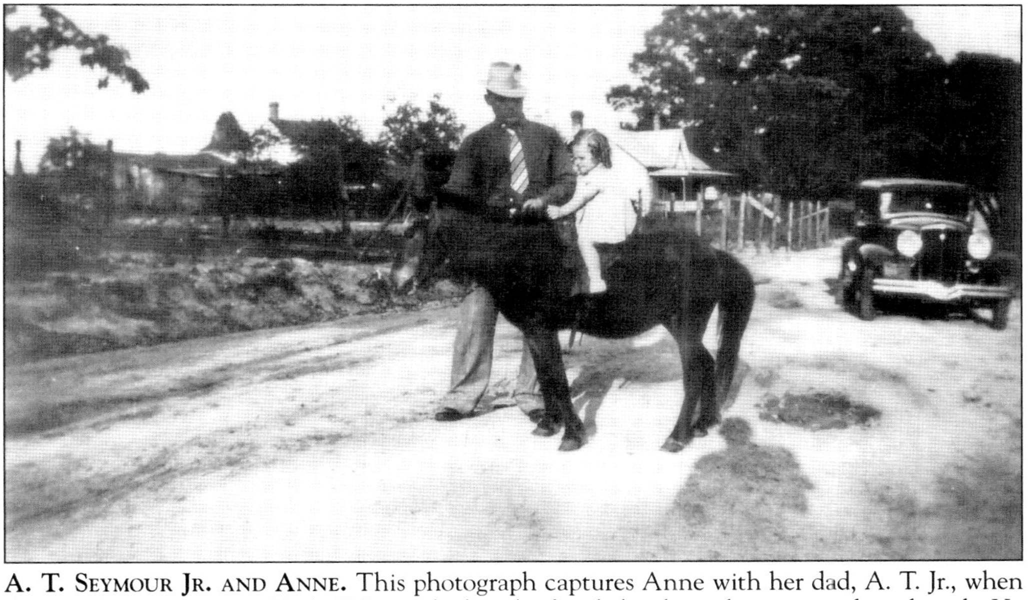

A. T. Seymour Jr. and Anne. This photograph captures Anne with her dad, A. T. Jr., when she was very young in 1937. A. T. Jr. worked in the family hardware business and stockyards. He also owned stables where the police station sits today. (Courtesy of Susan Mills.)

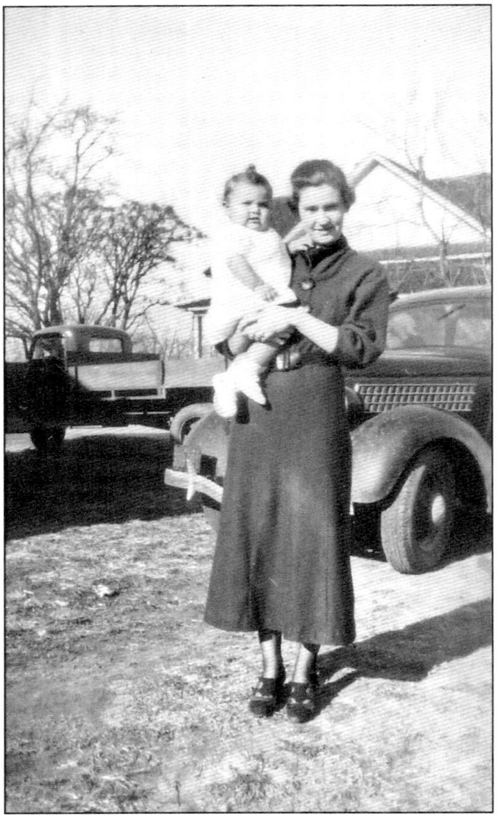

DORIS AND ANNE SEYMOUR. Here is Doris showing off her new baby girl, Anne, in 1937. (Courtesy of Susan Mills.)

BABY CARRIAGE, 1950. This is Susan Seymour-Mills enjoying her new, sporty baby carriage in the backyard. (Courtesy of Susan Mills.)

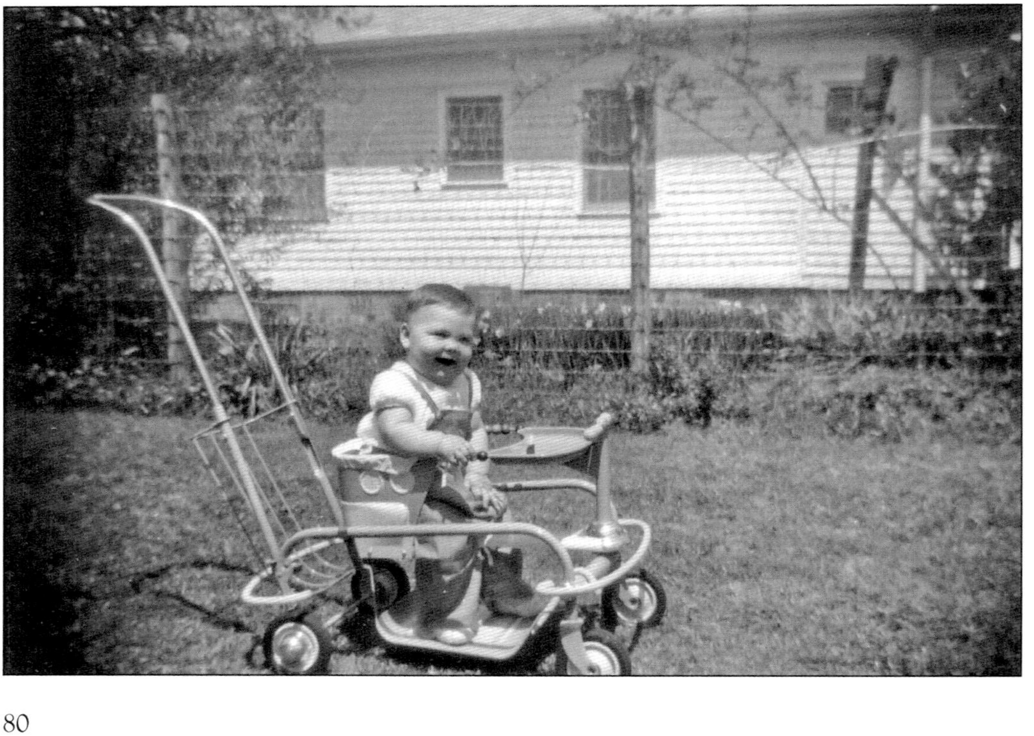

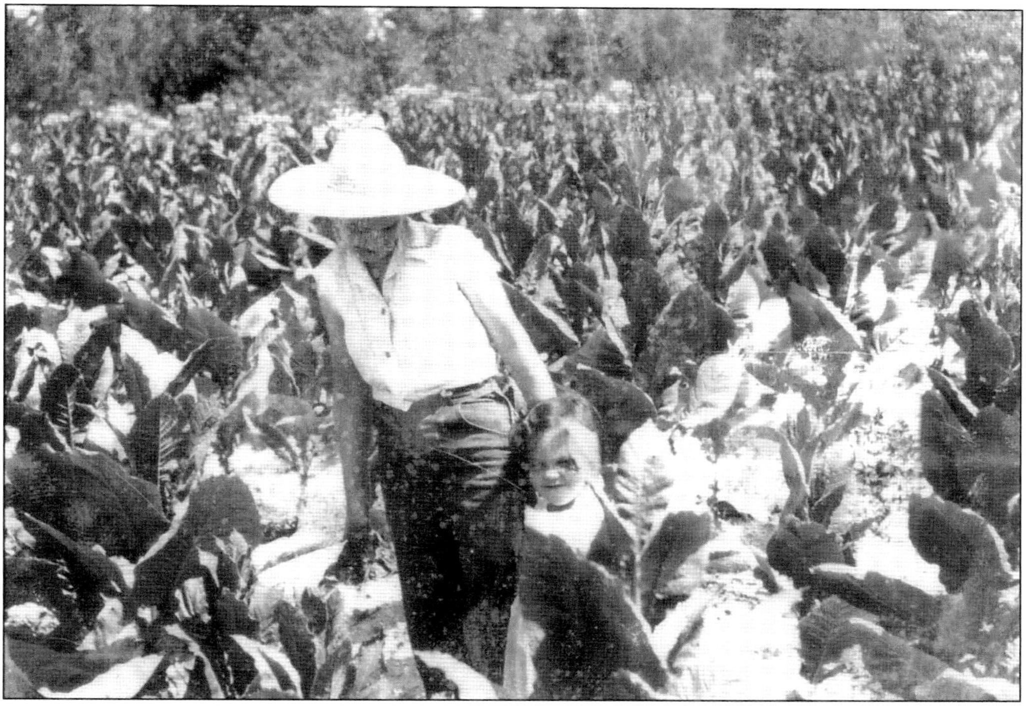

DORIS AND SUSAN SEYMOUR. This 1953 photograph captures Susan and her mother walking in the tobacco field. (Courtesy of Susan Mills.)

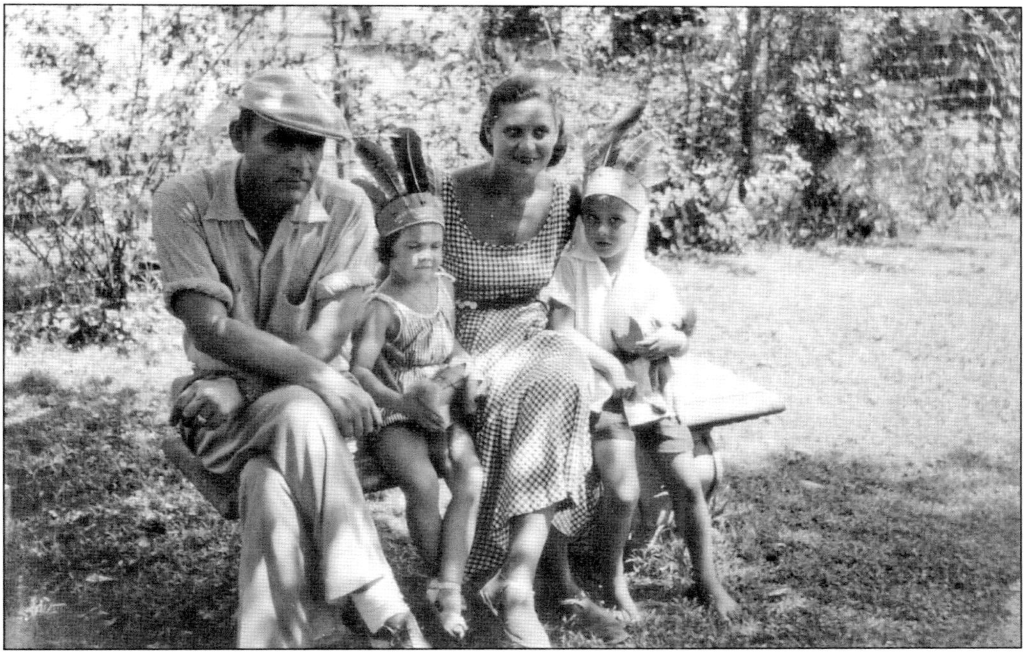

INDIANS IN APEX. Susan Seymour and her cousin Tommy are dressed to play Indians. Susan's father, A. T. Seymour, and his sister-in-law, Margaret, are also seated with them. (Courtesy of Susan Mills.)

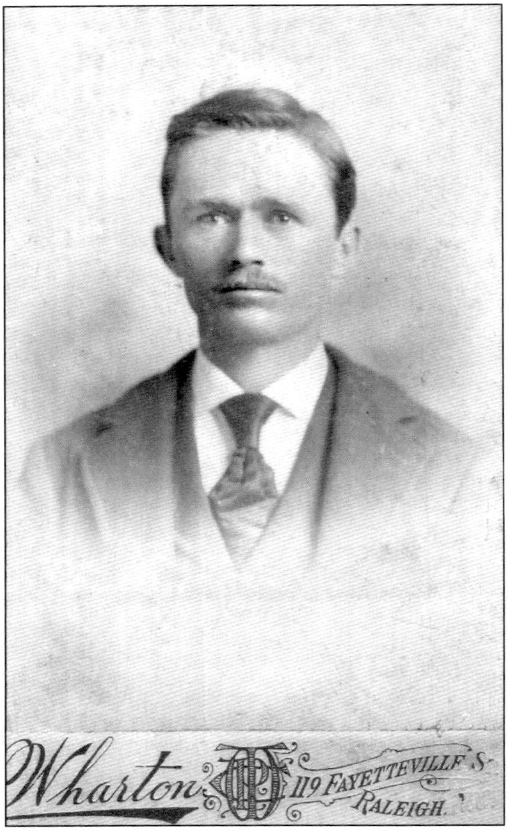

John and Pearl Mann-Seagroves. John and Pearl lived at 241 Swift Creek Road, where John was a farmer. Pearl was also known as Nevada P. They later moved to Center Street, where they raised four children, Walter G., Esther, Lelia, and John Q. Pearl. Her sister, Allie, and brother-in-law, Henry Rhodes, lived next door to the Seagroves on Swift Creek Road. (Both, courtesy of Diane Long.)

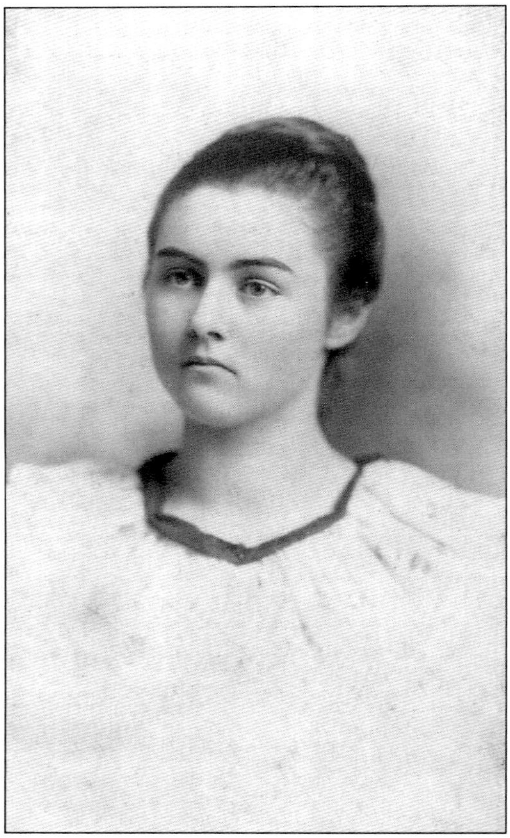

THOMAS EDISON SEAGROVES. Little is known about Thomas other than he was likely a cousin, and this photograph was taken in the early 1900s. (Courtesy of Diane Long.)

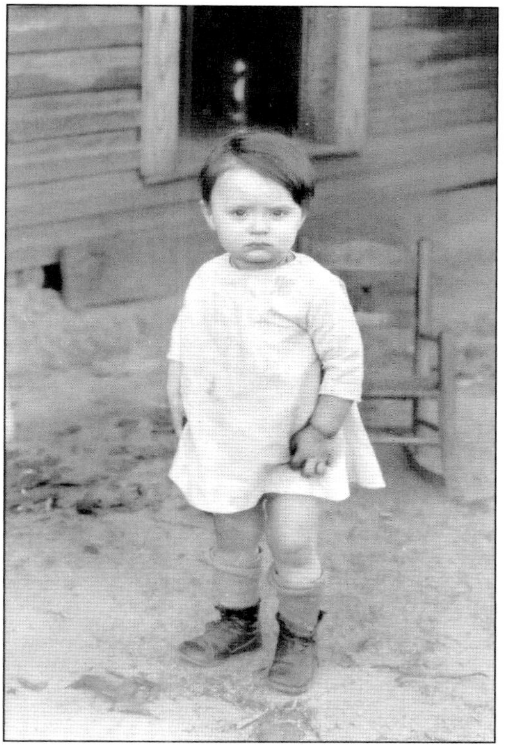

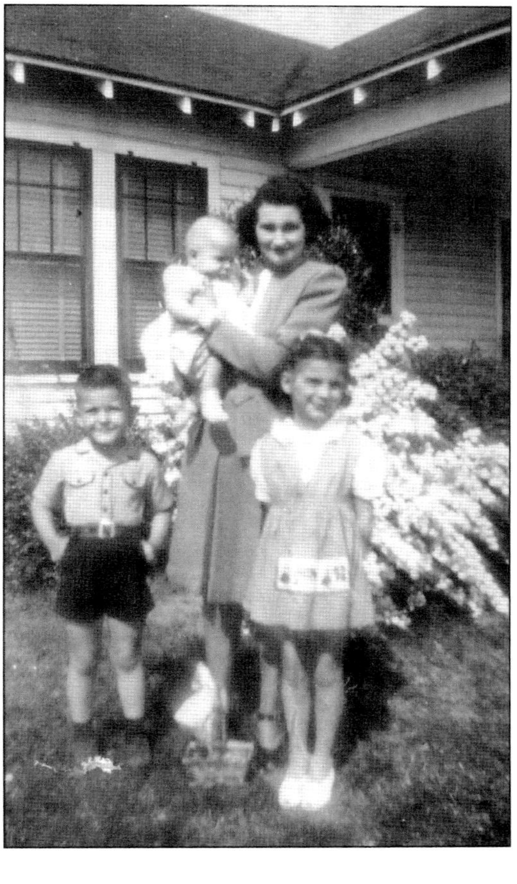

MABEL MANN-LONG. This 1940s photograph shows Mabel Mann-Long and her three children, (from left to right) Moody Allen Long, Blake, and Lawrence. Mabel is the daughter of Adolphus Mann, who was Daniel's youngest son. Mabel was accepted to the Duke University School of Nursing but did not attend. Instead, she married E. M. Long. Her son, Moody, was named after the evangelist Dwight L. Moody. (Courtesy of Diane Long.)

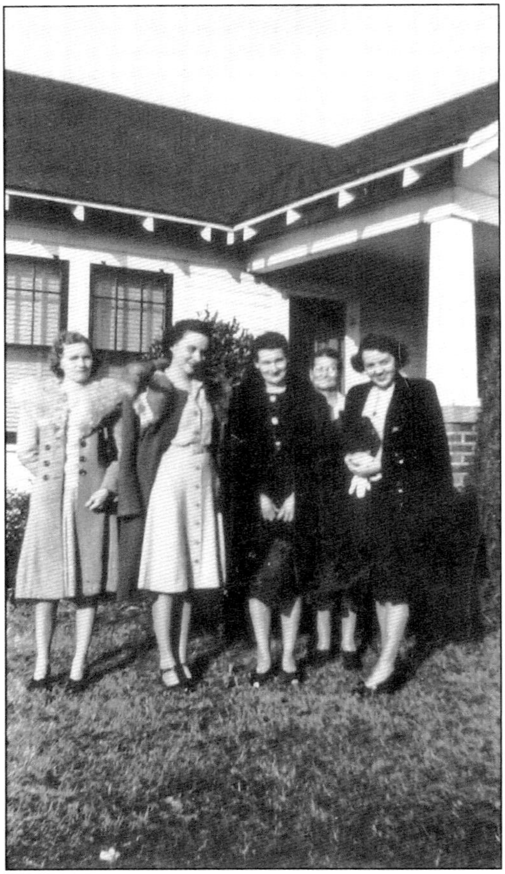

The Girls, 1940s. Houses tend to make great backdrops for family photographs. The Seagroves sisters thought so, too. Pictured from left to right are Esther, Lelia, Mabel Mann-Long, Vera Mann (Mabel's mother), and Margaret Seagroves, who was Esther and Lelia's sister-in-law. (Courtesy of Diane Long.)

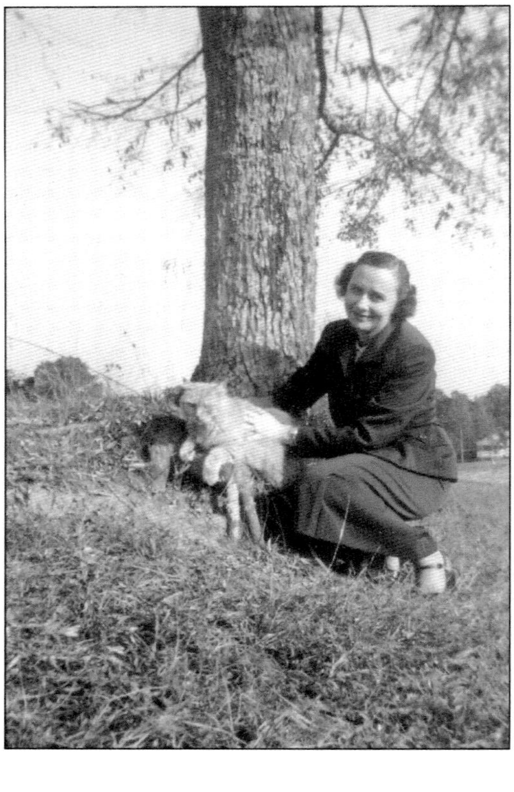

Lelia Seagroves. Lelia was the daughter of John and Pearl Seagroves. She was a beautician and worked in Pinehurst and Raleigh. She adored cats and was often photographed with her pets. (Courtesy of Diane Long.)

WALTER G. SEAGROVES, 1920S. Walter was the eldest son of John and Pearl Seagroves and was born in 1906. (Courtesy of Diane Long.)

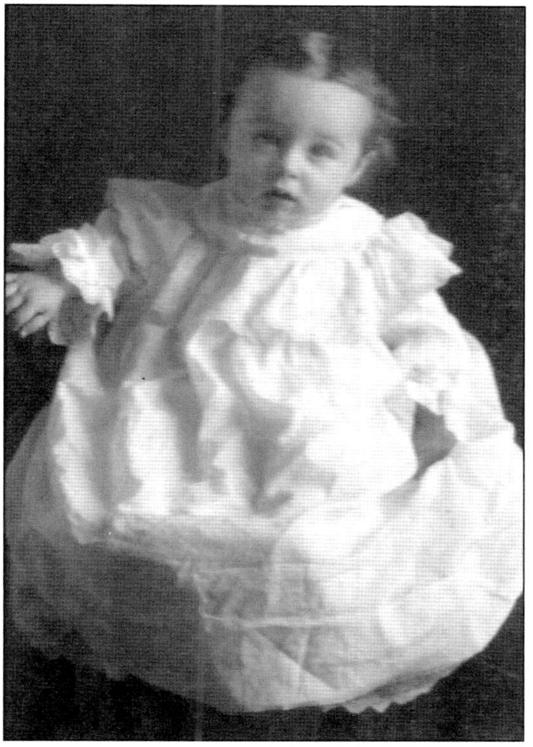

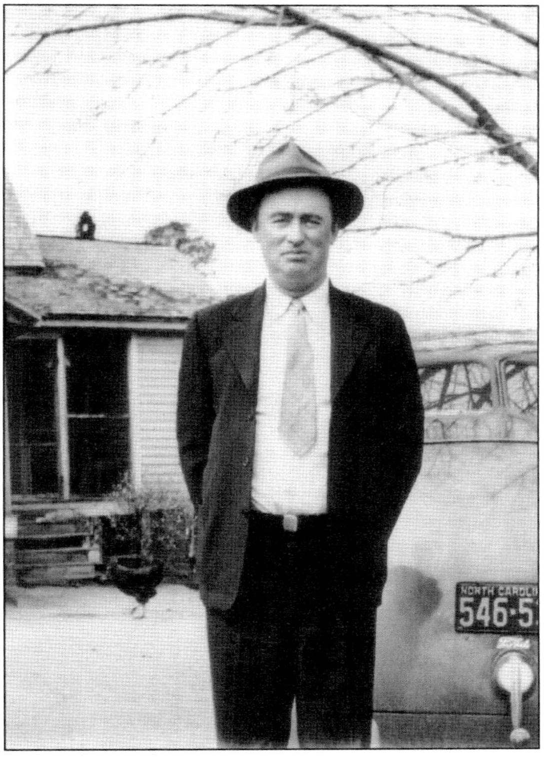

WALTER G. SEAGROVES, 1940S. This is a later photograph of Walter from the 1940s. (Courtesy of Diane Long.)

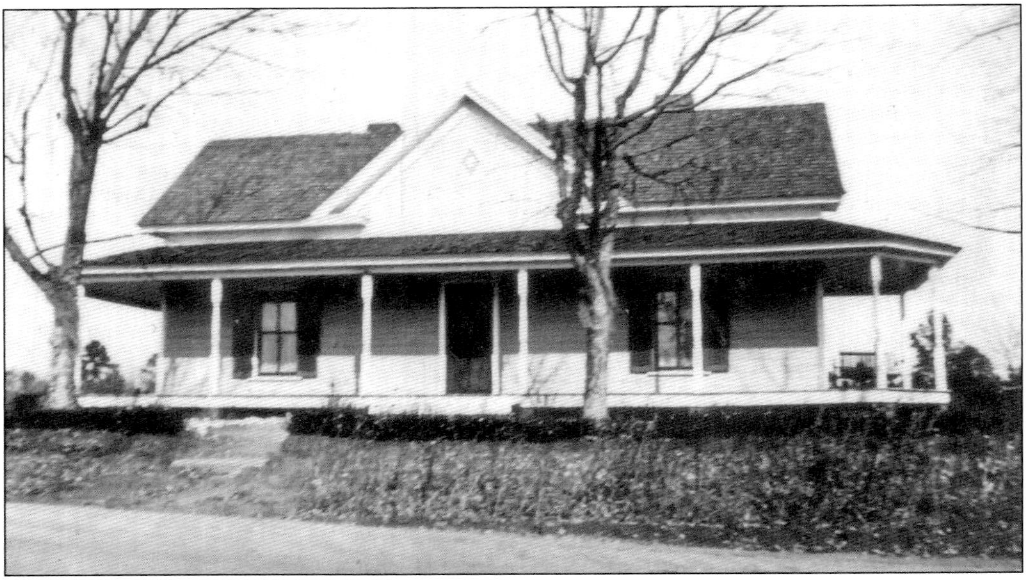

Seagroves Family Home, 1920s. John and Pearl Seagroves had this house built in 1910. This is where they raised their four children. The house still stands on Highway 1010. (Courtesy of Diane Long.)

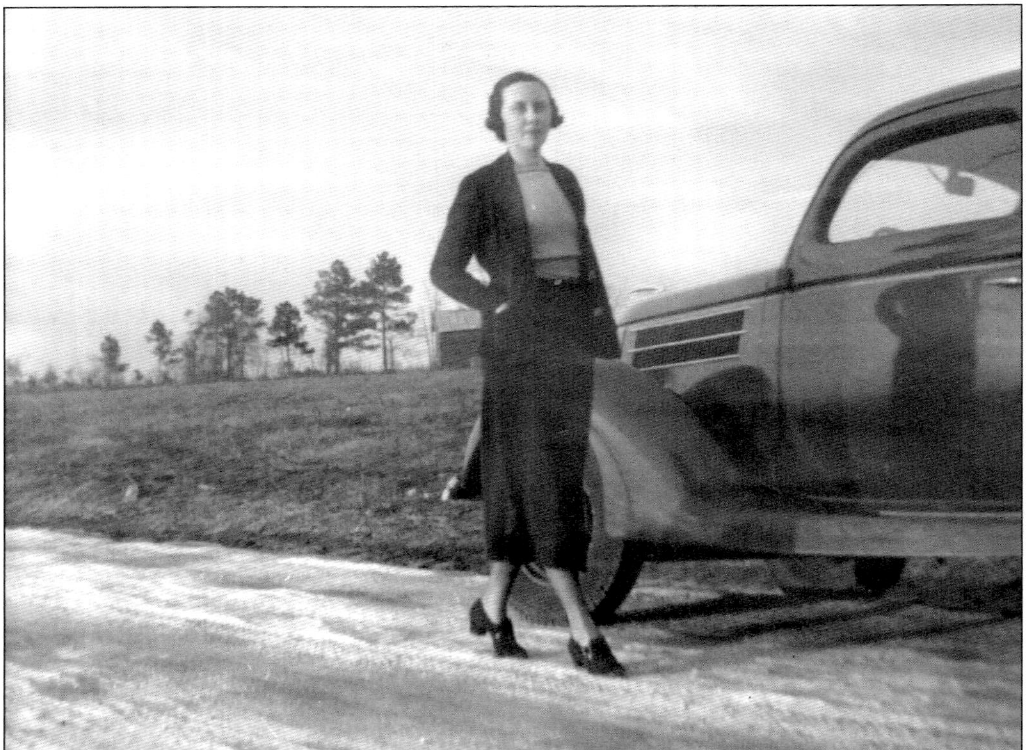

Lelia Seagroves on the Move. Lelia, one of the four children to grow up in the Seagroves' family home, traveled around North Carolina. (Courtesy of Diane Long.)

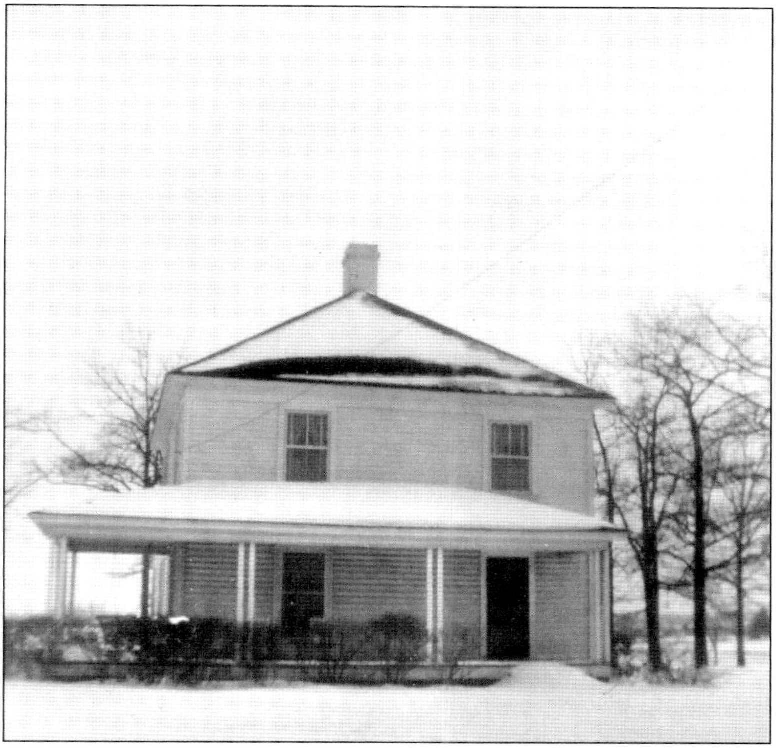

LELIA AND ESTHER SEAGROVES' HOME, 1950S. Lelia and her sister Esther moved into this house together. Not only was this their home, but Lelia had a room that served as her beauty parlor. (Courtesy of Diane Long.)

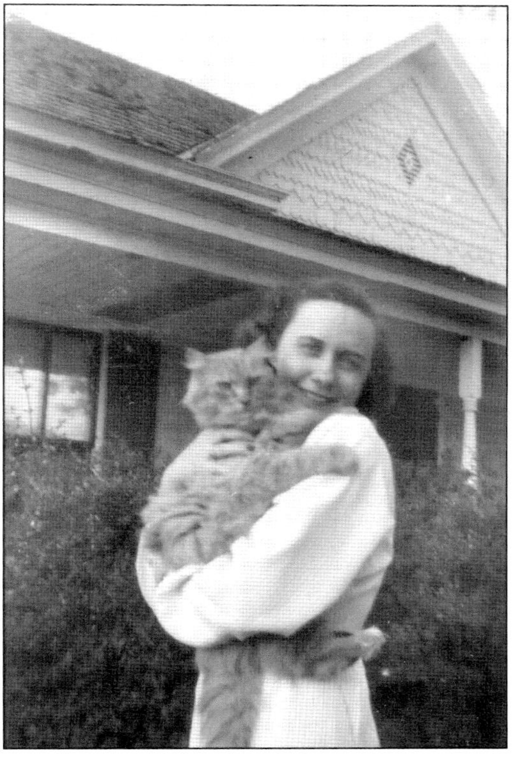

LELIA SEAGROVES AND KITTY. Lelia Seagroves poses for another photograph with her yellow tabby in front of the 1910 Seagroves' home. (Courtesy of Diane Long.)

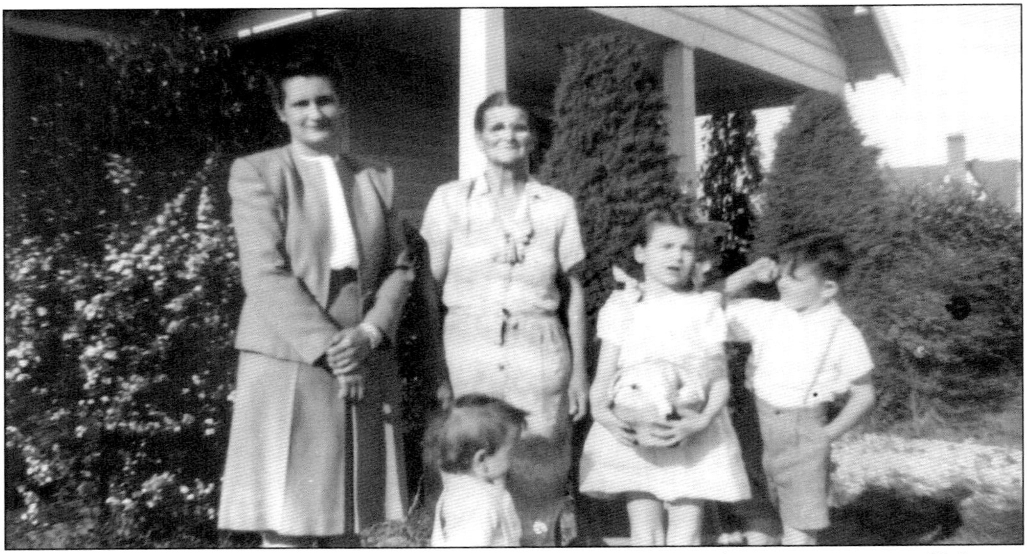

Three Generations of Manns. This 1940s photograph shows three generations of Manns. Pictured from left to right are Mabel Mann-Long, Lawrence Long (in front), Vera Mann (Mabel's mother), Blake Long, and Moody Allen Long. (Courtesy of Diane Long.)

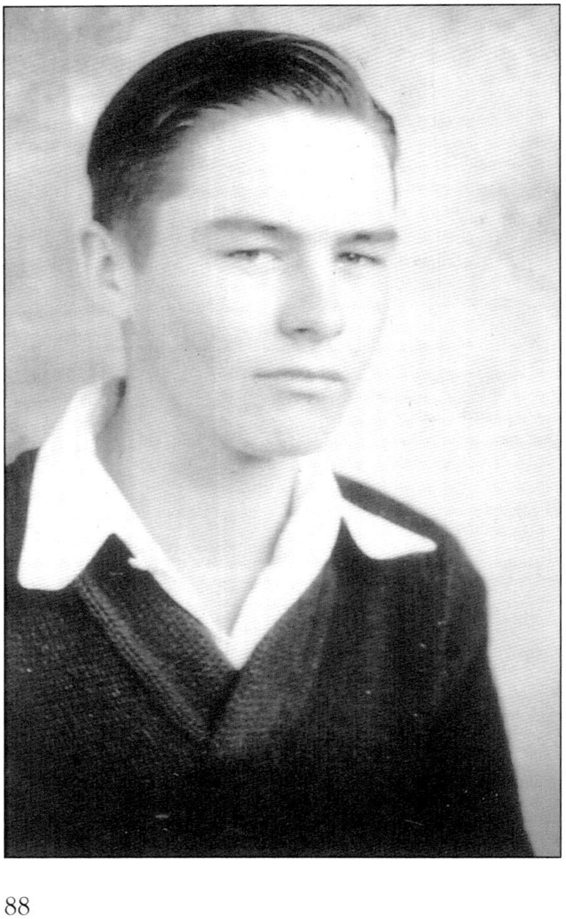

John "J. Q." Seagroves. John Q. was called J. Q. to avoid confusion with his father, John. This is his 1935 school picture. J. Q. was in World War II, and when he returned, he became a rural mail carrier. (Courtesy of Diane Long.)

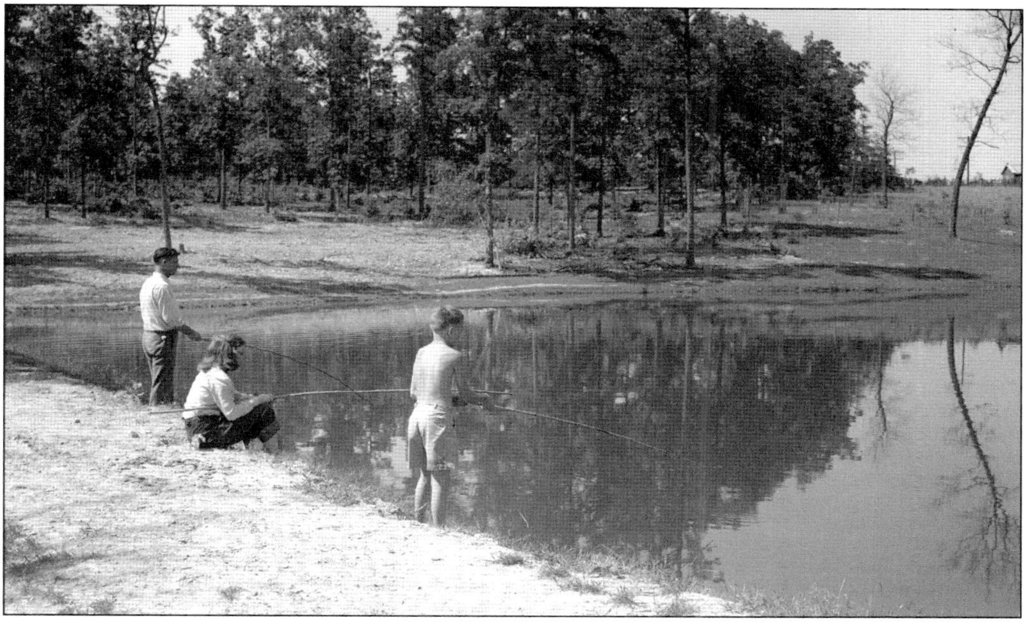

FISHING. Betty Lou Sharpe and friends are fishing in a pond in Apex. The Division of Conservation and Development took these pictures in 1945. The division's workers traveled the state capturing various images in an effort to promote tourism for North Carolina. (Both, courtesy of the North Carolina State Archives.)

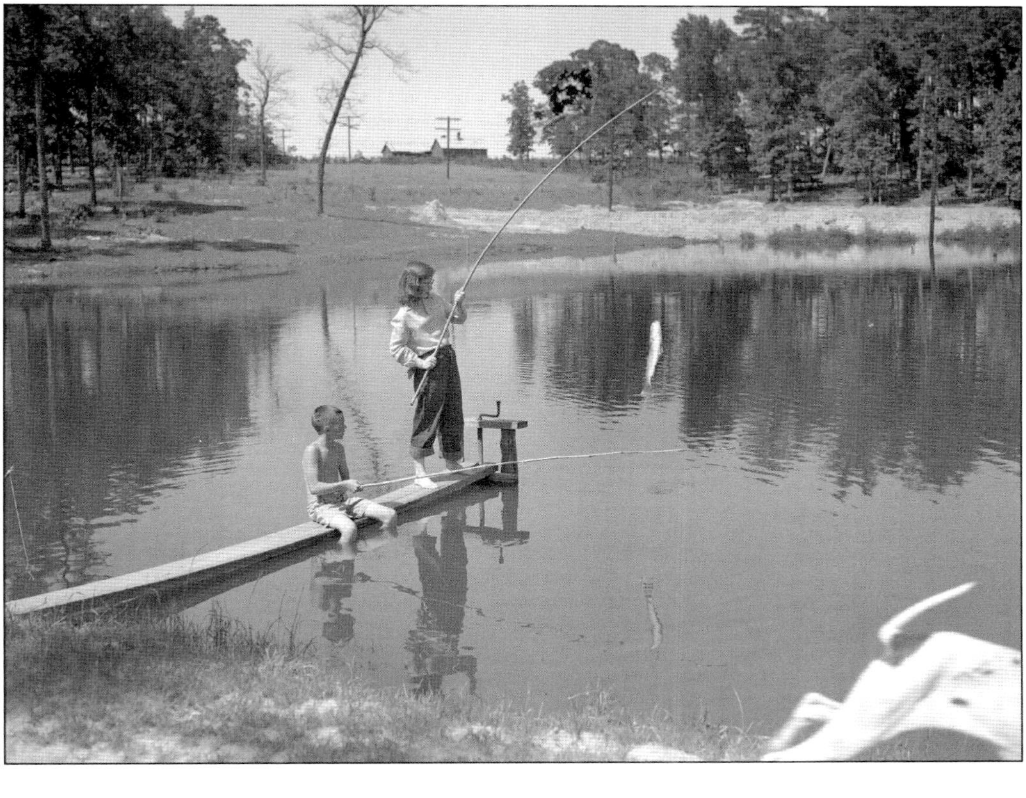

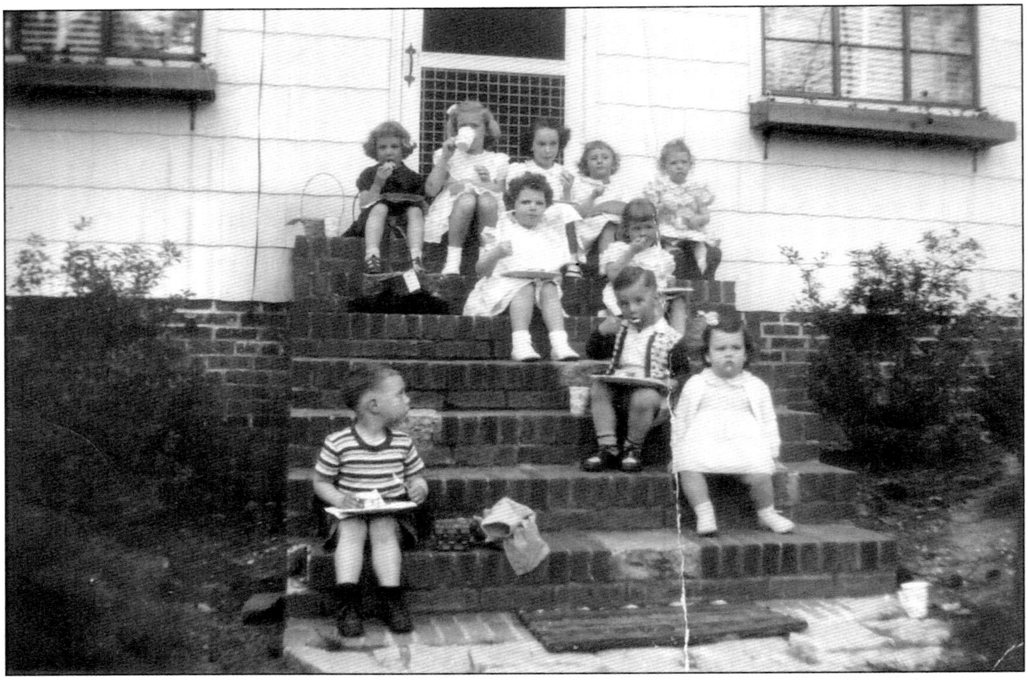

Birthday Party, 1952. This is a candid shot of some Apex children enjoying cake and ice cream on the steps. Susan Seymour is the little girl on the bottom step wearing a white dress with ice cream on her chin. (Courtesy of Susan Mills.)

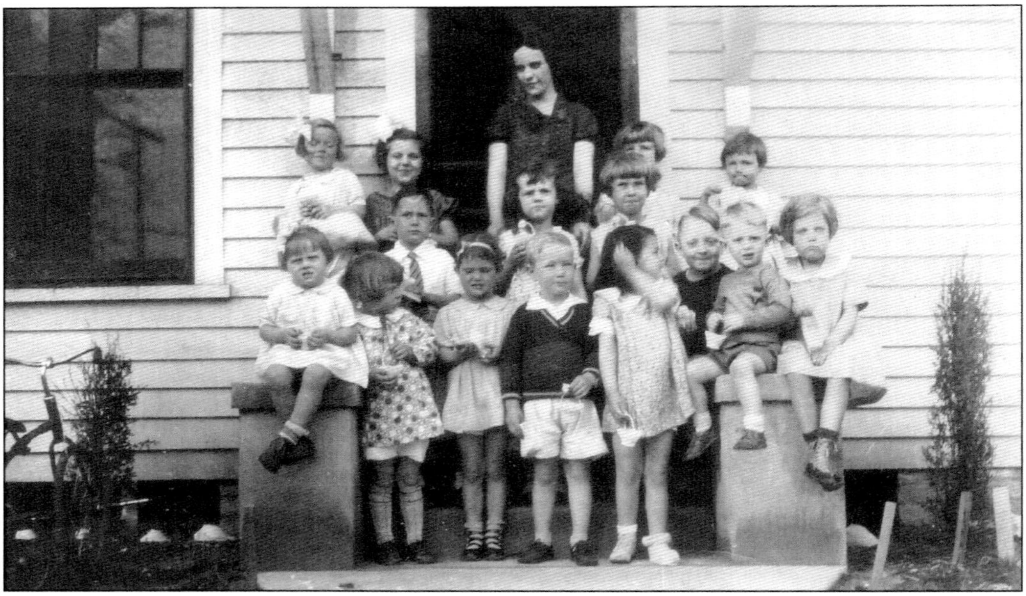

Birthday Party, 1932. This was Grace-Marie Blades's birthday party. Pictured from left to right are (first row) Ruby Bryan, Yvette Maynard, Charlotte Martin, Bobby Benton, Grace-Marie Blades, Billy Lassiter, Freddy Cash, and Edna Earl Stephens; (second row) Roy B. Martin, Nancy Weaver, and Helen Upchurch; (third row) Jacque Goodwin, Vivian Ann McNeil, a Miss Cain, Elizabeth Rogers, and unidentified. (Courtesy of Jacque Goodwin Burgess.)

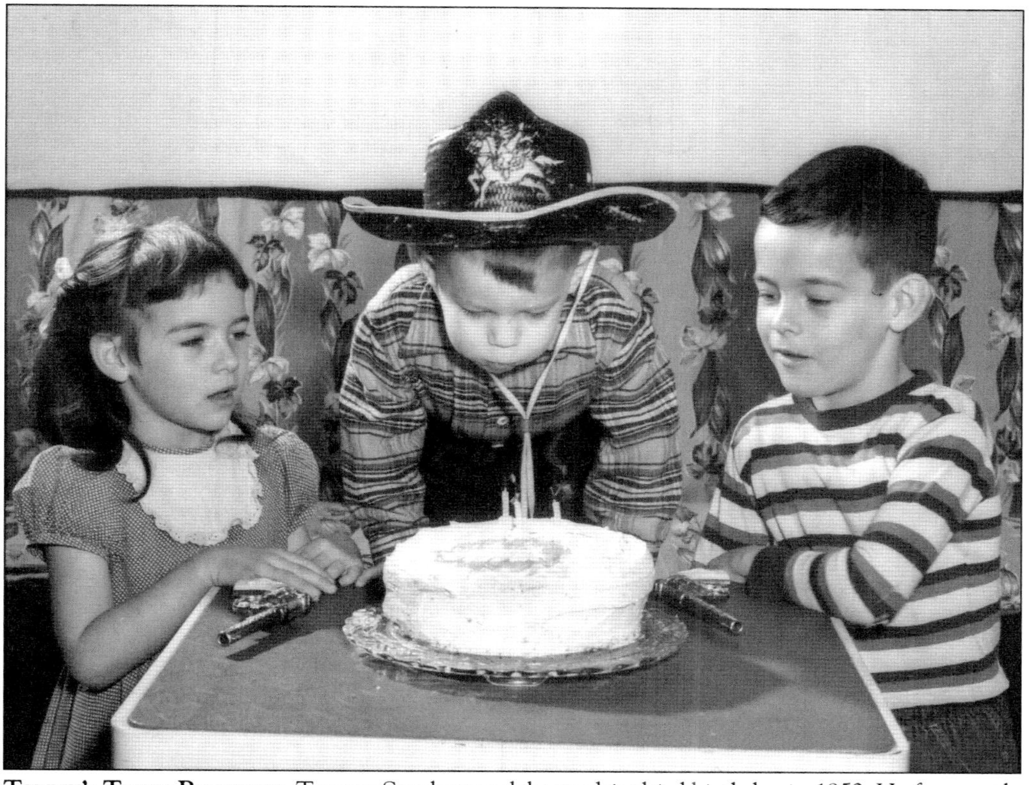

TOMMY'S THIRD BIRTHDAY. Tommy Stephens celebrates his third birthday in 1953. He frequently wore his Hopalong Cassidy hat and outfit. His sister Janet and brother Billy are helping him blow out his birthday candles. (Courtesy of Tommy Stephens and Janet Davis.)

JANET STEPHENS'S BIRTHDAY. Janet Stephens celebrates her fourth birthday in 1951 with a party. Her friends are, from left to right, Barbara Benton, Lynn Cooke, unidentified, Doug Poe, David Sykes, Billy Stephens, Mishew Tillerson, and Judy Yates-Hooks. (Courtesy of Tommy Stephens and Janet Davis.)

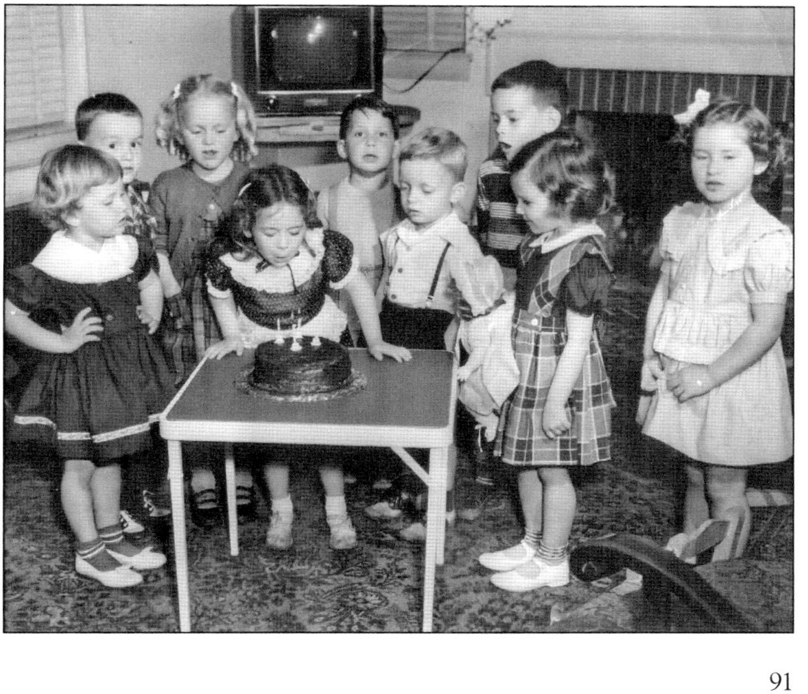

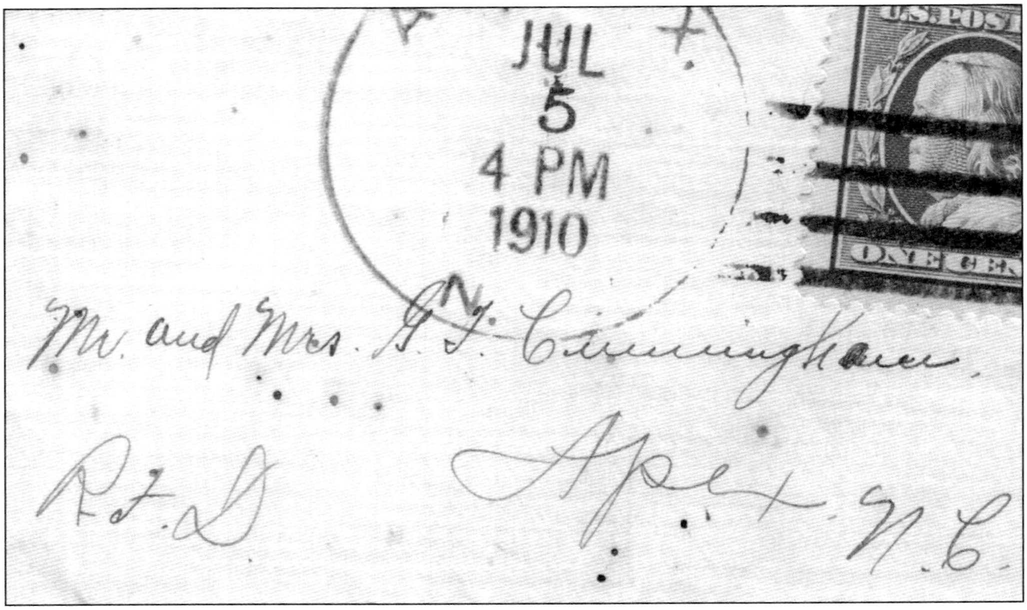

Party Invitation. Mamie and George Cunningham received this invitation in 1910 to attend an ice cream supper at the Hotel Poe. The supper was held by the Apex Baraca Class and was from 8:30 to 10:30 in the evening. The World Wide Baraca Union was founded in 1890 as a young men's Bible class. The name Baraca comes from the Hebrew word *beracha*, meaning blessedness or happiness. Its platform was, "young men at work for young men, and all standing by the Bible, and the Bible School." (Both, courtesy of the Wake County Public Library.)

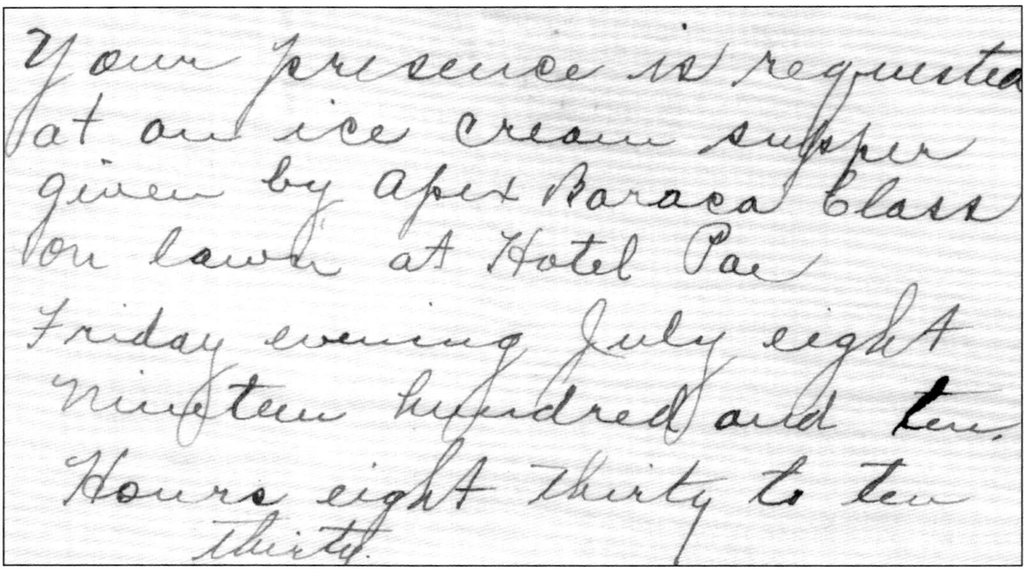
Your presence is requested
at an ice cream supper
given by Apex Baraca Class
on lawn at Hotel Poe
Friday evening July eight
nineteen hundred and ten.
Hours eight thirty to ten
thirty.

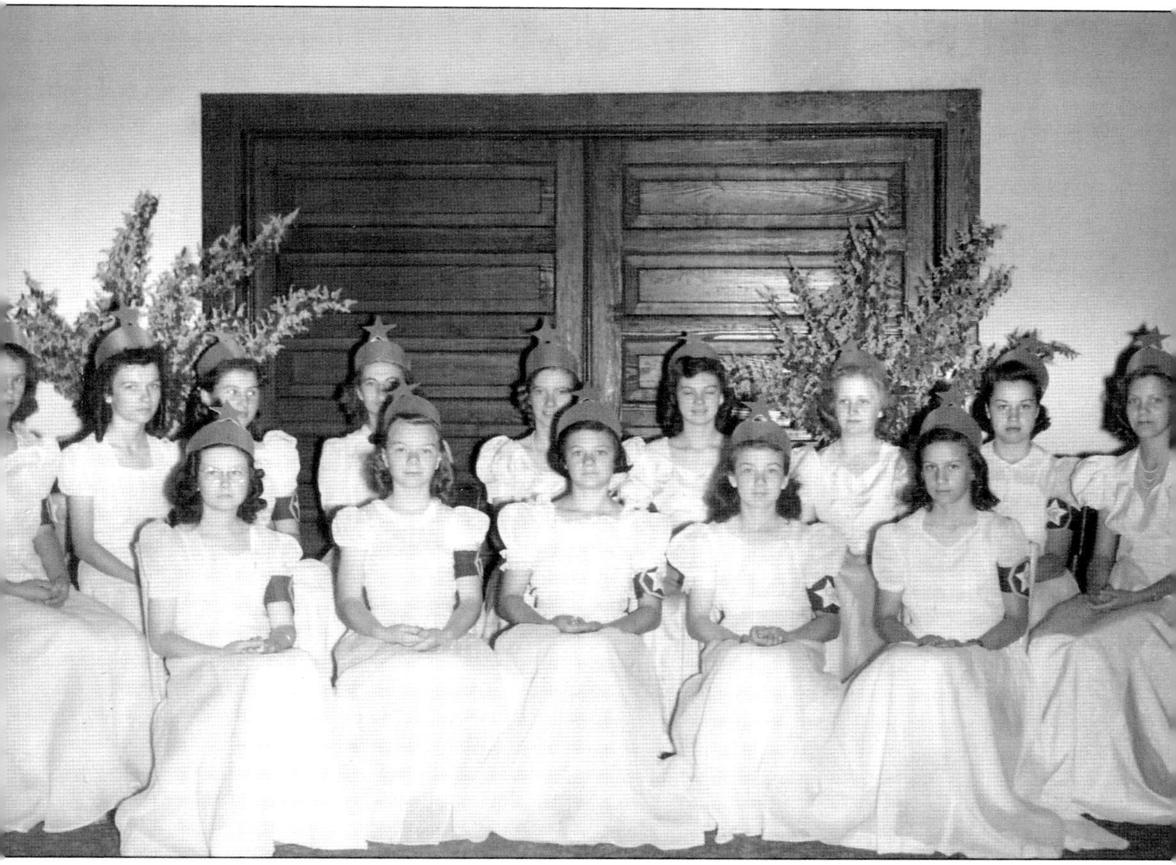

GIRLS AUXILIARY CORONATION. In 1941, Jacque Goodwin was one of the girls crowned queen. In this photograph from left to right are (first row) Frances Walls, Frances Upchurch, Melba Miller, Jacque Goodwin, and Yvette Maynard; (second row) Doris Pendergraph, Jean Glass, Lib Rogers, Mary Elizabeth Banks, Edna Earl Stephens, Carol Martin, Jean Maynard, Polly Upchurch, and Elizabeth Holland. (Courtesy of Jacque Goodwin Burgess.)

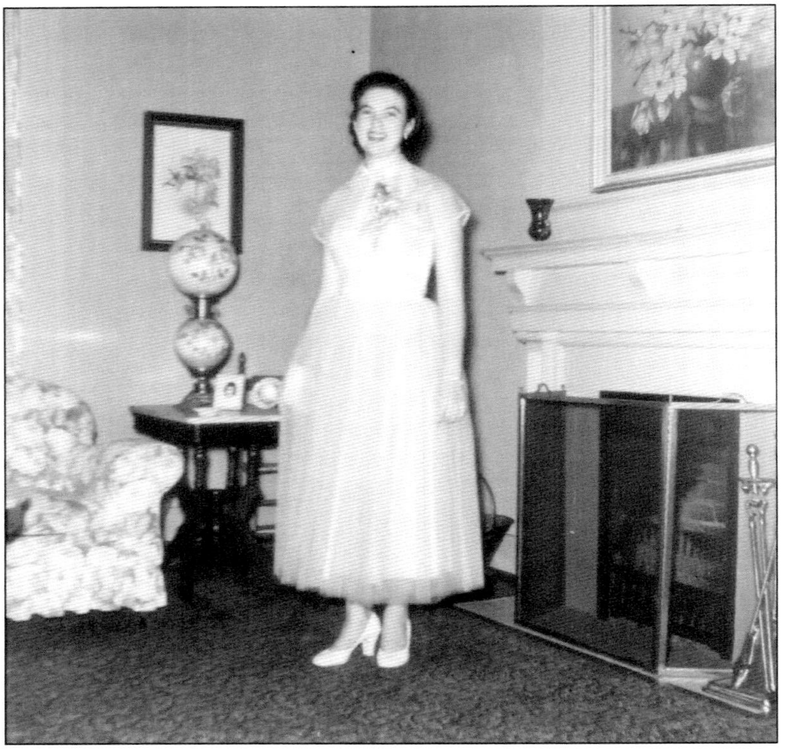

JOYCE HERNDON GOODWIN. Joyce is posing for this picture on her prom night in 1953. (Courtesy of Susan Mills.)

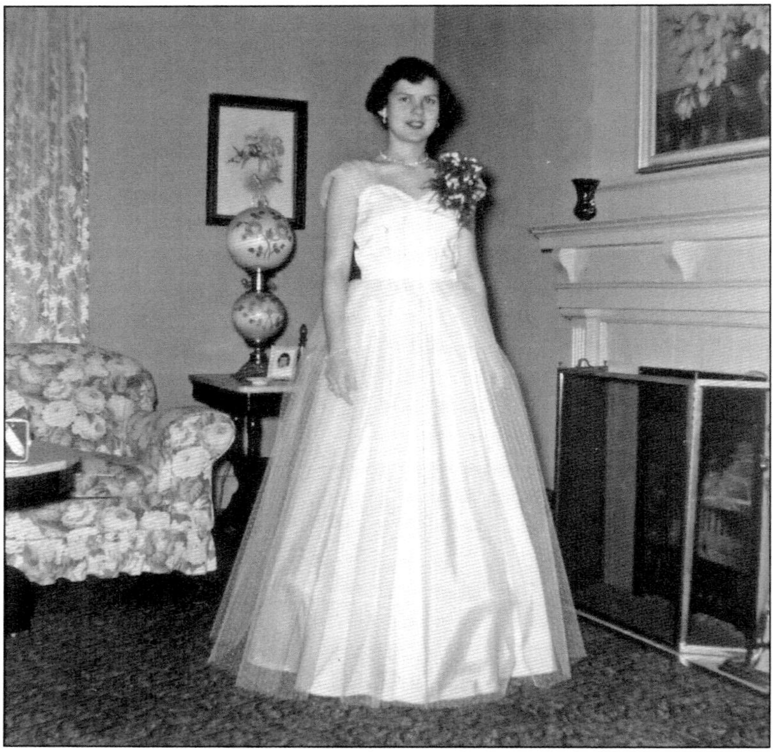

PHYLLIS MARTIN. Phyllis is posing for this picture on her prom night in 1953. She and Joyce got ready together. (Courtesy of Susan Mills.)

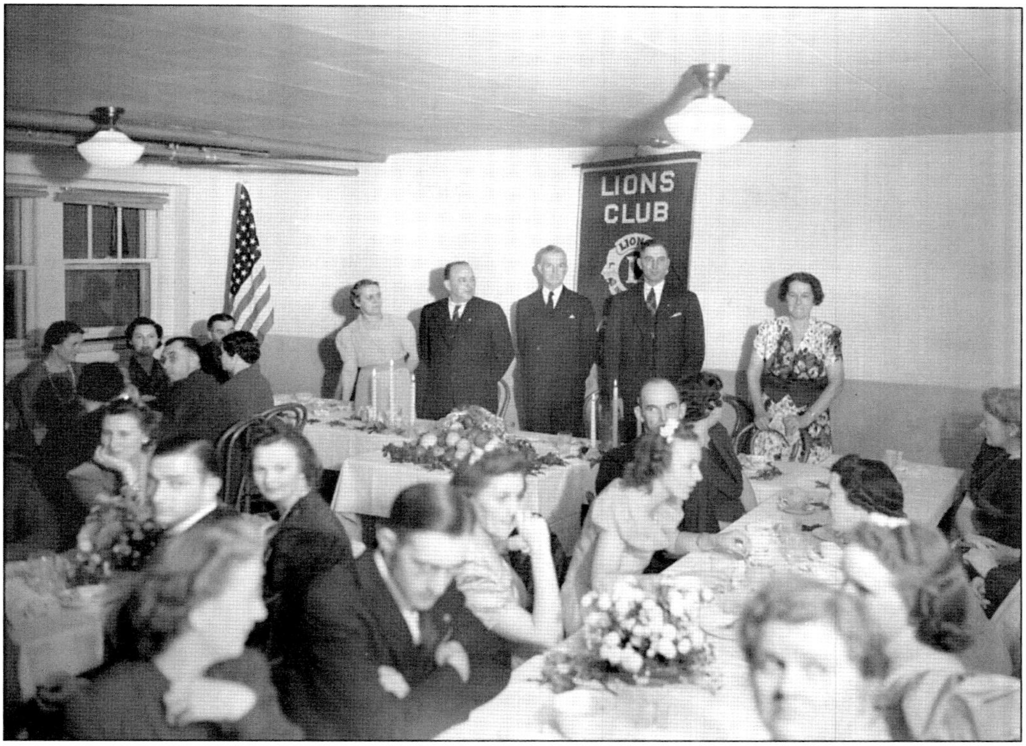

Apex Lions Club. The Apex Lions Club was chartered in 1937 by a group of local businessmen who wanted to make Apex a better place to live. The charter club members included a teacher, a lawyer, a doctor, a postman, a druggist, a dentist, a grocer, an auto dealer, a railroad agent, a mayor, a banker, a garage owner, and others who saw a need to come together and serve the local needs of the community. This is their 1942 banquet. (Courtesy of the North Carolina State Archives.)

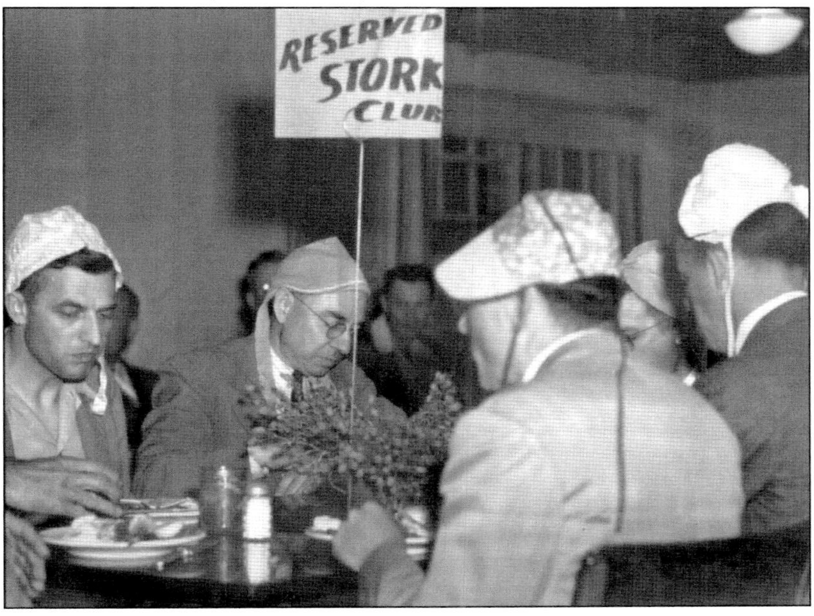

Apex Lions Club, 1940s. This photograph is of an Apex Lions Club event. The Lions Club consists of men and women who are committed to making their community a better place for all. (Courtesy of Ann Grebing.)

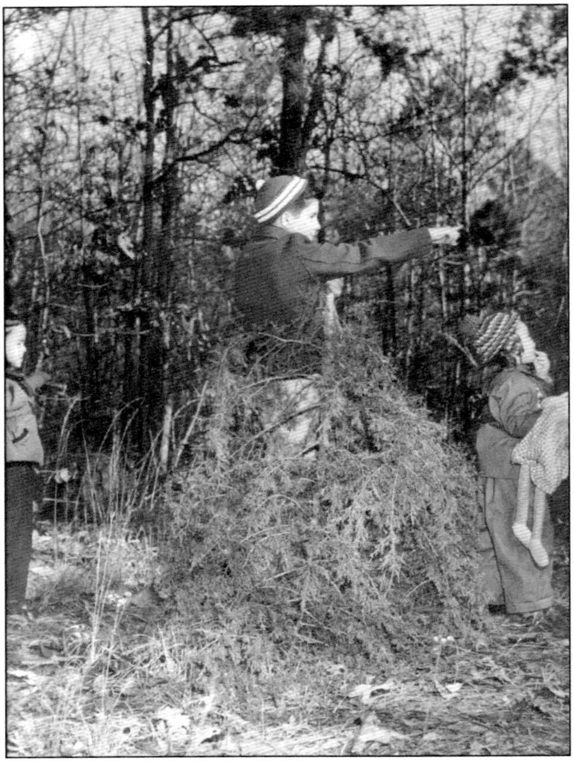

CUTTING DOWN THE TREE. From left to right, Billy Stephens, Theodore Sewell, and Janet Stephens, with her doll, went out in the woods to cut down a Christmas tree. (Courtesy of Tommy Stephens and Janet Davis.)

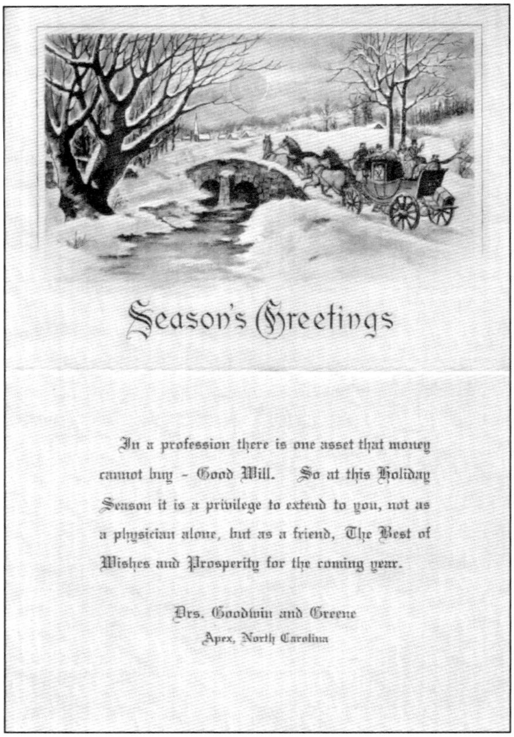

THE CHRISTMAS CARD. Dr. Oscar Goodwin partnered with a Dr. Greene to serve the needs of Apex's residents. This was a Christmas card they sent to their patients. (Courtesy of the Wake County Public Library.)

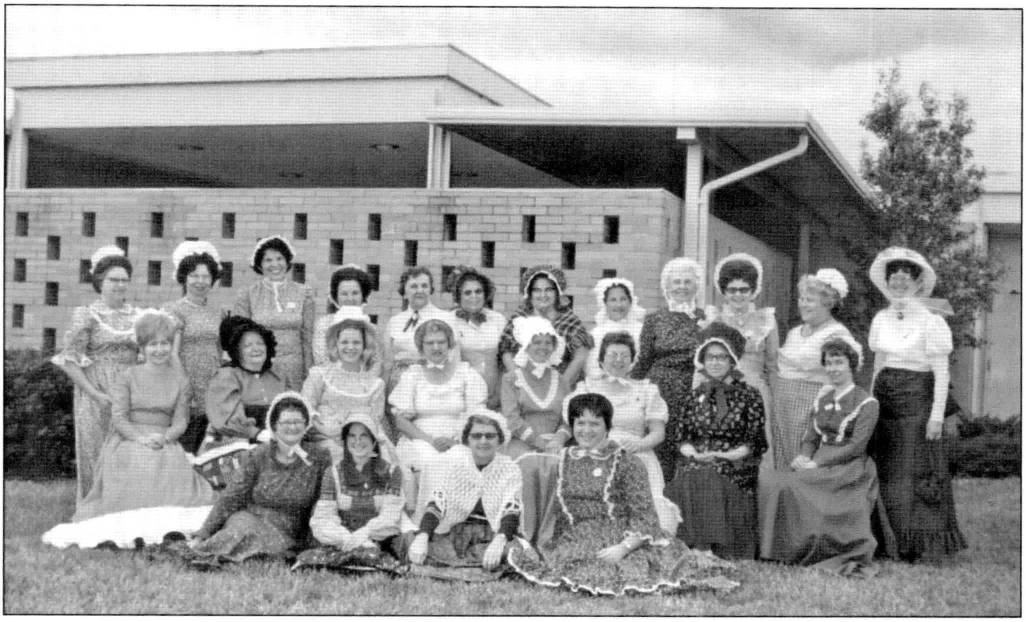

CENTENNIAL NIGHTINGALES. In 1973, the town of Apex celebrated its 100th birthday. To celebrate, various centennial committees dressed up in period clothing. Pictured from left to right are (first row) Bessie Pittman, Rebecca Watson, Lois Pendergraft, and Nancy Jones; (second row) Judy Seagroves, Lola Franks, Lenora Hines, Gladys Cash, Dorothy Banks, Verna Holder, a Mrs. Yates, and Lydia Smith; (third row) Elsie Scott, Barbara Brooks, Jane Grizzard, Betty Kirks, Alease Horton, Marie Walls, Polly Denson, Helen Baucom, Margaret Dickens, La Velle Mann, Nancy Matthews, and Diane Long. (Courtesy of Diane Long.)

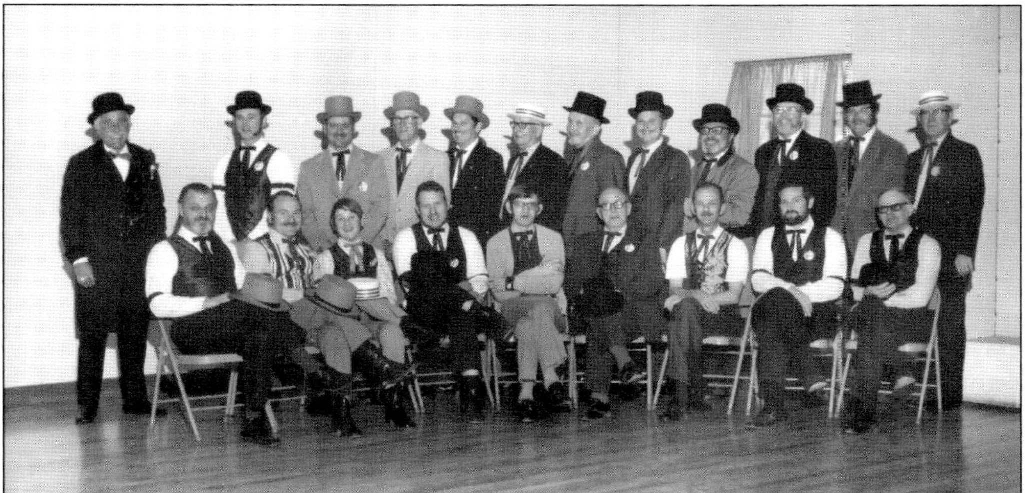

CENTENNIAL LIONS. In 1973, the town of Apex celebrated its 100th birthday. To celebrate, various centennial committees dressed up in period clothing. Pictured from left to right are (first row) Frank Spittler, Bob McIver, Kent McIver, Larry Jordan, Jim Ritchie, L. G. Jordan, Dr. L. A. Raynor, Talmadge Mills, and Bill Goodwin; (second row) Joe Hack, Charles Bennett, Brantley Murray, R. E. Truelove, T. B. Holland, M. D. Johnson, E. B. Tindal Jr., W. C. Mills Jr., W. C. Rodgers, Rev. Henry Morgan, Ken Leonard, and Dr. M. T. Jones. (Courtesy of Jacque Goodwin Burgess.)

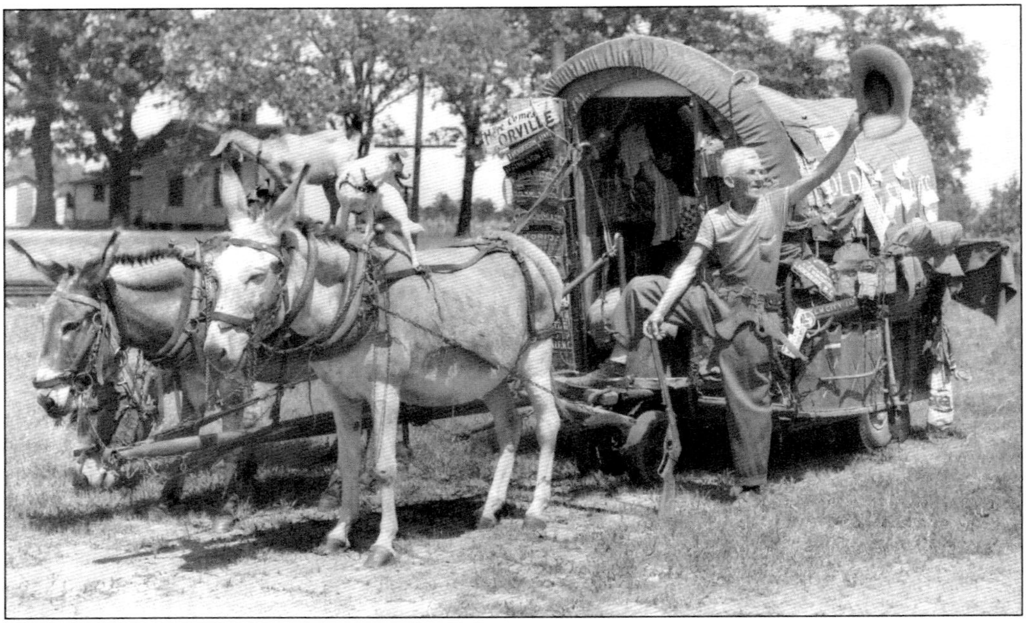

Putting on a Show. Orville seems to enjoy entertaining passersby with all his trinkets. Note his wooden gun around his waist and the dog and goat standing on the mules. (Courtesy of Tommy Stephens and Janet Davis.)

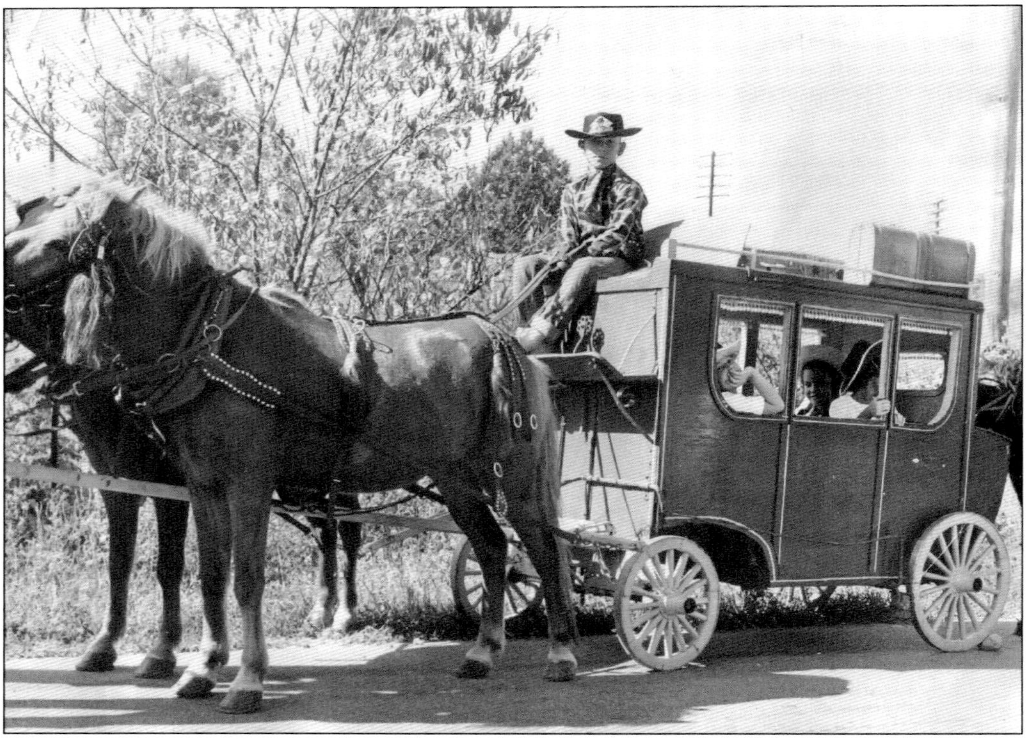

Another Parade. Billy Simms sits atop this wagon during a town parade. His passengers seem to be having fun. (Courtesy of Susan Mills.)

Five

FIRE AND BRIMSTONE

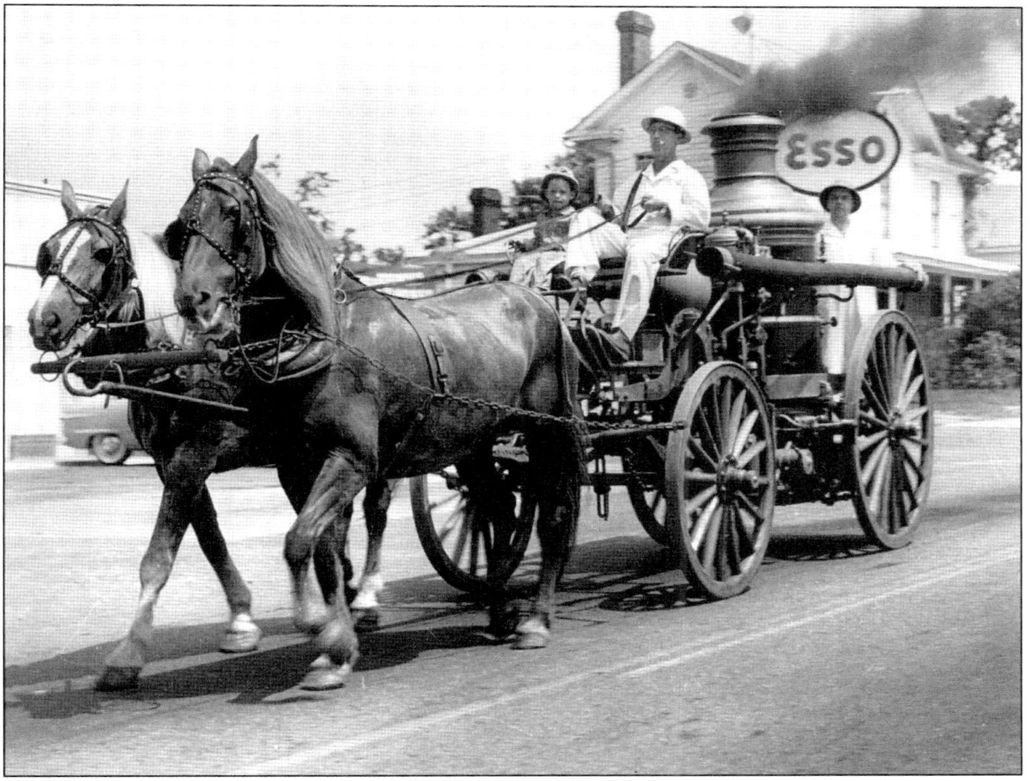

APEX PARADE, 1950s. The old fire truck is paraded through Apex to celebrate the newly built fire station. At the reins are Romulus Stephens Sr. along with his grandson Tommy. The man in the back in Charles Baucom. Charles and Romulus were two of the charter members of the Apex fire department. (Courtesy of Tommy Stephens and Janet Davis.)

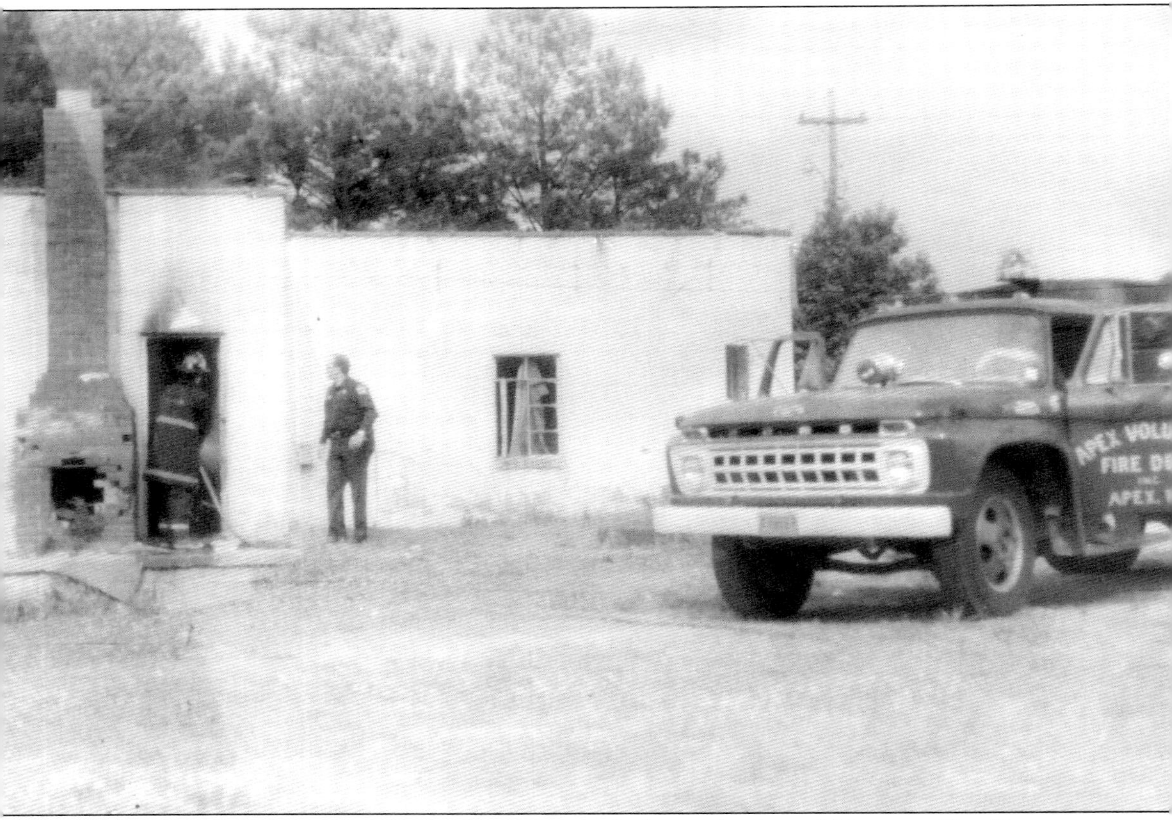

Old Fire Photograph. This 1950s photograph shows the Apex Volunteer Fire Department responding to a call. (Courtesy of the Apex Volunteer Fire Department.)

FIREHOUSE, 1950S. These photographs were taken in the early 1950s when the firehouse was still in the old town hall building. In 1949, the town hall caught fire when the courtroom stove broke loose from the flue. The two fire trucks were moved outside so they could fight the fire. The trucks were moved into position and had the fire under control in about 15 minutes. (Both, courtesy of the Apex Volunteer Fire Department.)

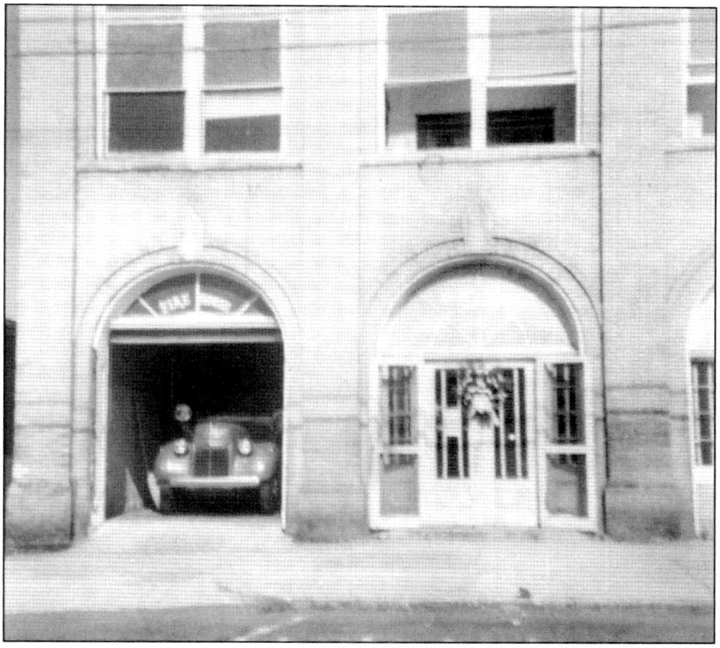

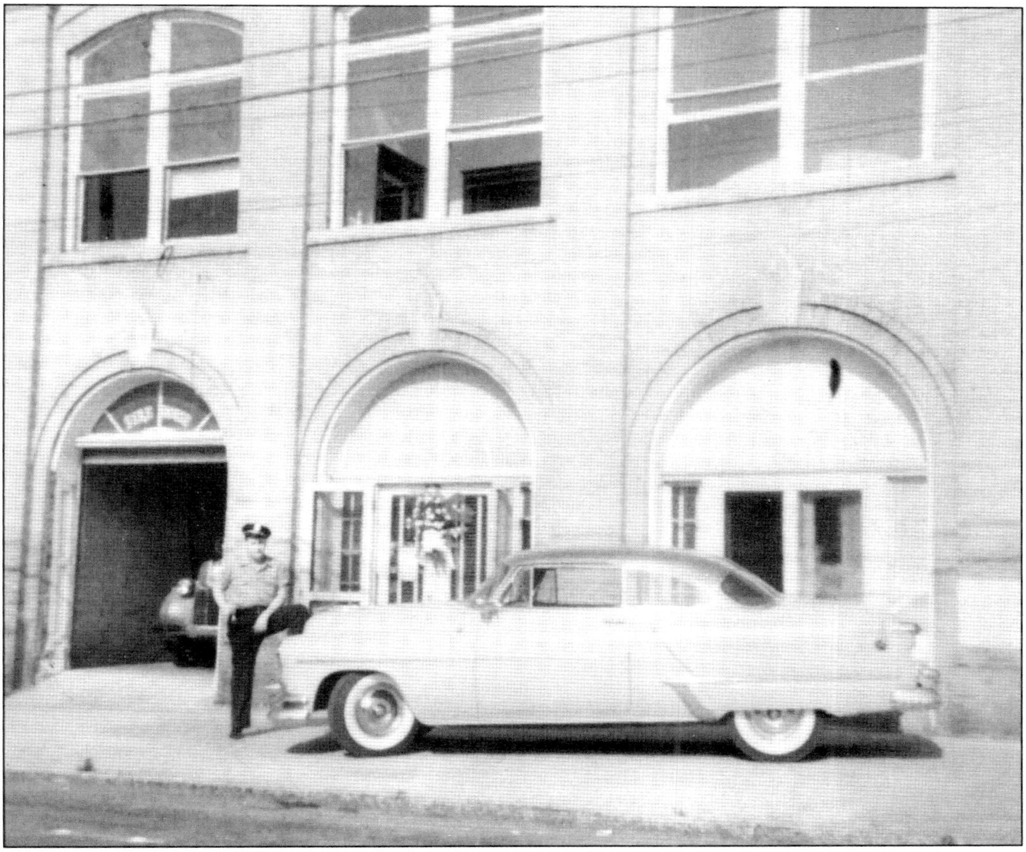

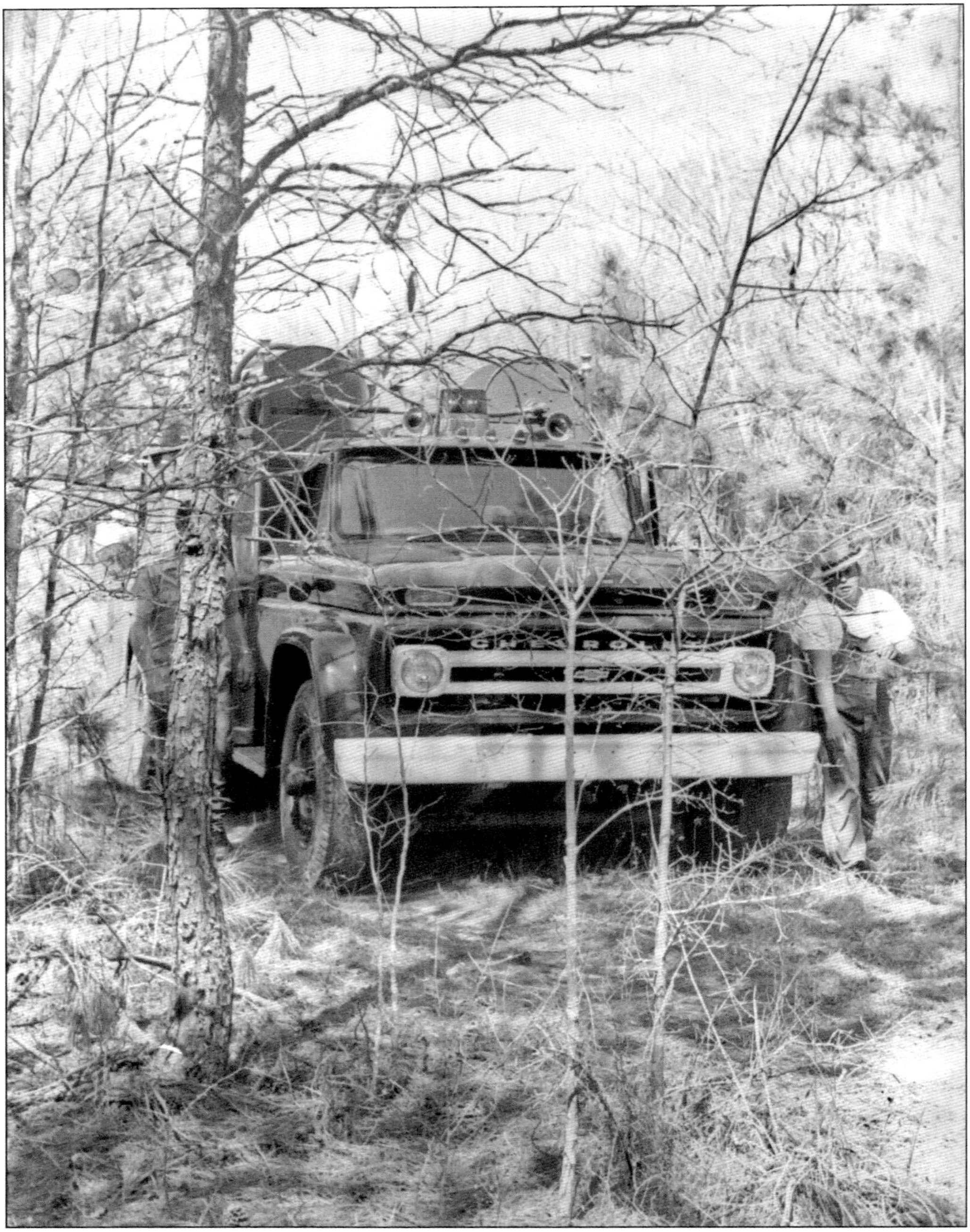

Tanker in the Woods. In 1952, Wake County's rural fire department formed. It was incorporated as the Apex Volunteer Fire Department, Rural Service, Inc. This is one of the tankers that served the rural community. (Courtesy of the Apex Volunteer Fire Department.)

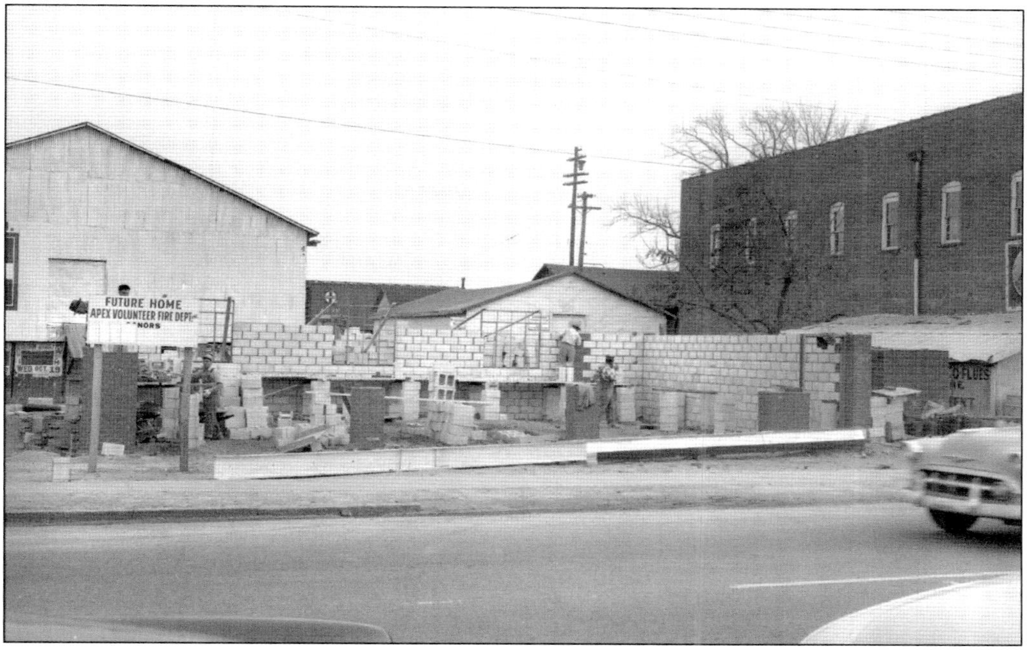

New Fire Station. In 1955, the volunteer firefighters began construction on a new station at 210 North Salem Street. The building measures 50-by-32 feet and is made of brick veneer construction with a 15-foot apron and three bays. Facilities include an area for hose drying, mechanical maintenance and storage, and a meeting room. The cost was $20,000, and the building was completed in 1956. (Both, courtesy of the Apex Volunteer Fire Department.)

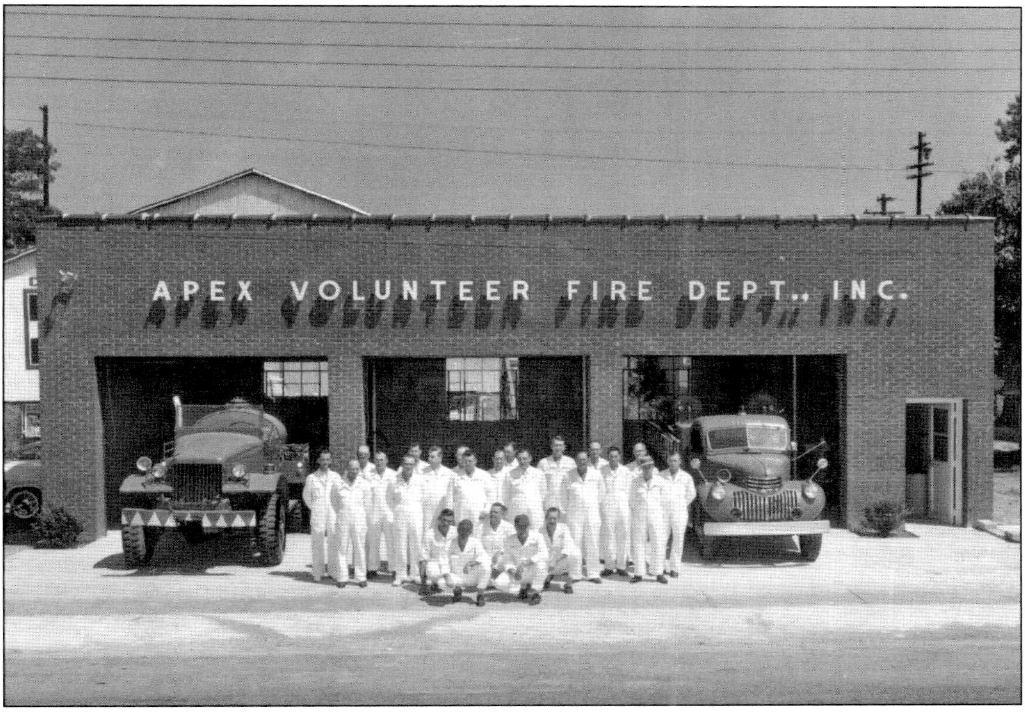

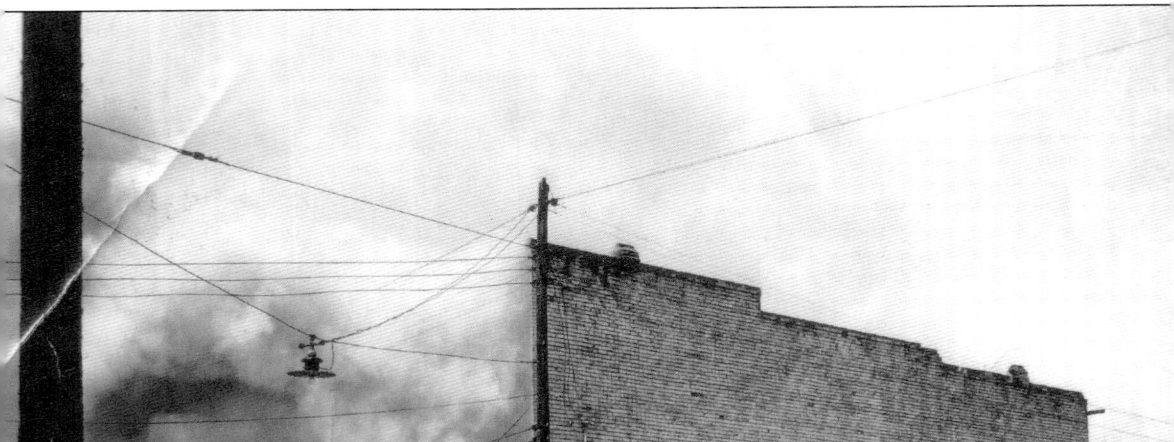

MOVIE HOUSE FIRE. In 1954, Apex's downtown movie theater burned to the ground. The entire inside of the theater burned out and quickly destroyed a wood partition between the theater balcony and the storeroom over a feed store. Fire departments in Cary and Raleigh were called when it appeared the fire was about to get out of control. The fire was finally tamed with the assistance of Cary and Raleigh firefighters. The town was saved, but the theater was not. (Courtesy of Tommy Stephens and Janet Davis.)

RESIDENTS RACE. Once word of the movie house fire was out, Apex residents scrambled to see the fire or to get out of its path. (Courtesy of Tommy Stephens and Janet Davis.)

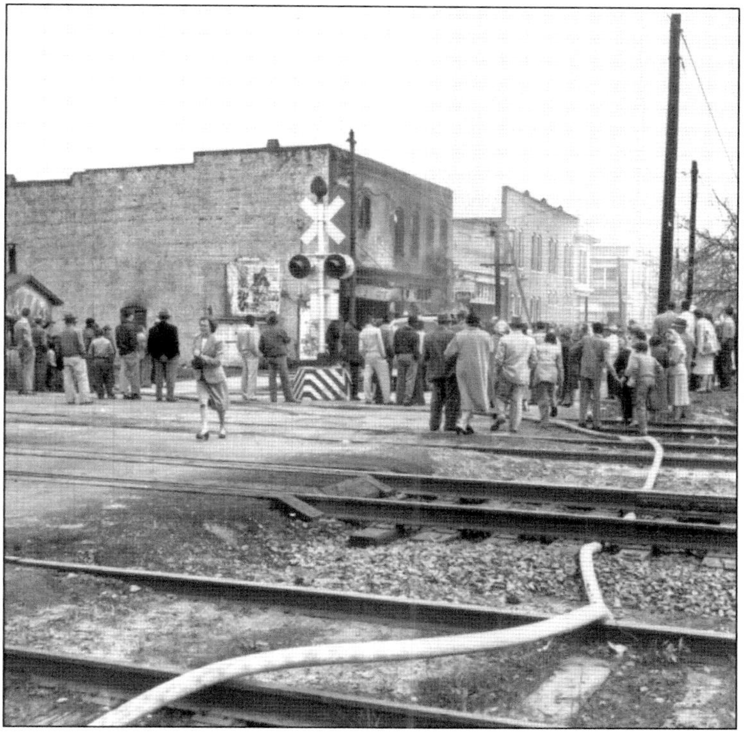

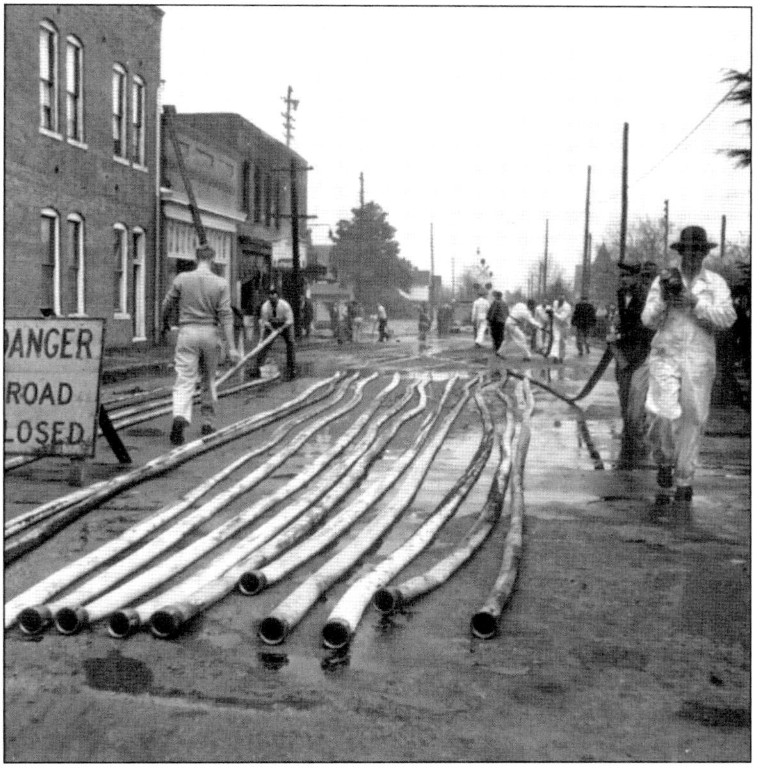

FIRE HOSES. The Apex Volunteer Fire Department lays out their hoses after fighting the movie house blaze. Note the water on the ground and the "road closed" sign due to the damage. (Courtesy of Tommy Stephens and Janet Davis.)

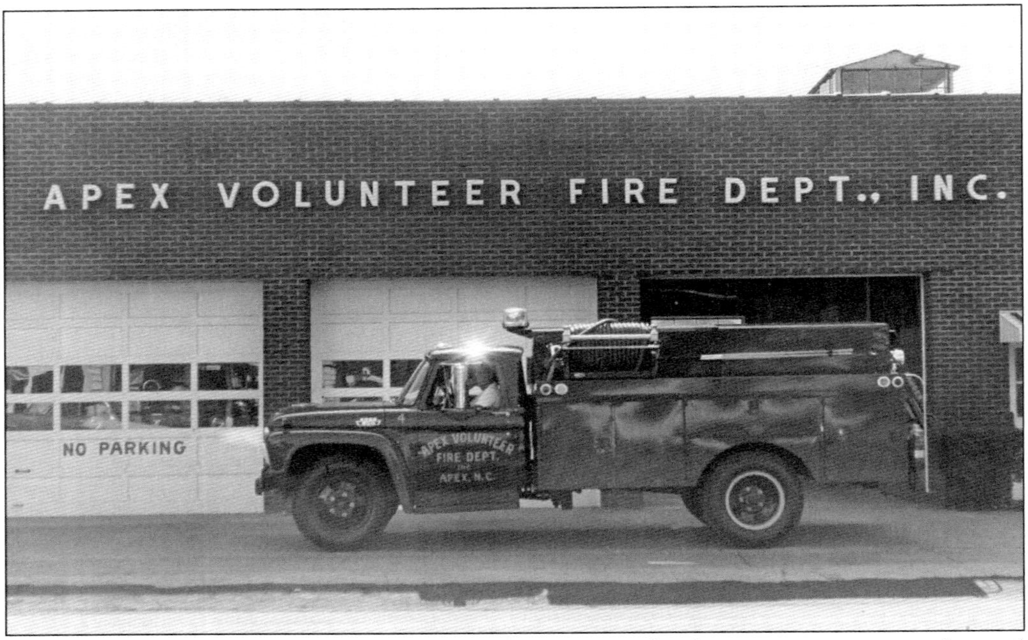

New Station. In February 1957, the board of directors voted to begin construction on the civil defense tower. There was to be a steel stairway (at 7¢ per pound, not to exceed $75) and a trap door leading to it. The civil defense tower can be seen on the right side of the station roof. (Courtesy of the Apex Volunteer Fire Department.)

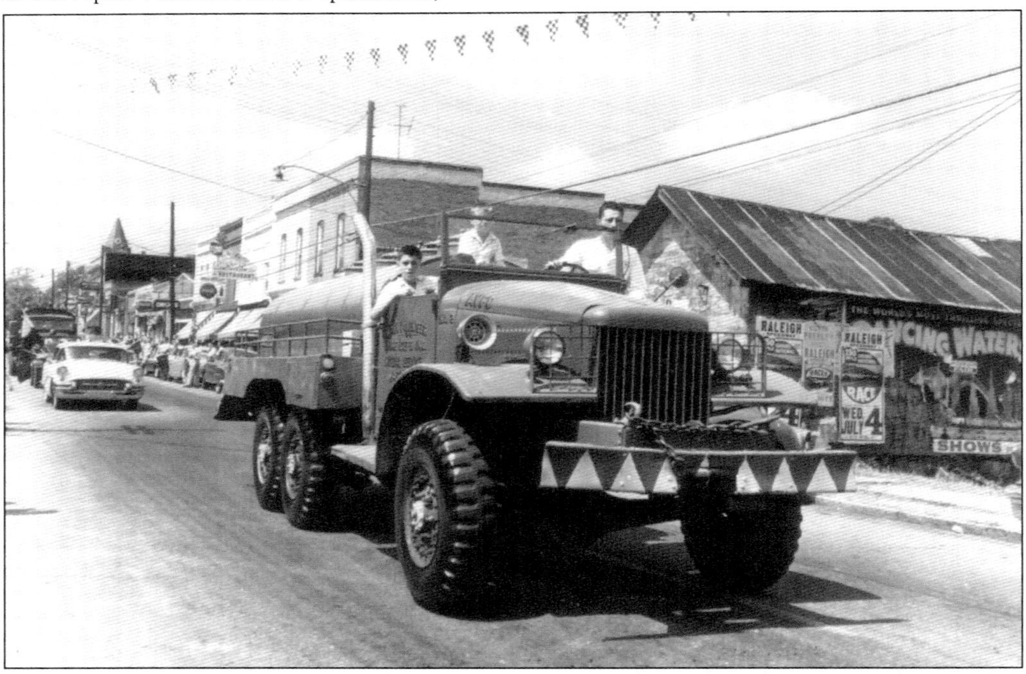

Fireman's Day Parade, 1950s. The Fireman's Day parade is when the Apex Volunteer Fire Department can display its equipment and have a little fun. (Courtesy of the Apex Volunteer Fire Department.)

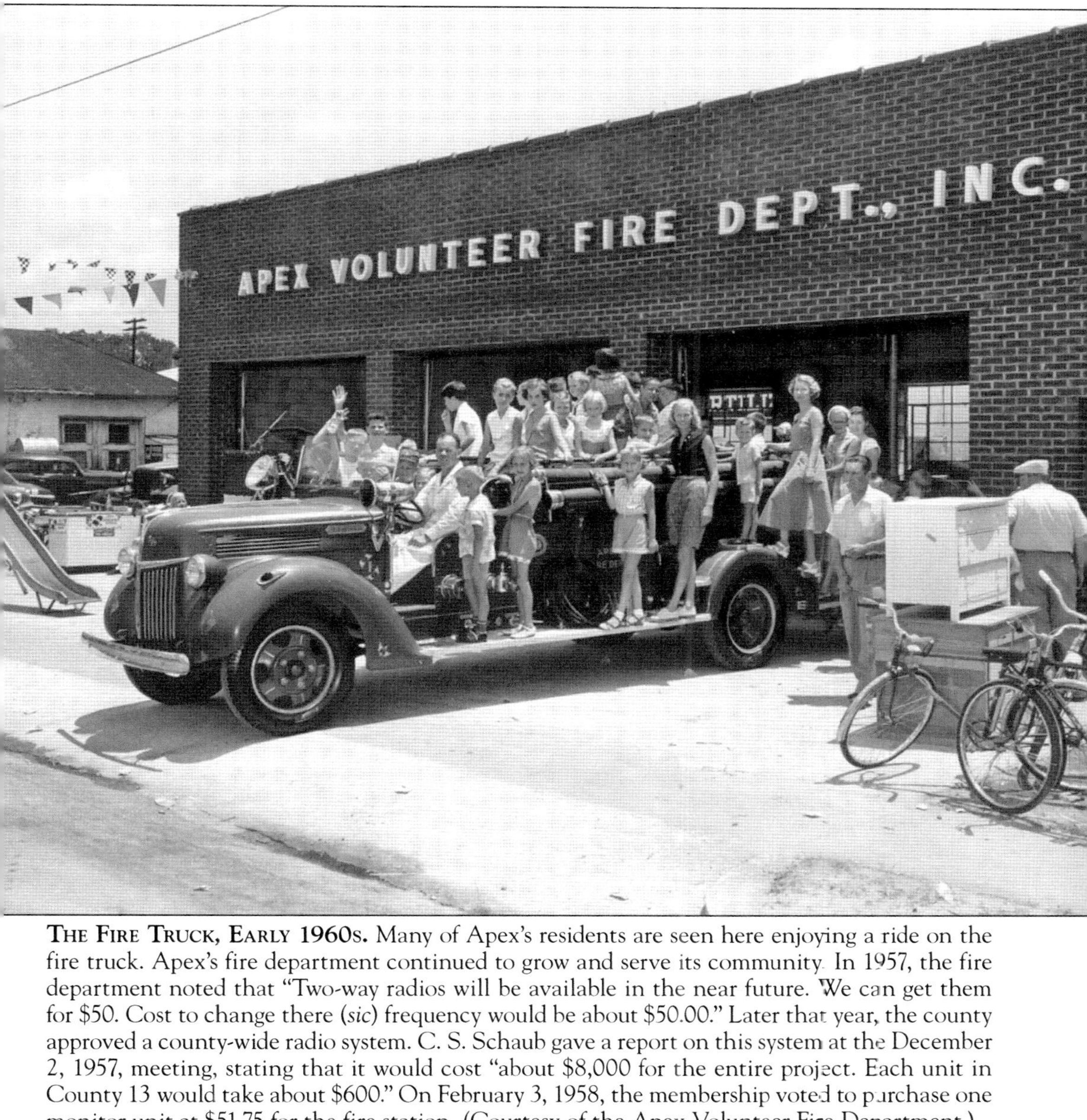

The Fire Truck, Early 1960s. Many of Apex's residents are seen here enjoying a ride on the fire truck. Apex's fire department continued to grow and serve its community. In 1957, the fire department noted that "Two-way radios will be available in the near future. We can get them for $50. Cost to change there (*sic*) frequency would be about $50.00." Later that year, the county approved a county-wide radio system. C. S. Schaub gave a report on this system at the December 2, 1957, meeting, stating that it would cost "about $8,000 for the entire project. Each unit in County 13 would take about $600." On February 3, 1958, the membership voted to purchase one monitor unit at $51.75 for the fire station. (Courtesy of the Apex Volunteer Fire Department.)

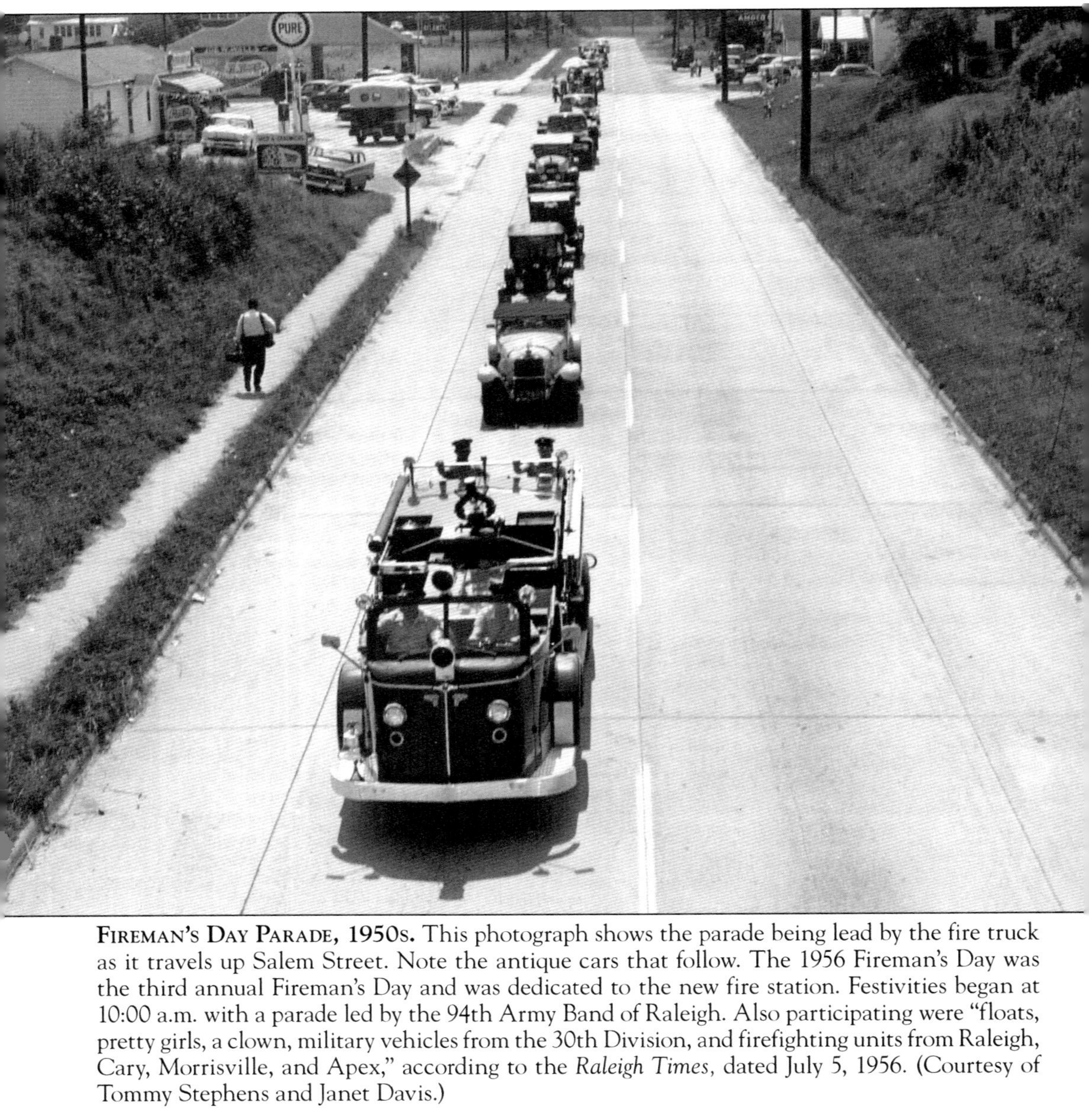

FIREMAN'S DAY PARADE, 1950S. This photograph shows the parade being lead by the fire truck as it travels up Salem Street. Note the antique cars that follow. The 1956 Fireman's Day was the third annual Fireman's Day and was dedicated to the new fire station. Festivities began at 10:00 a.m. with a parade led by the 94th Army Band of Raleigh. Also participating were "floats, pretty girls, a clown, military vehicles from the 30th Division, and firefighting units from Raleigh, Cary, Morrisville, and Apex," according to the *Raleigh Times*, dated July 5, 1956. (Courtesy of Tommy Stephens and Janet Davis.)

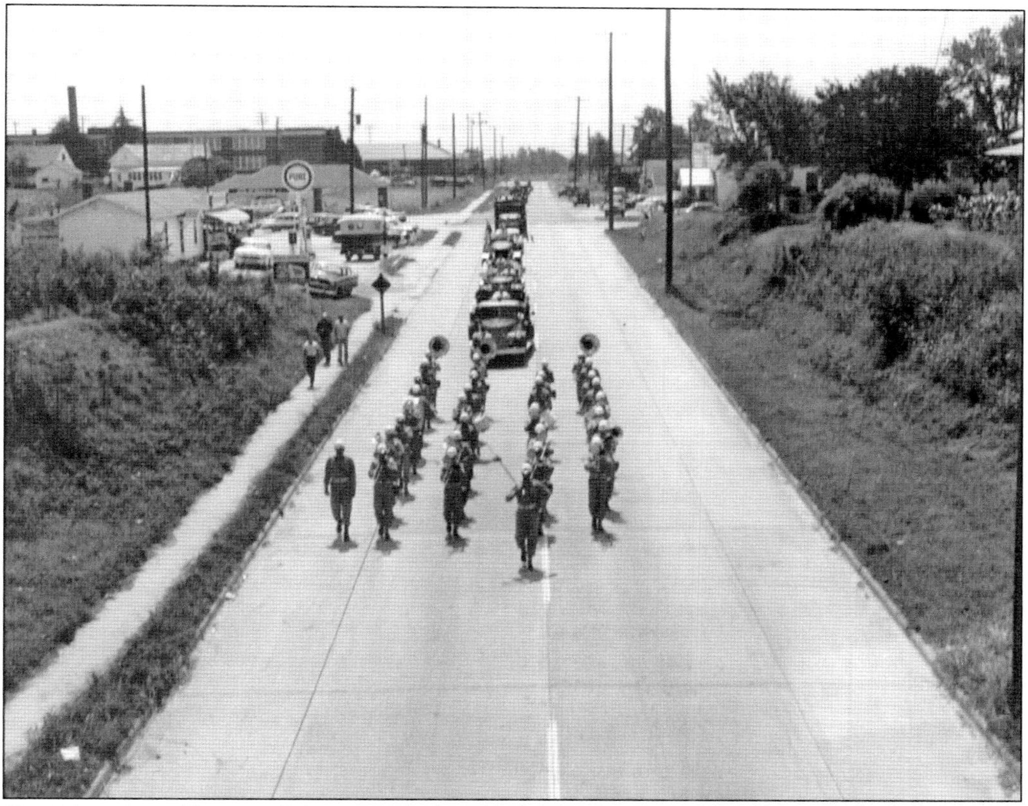

The 94th Army Band of Raleigh. The band led the 1956 Apex Fireman's Day parade. (Courtesy of Tommy Stephens and Janet Davis.)

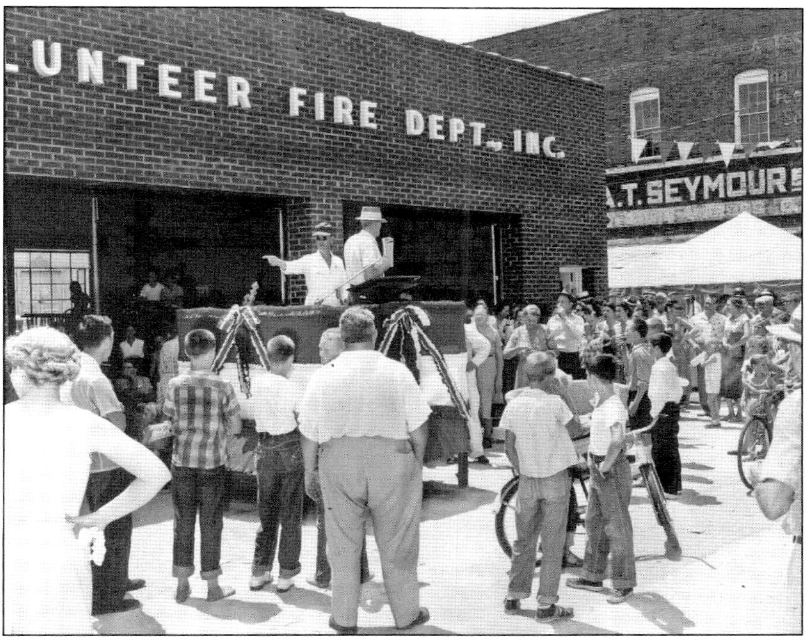

Fun in Town. Festivities abound at the Fireman's Day parade. (Courtesy of Tommy Stephens and Janet Davis.)

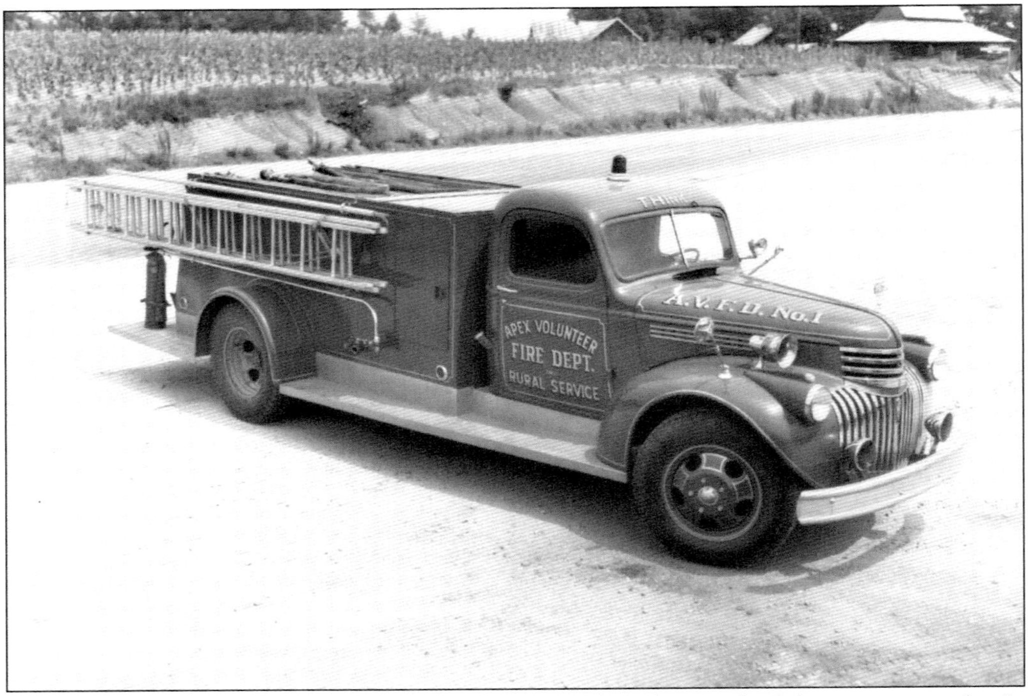

RURAL SERVICE. In a 1945 article in the *Raleigh Times*, the volunteer firefighters are praised as "a group of farsighted and enterprising men who on their own are attempting to eliminate rural fire protection as a problem in the Apex area." (Courtesy of the Apex Volunteer Fire Department.)

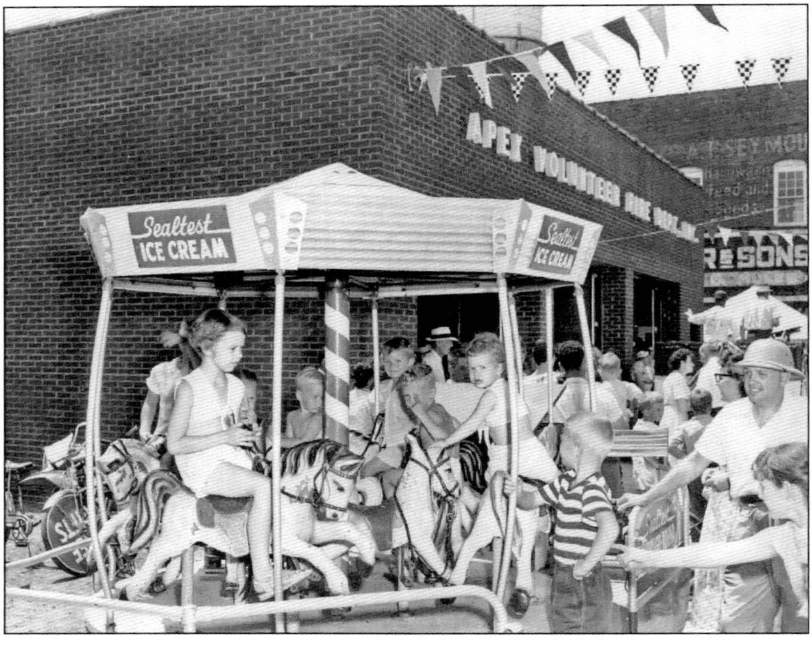

MERRY-GO-ROUND. Apex children are having fun at the Apex Fireman's Day parade. Charles Baucom is the gentleman in the hat on the right. (Courtesy of Tommy Stephens and Janet Davis.)

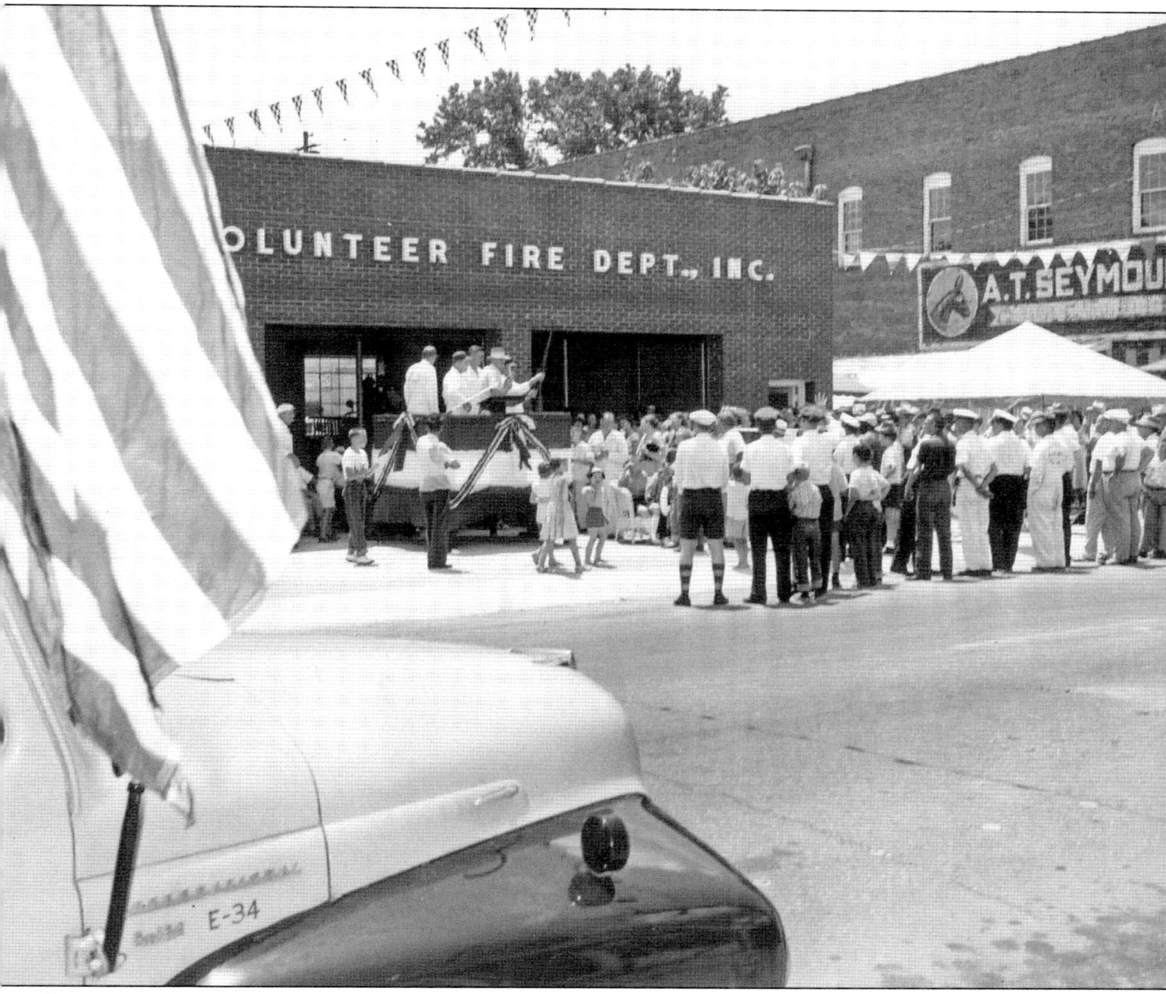

Let the Festivities Begin. Speeches are given to celebrate the annual Fireman's Day parade. Despite the fun scene witnessed here, the fire department remained troubled over finances. On June 24, 1957, it was noted, "The Fire Dept. Treasure is about to be depleted, so to keep from going broke, C. S. Schaub donated the sum of .01c to the Department." On April 7, 1958, "C. S. Schaub made motion, seconded by Nolan Cooke for the secretary to write each fire department in the county on the following subject: Bring up before the next meeting of the Wake County Firemen Association suggesting that they appoint a committee to go before the County Commissioners and ask for a $50.00 increase per month to take care of the increase in expenses of each Fire Dept." (Courtesy of Tommy Stephens and Janet Davis.)

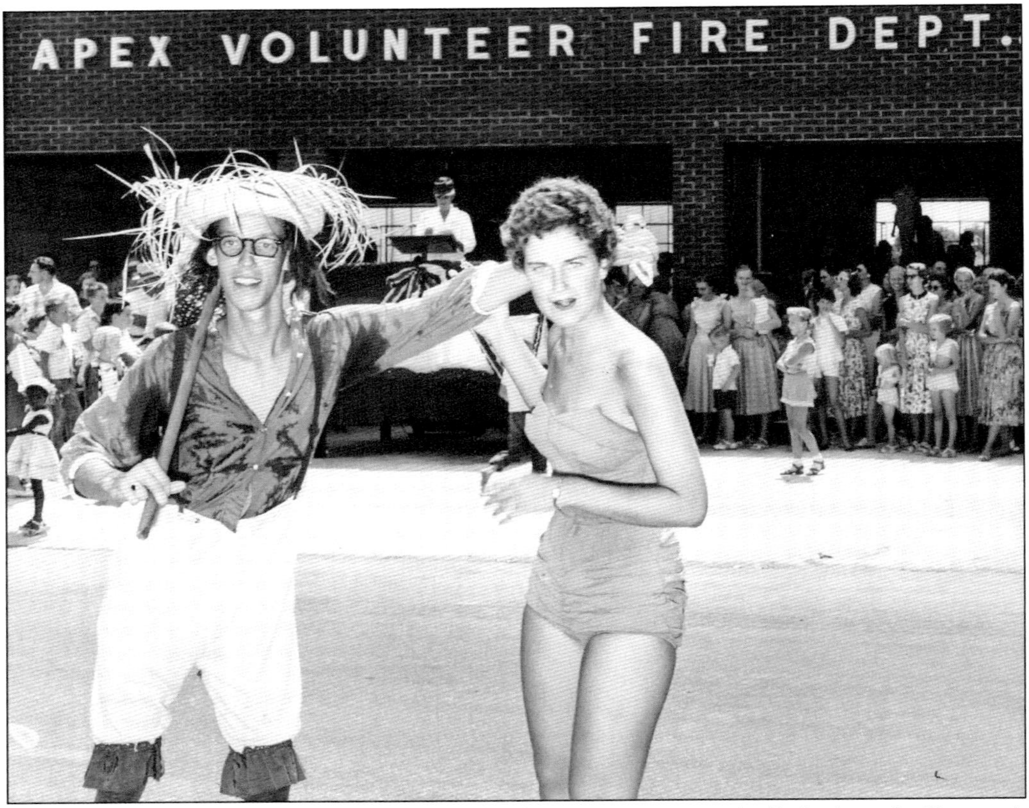

WATCH OUT FOR THE WATER. Buddy Holland and Margie Tingen cool off a little at the Fireman's Day parade. At first it looks all so innocent, but then Buddy decides that Margie needs to be cooled off. Margie appears to have been prepared, since she is in her bathing suit. (Both, courtesy of Tommy Stephens and Janet Davis.)

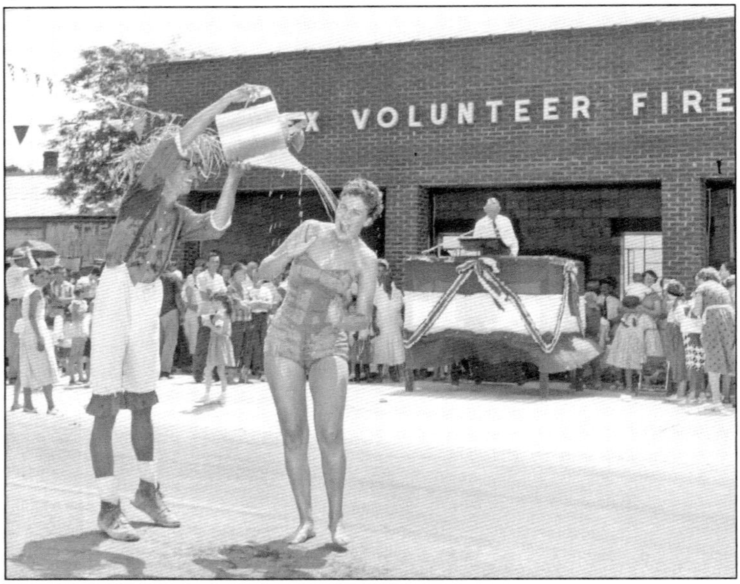

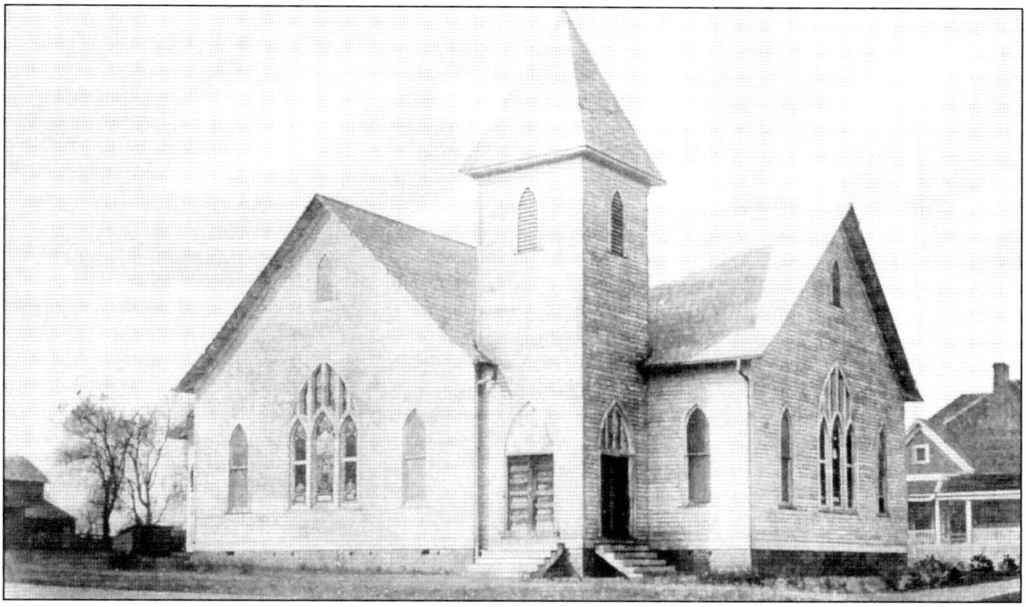

Apex United Methodist Episcopal Church, 1920s. This church began in 1870 as the Apex Methodist Episcopal Church, but after 1939, it dropped the "Episcopal." The church has had three locations since it began. In 1916, it moved to its current location at the corner of Hughes and Chatham Streets. (Courtesy of Apex United Methodist Church.)

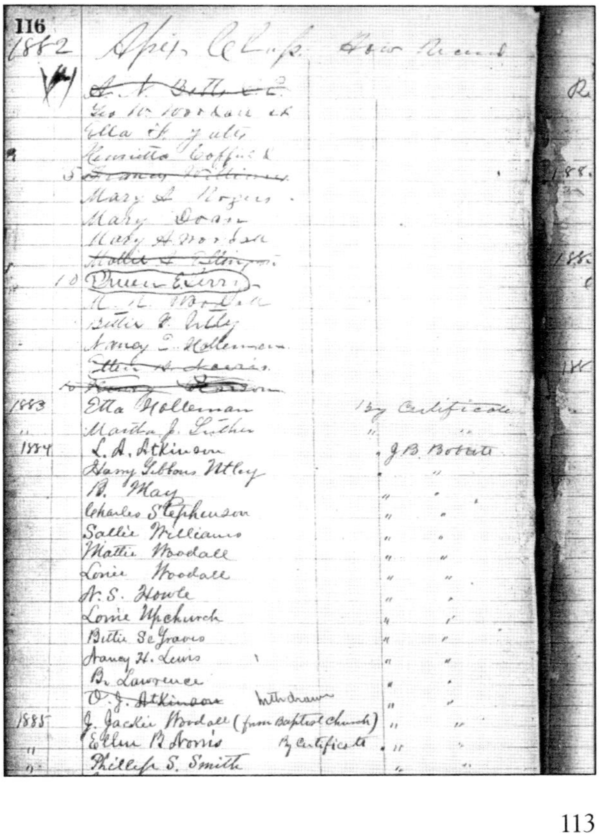

116
1882 Apex Class
Mary A. Rogers
1883 Etta Holleman — By Certificate
" Martha J. Luther — "
1884 L. A. Atkinson — J. B. Bobbitt
Mary Gibbons Utley
B. May
Charles Stephenson
Sallie Williams
Mattie Woodall
Lonie Woodall
N. S. Howle
Lonie Upchurch
Bettie SeGraves
Nancy H. Lewis
B. Lawrence
O. J. Atkinson — Withdrawn
1885 J. Jackie Woodall (from Baptist Church)
" Ellen B Norris — By Certificate
" Phillip S. Smith

Apex Methodist Episcopal Church Register. This is a page from the 1882 church member book. Some of the names shown are Etta and Nancy Holleman, Mary Rogers, Ella Yates, Charles Stephenson, Lonnie Upchurch, and Bettie Seagroves. (Courtesy of Apex United Methodist Church.)

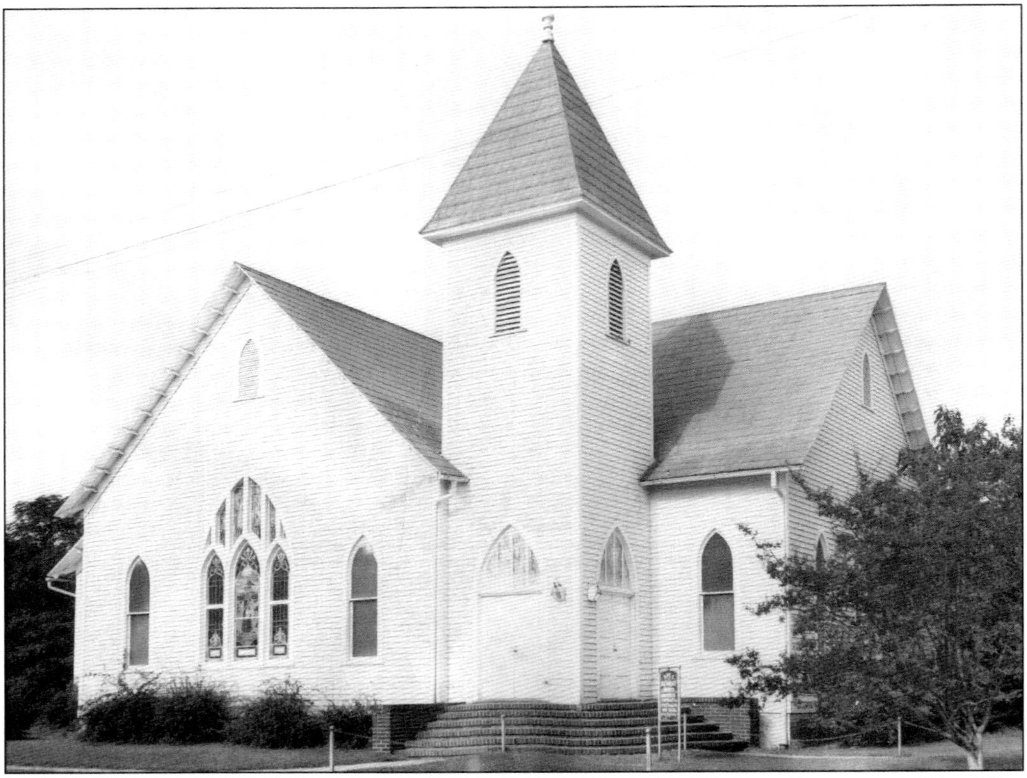

Apex United Methodist Church, 1950s. The Methodist church actually bought the corner lot that belonged to the Presbyterian church. For reasons unknown, the Presbyterians never built there. This church is well known for its stained-glass windows and still has the original pews. (Courtesy of Apex United Methodist Church.)

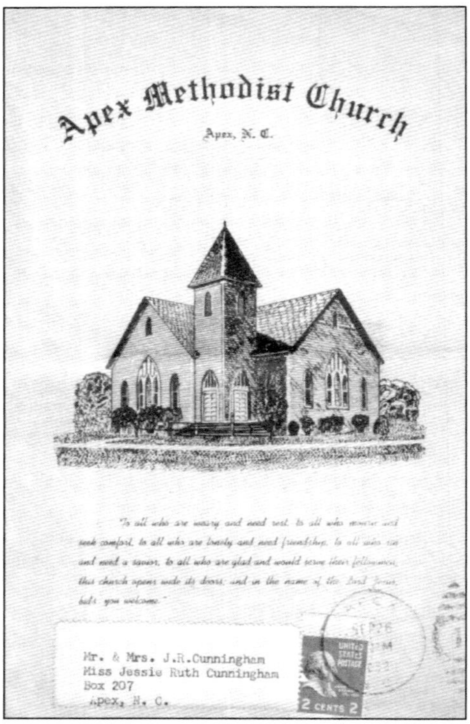

Apex United Methodist Church Bulletin. This 1952 church bulletin was mailed to its worshippers. James Reives and Lizzie Cunningham were prominent Apex citizens. Their daughter, Jesse Ruth, was an Apex schoolteacher for a number of years. (Courtesy of Apex United Methodist Church.)

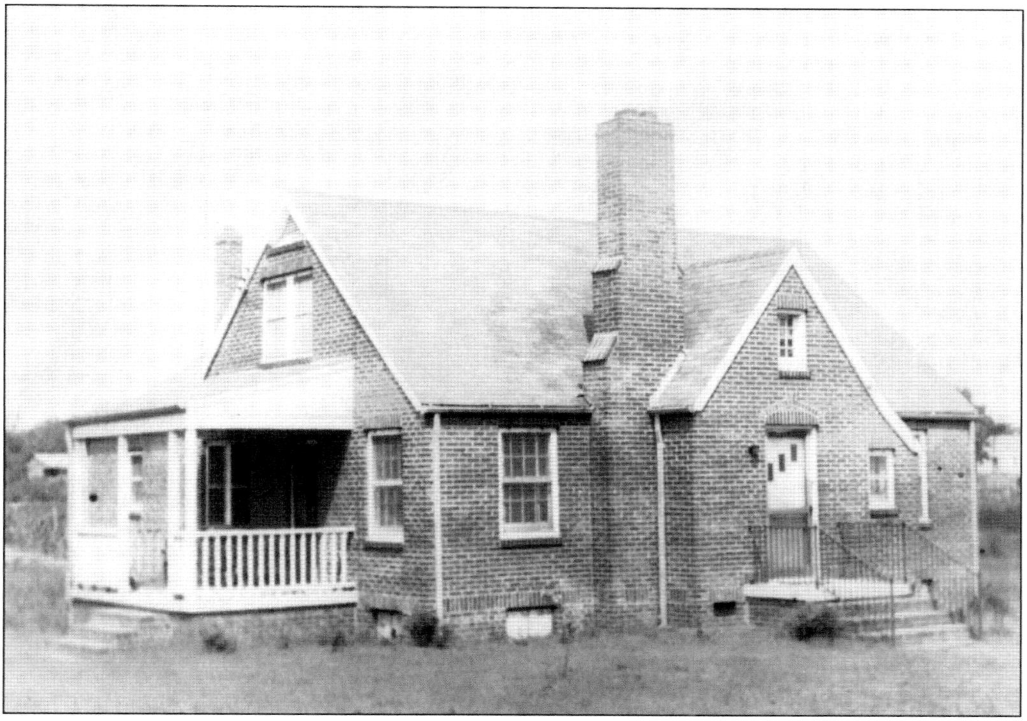

APEX UNITED METHODIST CHURCH PARSONAGE, 1940S. This is the house where the pastor of the church lived. It was just around the corner from the church. (Courtesy of Apex United Methodist Church.)

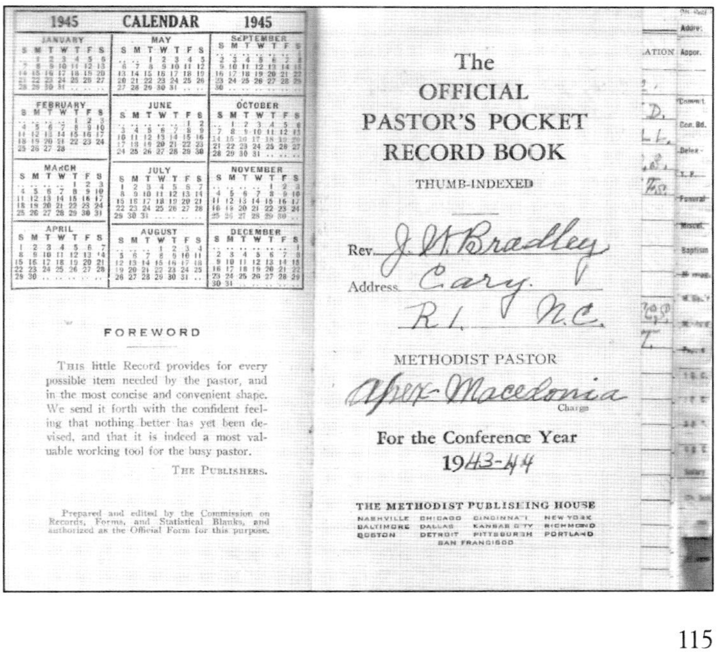

APEX UNITED METHODIST CHURCH PASTOR'S BOOK. The pastor of the Methodist church, J. W. Bradley, visited many members of his congregation throughout the years. This 1943 booklet belonging to him includes the names of church members with whom he visited. The pastor was based out of Cary but visited the church and its members on a regular basis. (Courtesy of Apex United Methodist Church.)

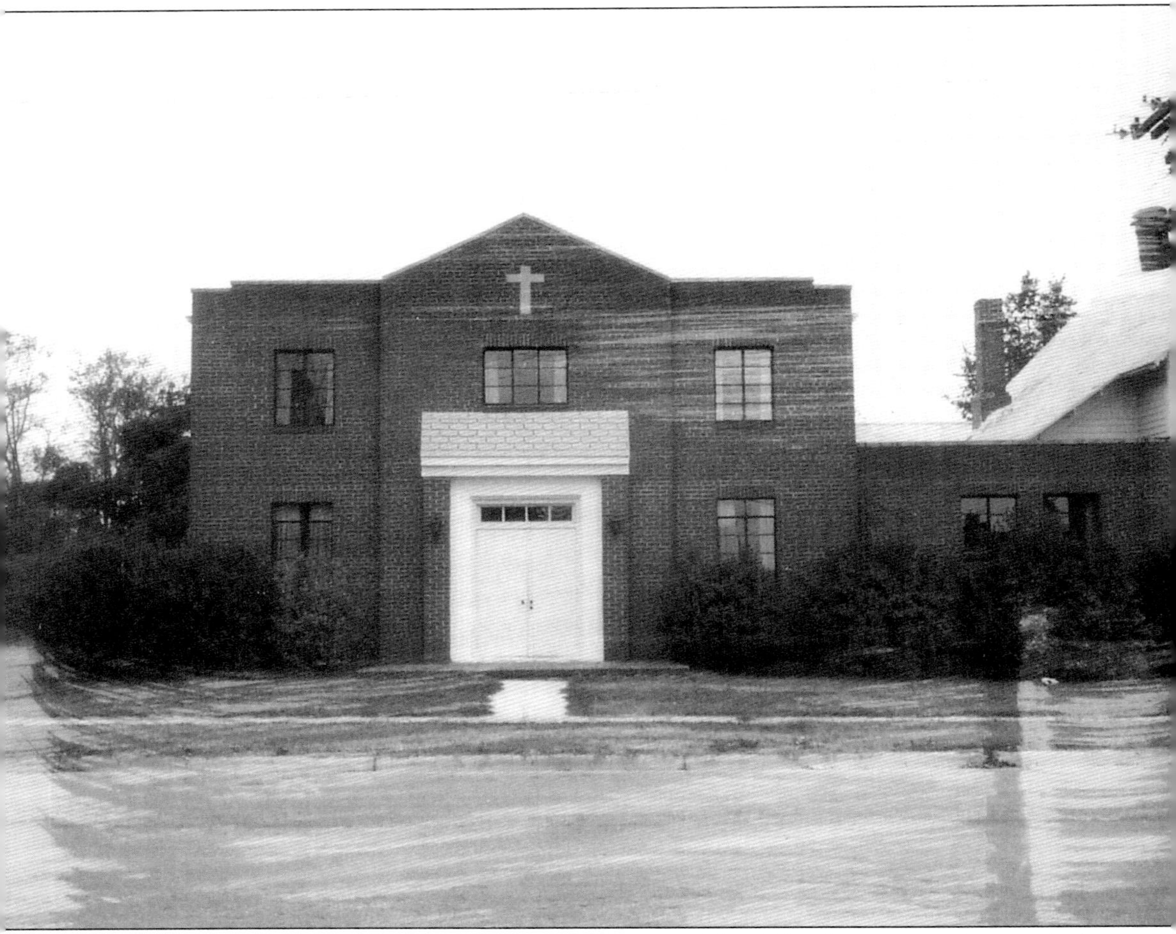

APEX UNITED METHODIST CHURCH EDUCATION BUILDING. This 1952 education building was built to offer Bible studies to the congregation's youth. (Courtesy of Apex United Methodist Church.)

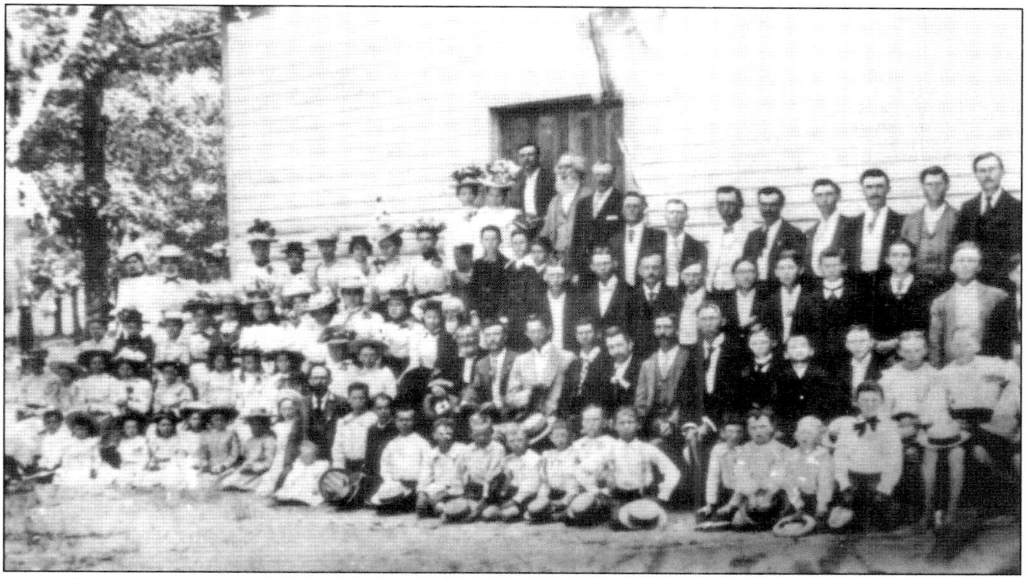

Salem Baptist Church. In 1840, the Salem Meeting House was officially designated a church. The residents of the local community had already been gathering there for worship prior to that time. Three families subsequently donated a total of 3 acres of land, and construction of the first building began. Enough support was raised to retain Rev. Stephen Senter as the first pastor. (Courtesy of the Salem Baptist Church.)

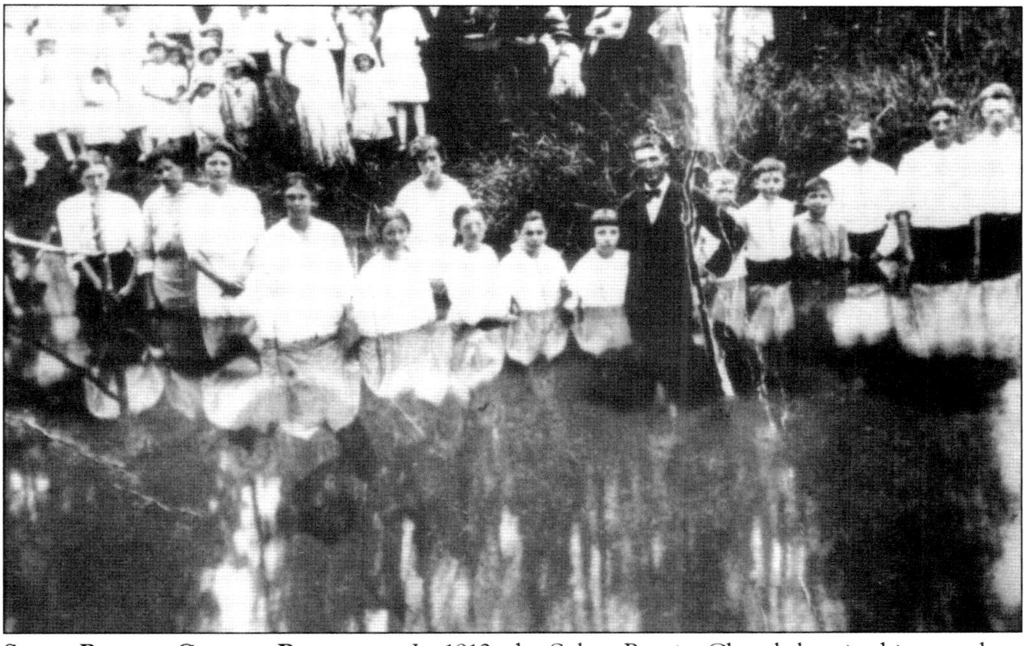

Salem Baptist Church Baptismal. In 1912, the Salem Baptist Church baptized its members in a nearby pond. As was written in the records of the 1840 meeting, "This church recently constituted under very favorable circumstances though their number is small, yet the prospects of an increase are very flattering for the work of the Lord is progressing in the neighborhood." (Courtesy of the Salem Baptist Church.)

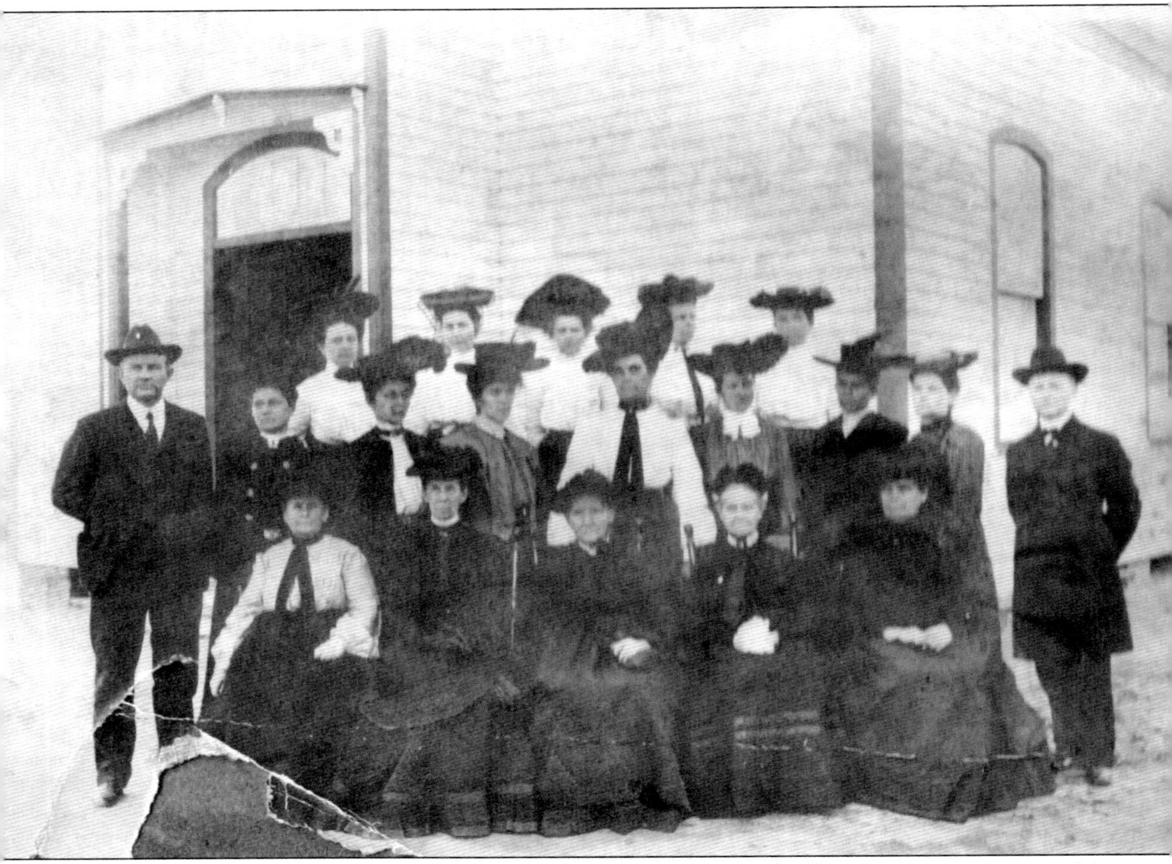

APEX BAPTIST CHURCH MISSIONARY, AROUND 1905. This was the first missionary society of the church. Pictured from left to right are (first row) Mrs. J. C. Burns, Mrs. John M. White, Mrs. Edith Ann Carter, Mrs. James Weaver, and Mrs. Rufus Smith (Margaret); (second row) Sebastian C. Olive, Mrs. A. B. Hunter (Alice), Edna Hudson, Margaret Bagley, Cora Honeycutt, Ida Lassiter, Mrs. W. H. Harward (Burlena), Mrs. C. V. Brooks, and Rev. C. V. Brooks; (third row) Mrs. A. V. Baucom (Anna), Mrs. Lou Olive, Mrs. Arch Wood (Bessie), Mrs. S. C. Olive (Corrine), and Ophelia Bell. (Courtesy of the Apex Baptist Church.)

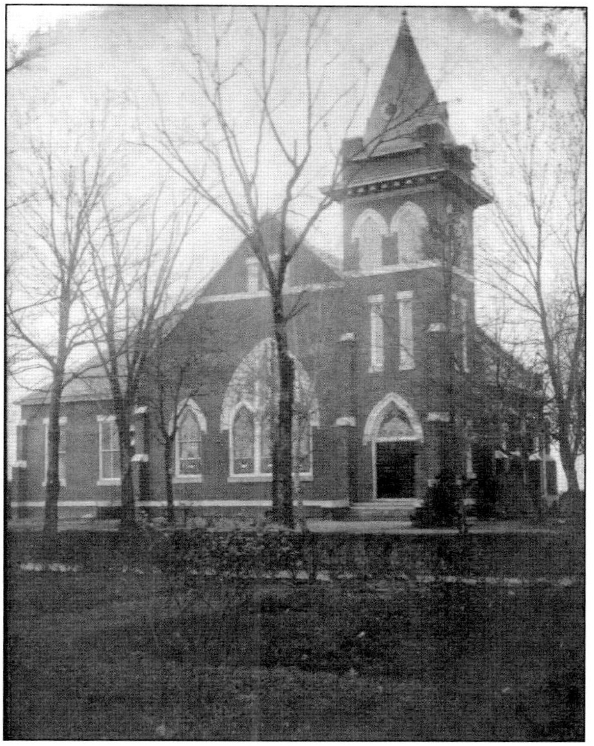

APEX BAPTIST CHURCH, AROUND 1912. The church began as a small, white, frame building with two rows of pews. It also had a bell tower over the front entrance. It was located between Moore and Williams Streets next to Lila Seymour's house. However, in 1911, the church building was deemed unsafe. It was relocated to its current location in 1912, where a grand, new brick edifice was erected. It cost between $15,000 and $20,000, and offered a seating capacity of about 350. (Both, courtesy of the Salem Baptist Church.)

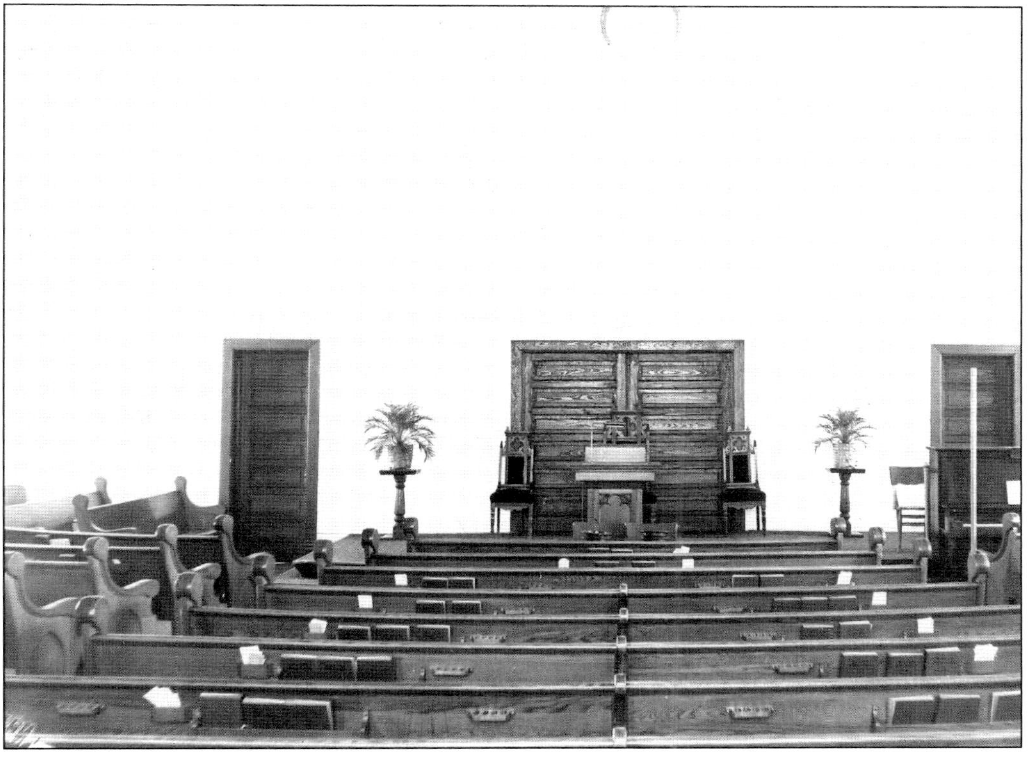

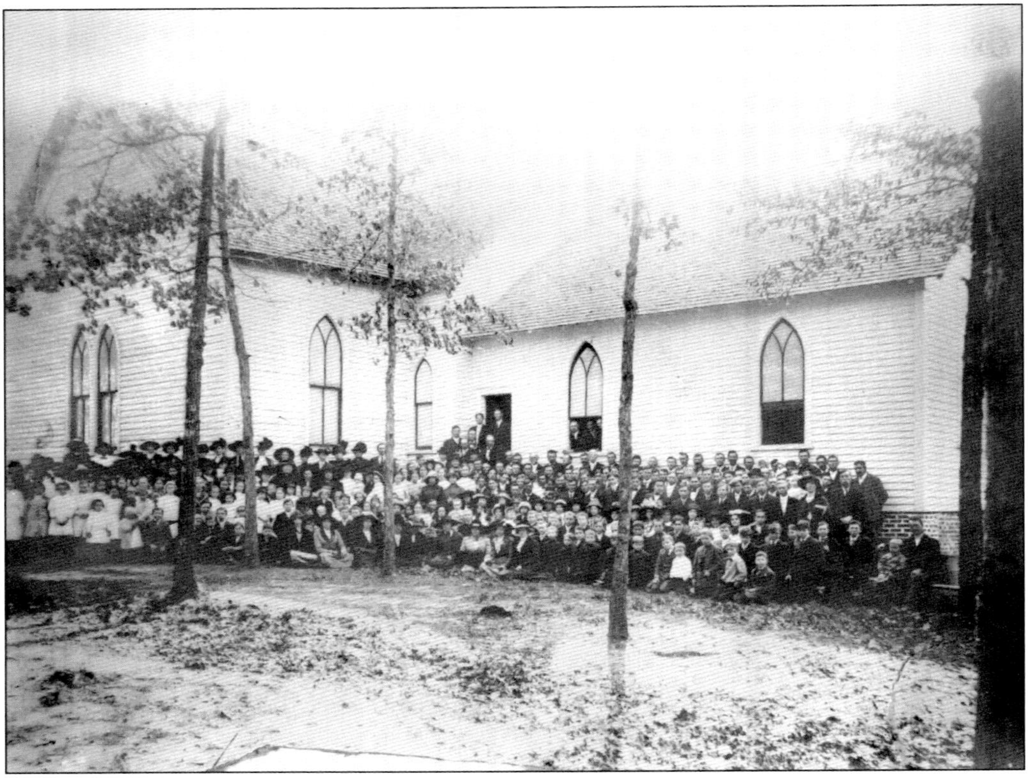

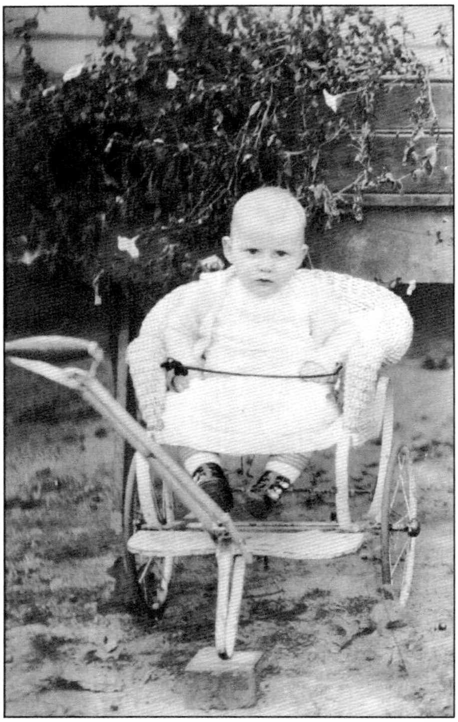

Olive Chapel Baptist Church. Johnson Olive and his nearby brethren began preaching the gospel around 1853 in Olive's Chapel, which is now known as Olive Chapel. This early-1900s congregation shows just how fast this small country church grew. (Courtesy of North Carolina State Archives.)

Eugene Olive. Eugene is the son of John and Ellen Olive. He grew up and became a minister at Olive Chapel. (Courtesy of North Carolina State Archives.)

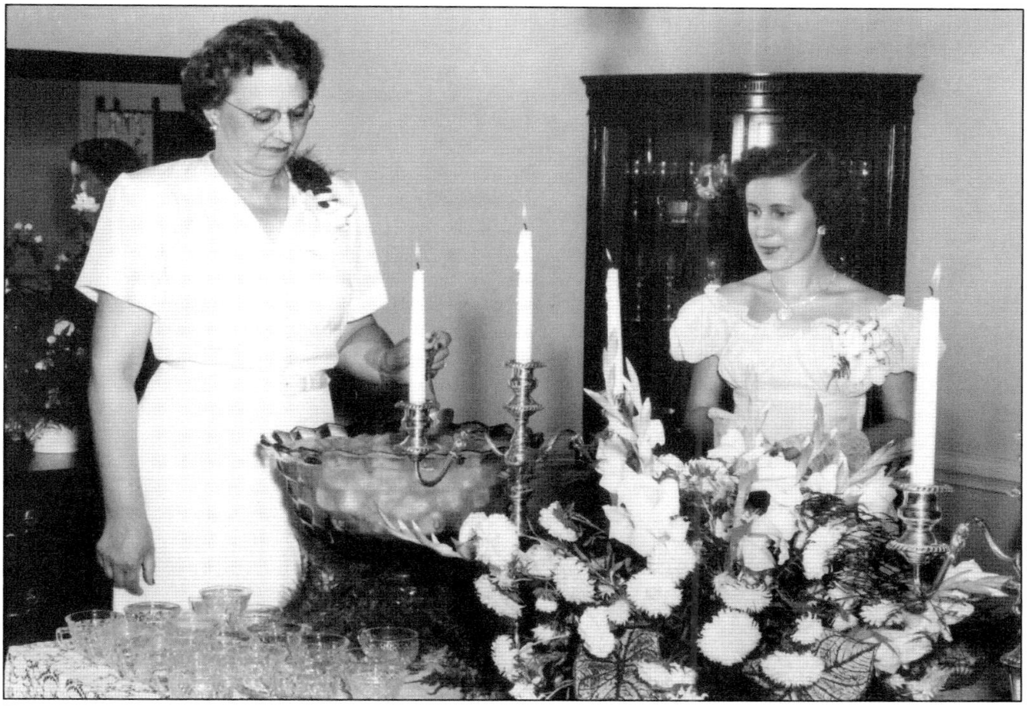

Burgess Rehearsal Dinner Preparation. Jacque Goodwin married Andrew Judson Burgess in 1943. This photograph shows Alice Bailey on the left and Gladys Smallwood on the right. (Courtesy of Jacque Goodwin Burgess.)

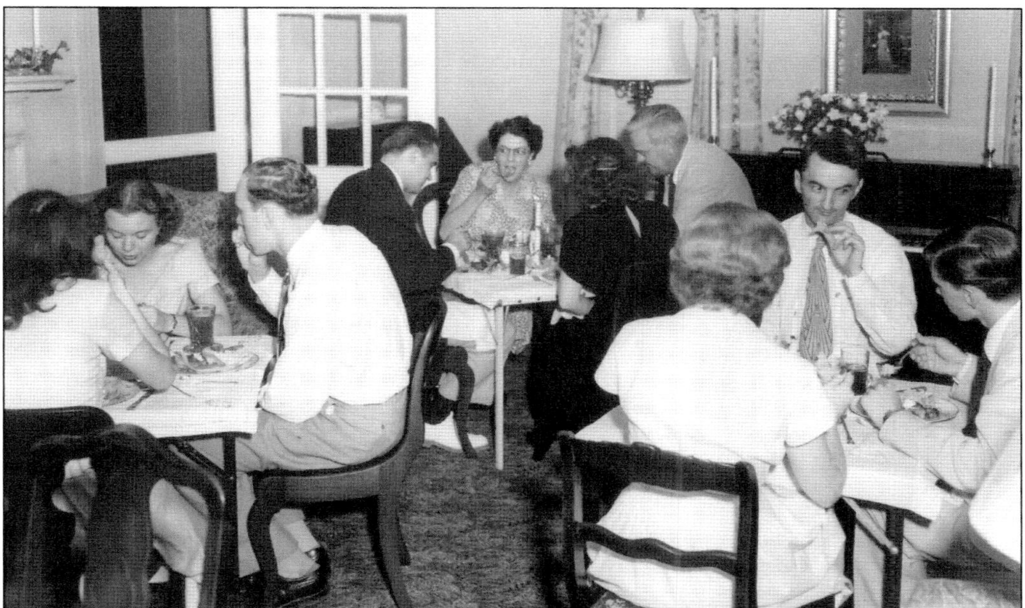

Burgess Rehearsal Dinner. Jacque Goodwin's parents had a large, newly built home that was just outside of downtown Apex. They called it Good Acres. Guests are enjoying the rehearsal dinner food. (Courtesy of Jacque Goodwin Burgess.)

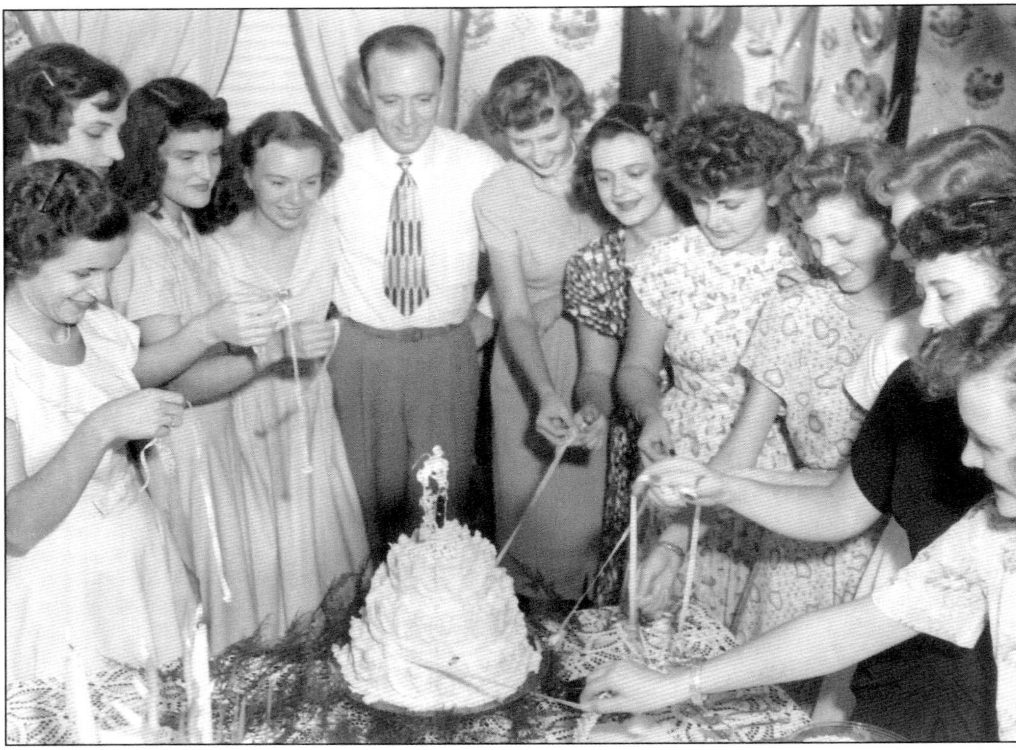

Burgess Rehearsal Favor Pull. During the rehearsal dinner, the bridesmaids stood around the rehearsal dinner cake. There were party charms or favors buried in the frosting with a ribbon tied to each. Each bridesmaid pulled a string to see which favor she got. Each favor signified something about her future as a bride. (Both, courtesy of Jacque Goodwin Burgess.)

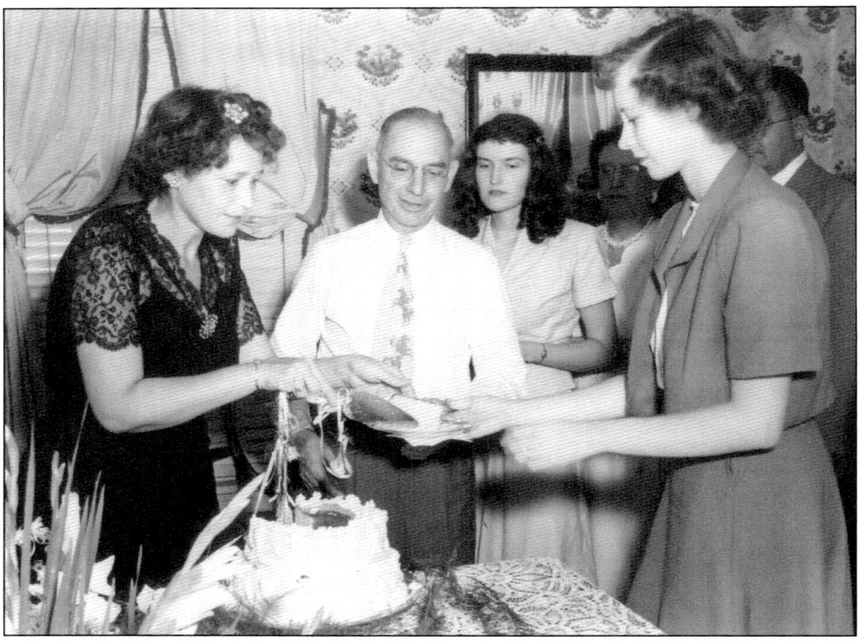

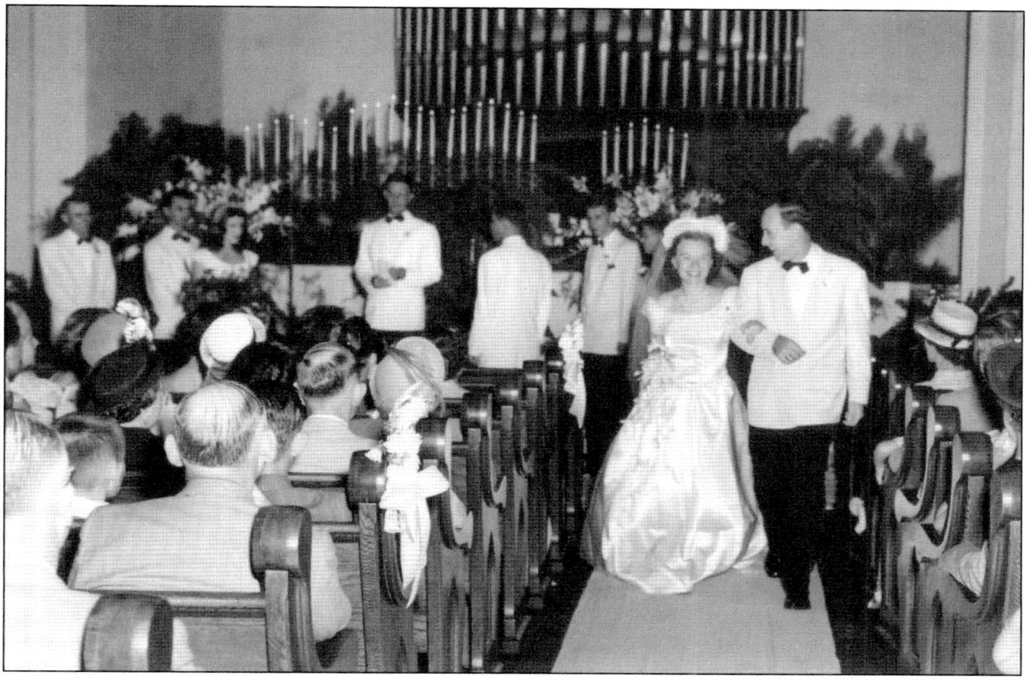

Burgess Wedding. Jacque Goodwin says "I do" to Andrew Judson Burgess in 1943. The smiling bride and groom leave the church for Good Acres. (Courtesy of Jacque Goodwin Burgess.)

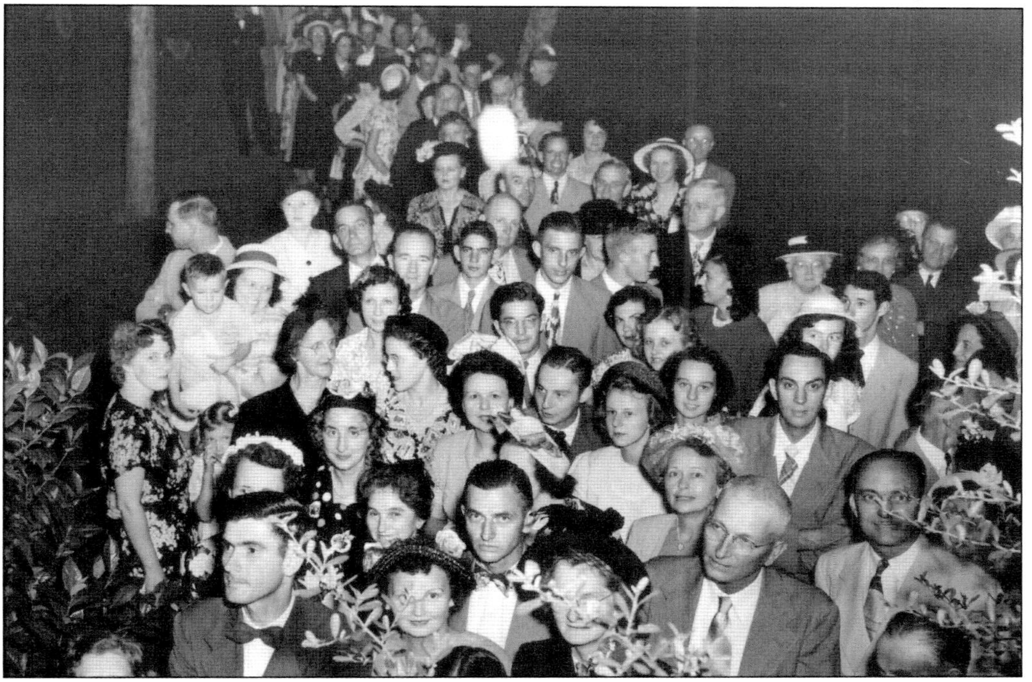

Burgess Wedding Reception. Jacque and Andrew Burgess's guests line up outside Jacque's family home, Good Acres, to offer congratulations to the bride and groom. (Courtesy of Jacque Goodwin Burgess.)

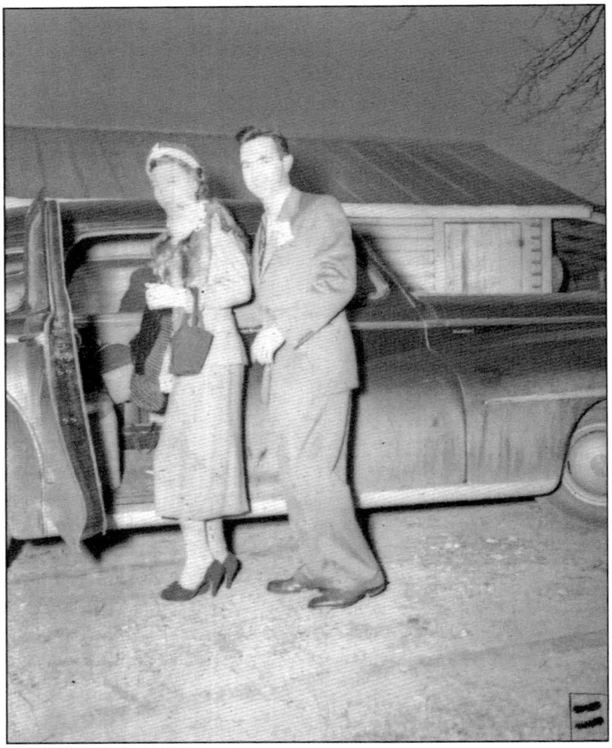

Ashworth Wedding. Jane Beasley and Wilton Durwood "Skinny" Ashworth head off for their honeymoon in Asheville, North Carolina, and Gatlinburg, Tennessee. Jane was from Apex, while Skinny was from Fuquay-Varina. These photographs were taken on July 26, 1946. (Both, courtesy of Tommy Stephens and Janet Davis.)

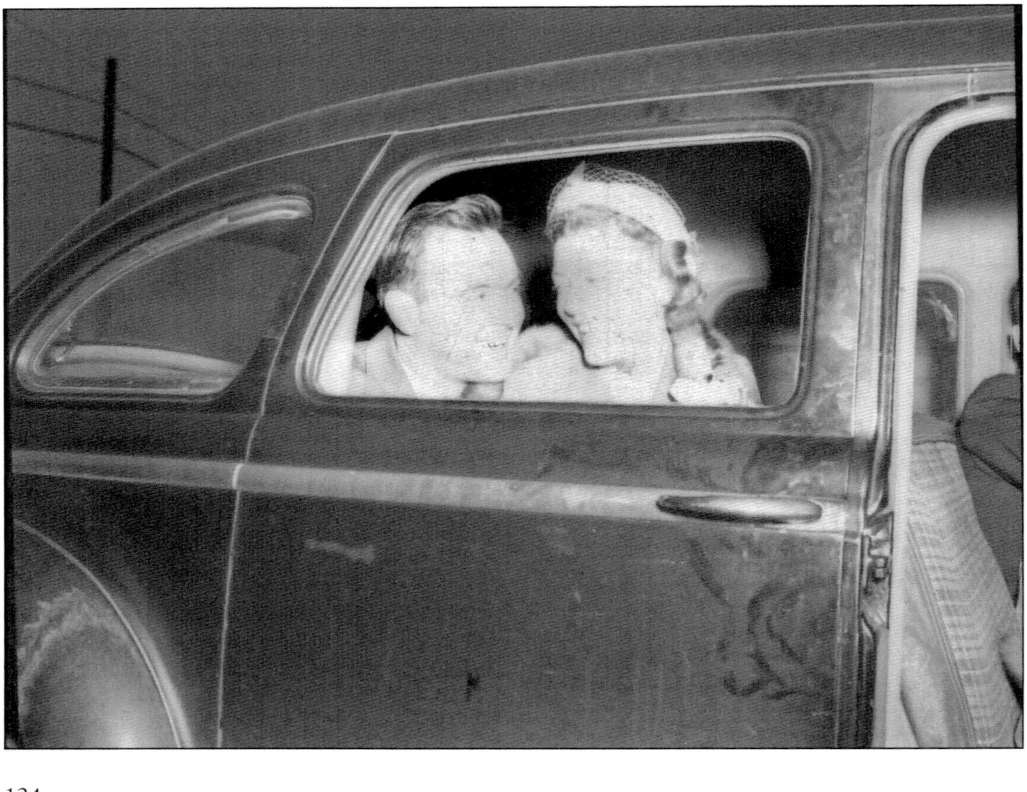

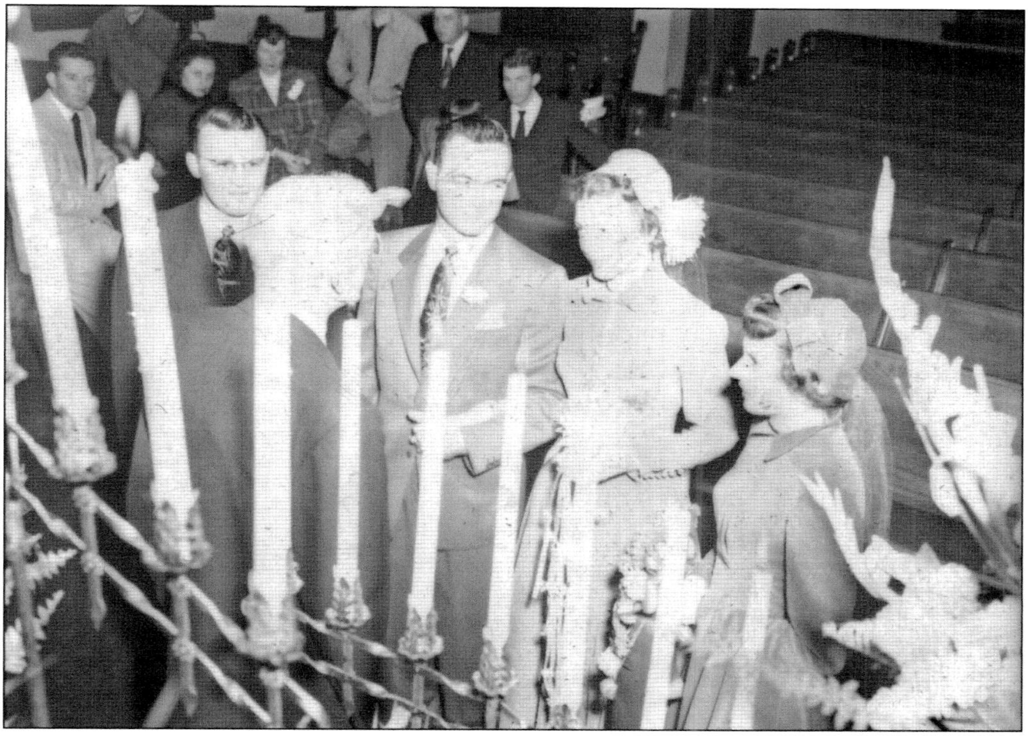

Ashworth Wedding Party. Jane Beasley and Wilton Durwood "Skinny" Ashworth have said "I do" at the Apex United Methodist Church on July 26, 1946. Below, they are at the reception, feeding cake to one another. (Both, courtesy of Tommy Stephens and Janet Davis.)

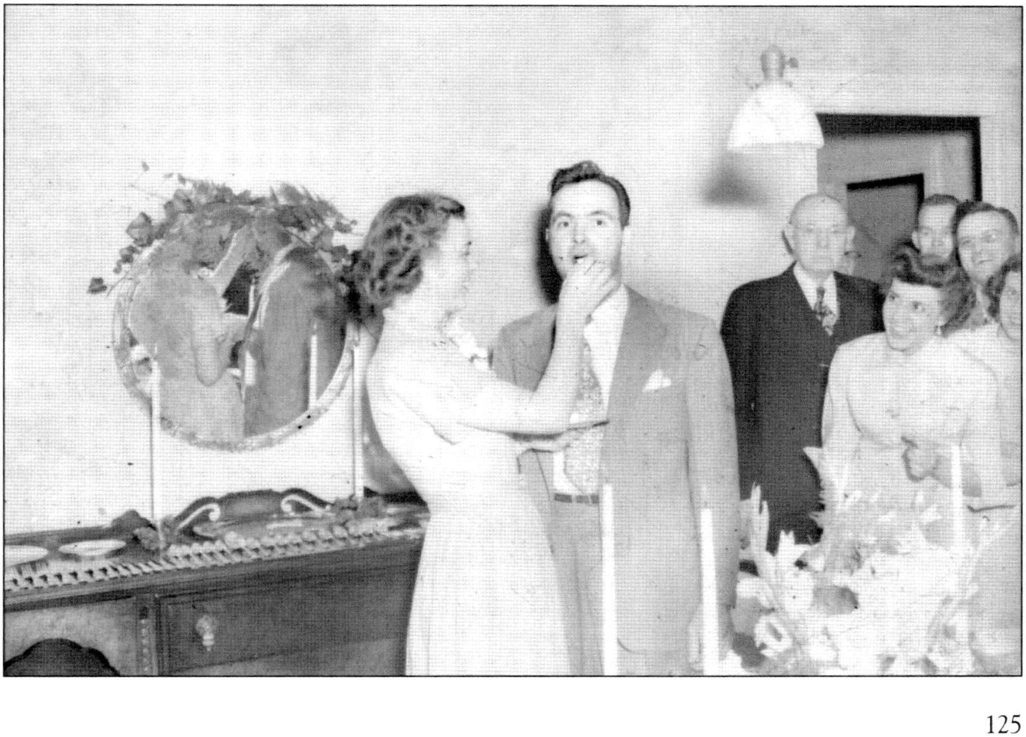

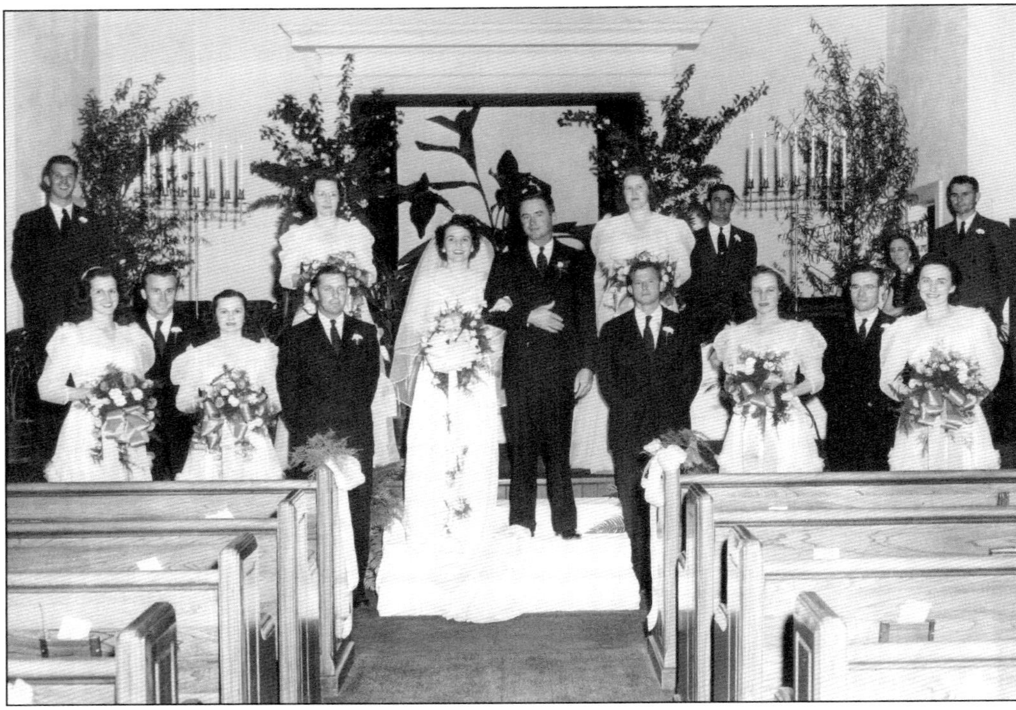

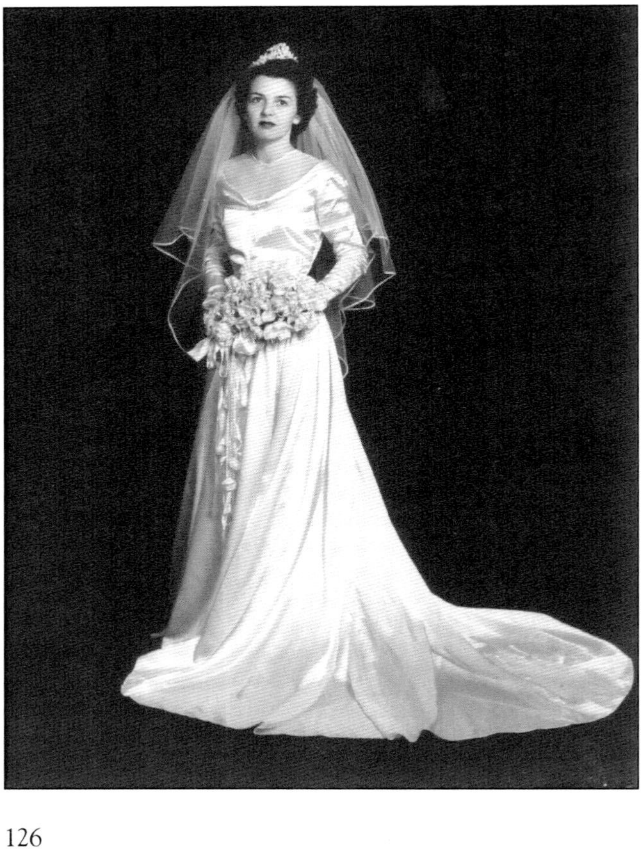

J. Q. SEAGROVES WEDDING. John Q. and Margaret Seagroves were married in the 1950s. (Both, courtesy of Diane Long.)

Resources

Apex Centennial Guide 1873–1973. Apex, NC: 1973.
Apex Journal, 1911 various issues, Wake County, Olivia Raney Library, Raleigh, NC.
Apex Lions Club, Web site history, Apex, NC.
Apex town council minutes and charter, 1875–1920, Town of Apex, Apex, NC.
Apex Volunteer Fire Department, history, Apex, NC.
Branson's North Carolina Business Directory, 1877–1878. Raleigh, NC: Branson and Farrar, NC State Archives.
Chataigne, J. H. *Chataigne's NC Directory and Gazetteer, 1883–1884*. Raleigh, NC: N.C. State Archives.
genforum.genealogy.com. Mann Family of Wake, Chatham, and Northampton Counties, NC Web site, last accessed 6/4/09.
Hendricks, Garland, *Biography of a Country Church*. Apex, NC.
News & Observer, various issues, Raleigh, NC.
Olive, Anne Lydia. *Apex Journal* transcription, September 15, 1911, Apex, NC.
Salem Baptist Church. *150 Years*. Apex, NC: Salem Baptist Church, 1990.
Sentinel, October 25, 1875, Raleigh, NC.
U.S. Census, various years, online from Wake County Public Library, Raleigh, NC.
Wake County, Olivia Raney Library, Elizabeth Reid Murray collection, Raleigh, NC.
Winter, Richard, U.S. postal history, Apex, NC.

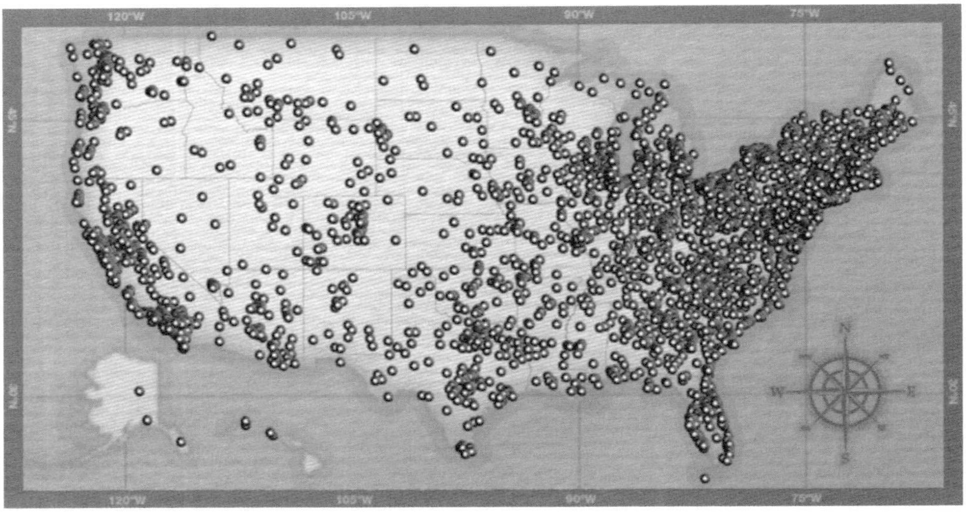